The Global Governance of Precarity

'Standard' employment relationships, with permanent contracts, regular hours, and decent pay, are under assault. Precarious work and unemployment are increasingly common, and concern is also growing about the expansion of informal work and the rise of 'modern slavery'. However, precarity and violence are in fact longstanding features of work for most of the world's population. Lamenting the 'loss' of secure, stable jobs often reflects a strikingly Eurocentric and historically myopic perspective.

This book argues that standard employment relations have always co-existed with a plethora of different labour regimes. Highlighting the importance of the governance of irregular forms of labour the author draws together empirical, historical analyses of International Labour Organisation (ILO) policy towards forced labour, unemployment, and social protection for informal workers in sub-Saharan Africa. Archival research, extensive documentary research, and interviews with key ILO staff are utilized to explore the critical role the organization's activities have often played in the development of mechanisms for governing irregular labour.

Addressing the increasingly widespread and pressing practical debates about the politics of precarious labour in the world economy this book speaks to key debates in several disciplines, especially IPE, global governance, and labour studies. It will also be of interest to scholars working in development studies and critical political economy.

Nick Bernards is Assistant Professor of Global Sustainable Development at the University of Warwick.

RIPE Series in Global Political Economy
Series Editors: James Brassett
University of Warwick, UK
Eleni Tsingou
Copenhagen Business School, Denmark
and
Susanne Soederberg
Queen's University, Canada

The RIPE Series published by Routledge is an essential forum for cutting-edge scholarship in International Political Economy. The series brings together new and established scholars working in critical, cultural, and constructivist political economy. Books in the RIPE Series typically combine an innovative contribution to theoretical debates with rigorous empirical analysis.

The RIPE Series seeks to cultivate:

- Field-defining theoretical advances in International Political Economy
- Novel treatments of key issue areas, both historical and contemporary, such as global finance, trade, and production
- Analyses that explore the political-economic dimensions of relatively neglected topics, such as the environment, gender relations, and migration
- Accessible work that will inspire advanced undergraduates and graduate students in International Political Economy.

The *RIPE Series in Global Political Economy* aims to address the needs of students and teachers.

Recent titles:

A Global Political Economy of Democratisation
Beyond the Internal-External Divide
Alison J. Ayers

The Global Governance of Precarity
Primitive Accumulation and the Politics of Irregular Work
Nick Bernards

Polanyi in Times of Populism
Vision and Contradiction in the History of Economic Ideas
Christopher Holmes

For a full list of titles in this series, please visit www.routledge.com/RIPE-Series-in-Global-Political-Economy/book-series/RIPE

The Global Governance of Precarity

Primitive Accumulation and the Politics of Irregular Work

Nick Bernards

LONDON AND NEW YORK

First published 2018
by Routledge
2 Park Square, Milton Park, Abingdon, Oxon OX14 4RN

and by Routledge
711 Third Avenue, New York, NY 10017

Routledge is an imprint of the Taylor & Francis Group, an informa business

© 2018 Nick Bernards

The right of Nick Bernards to be identified as author of this work has been asserted by him in accordance with sections 77 and 78 of the Copyright, Designs and Patents Act 1988.

All rights reserved. No part of this book may be reprinted or reproduced or utilised in any form or by any electronic, mechanical, or other means, now known or hereafter invented, including photocopying and recording, or in any information storage or retrieval system, without permission in writing from the publishers.

Trademark notice: Product or corporate names may be trademarks or registered trademarks, and are used only for identification and explanation without intent to infringe.

British Library Cataloguing-in-Publication Data
A catalogue record for this book is available from the British Library

Library of Congress Cataloging-in-Publication Data
A catalog record for this book has been requested

ISBN: 978-1-138-30372-0 (hbk)
ISBN: 978-0-203-73084-3 (ebk)

Typeset in Times New Roman
by Apex CoVantage, LLC

For Laura and Max

Contents

Acknowledgements	ix
List of abbreviations	xi
Introduction	1
Irregular labour and residualism 6	
History, scale, and method 10	
Plan of the book 12	
1 Irregular labour in global capitalism	17
Irregular labour and the undercurrents of primitive accumulation 18	
Political relations of force, the subaltern, and governance 26	
Conclusion 33	
2 The governance of forced labour and the antinomies of colonialism	37
Colonial world order and the origins of the ILO 39	
African labour and the antinomies of colonialism 41	
The ILO and 'Native Labour', c. 1919–1930 43	
The Witwatersrand gold fields and the limits of freedom 48	
Conclusion 54	
3 Urbanization, colonial crisis, and social policy	59
War, depression, and colonial crisis 60	
Migration and productivity, 1948–1960 63	
Conclusion 74	

4 Irregular work in the postcolonial social order: the World Employment Programme discovers the 'informal' 77

The antinomies of decolonization 79
WEP and the 'discovery' of employment 82
Informality, the state, and the politics of poverty in Kenya 88
Conclusion 93

5 Neoliberal crises and the politics of informality 97

Irregular labour in neoliberal Africa 99
From social security to microinsurance for informal workers 102
Governing informal apprenticeships in Tanzania 110
Conclusion 114

6 Reviving the governance of forced labour: 'traditional slavery' and child trafficking in West Africa 117

Governing unfree labour in the twenty-first century 119
Governing 'traditional' slavery in Niger 123
Governing child trafficking in West Africa 128
Conclusion 133

Conclusion 135

IPE, work, and the making of class 136
Neoliberalism and its limits 137
Precarious politics? 140

References 145
Index 161

Acknowledgements

This book started life during my PhD research at McMaster University. I am grateful to my doctoral supervisor, Robert O'Brien, as well as my advisory committee Bonny Ibhawoh, Stephen McBride, and Tony Porter, for their encouragement, guidance, and criticisms throughout this project. Without their support, I'd probably still be at McMaster trying to finish my dissertation.

The (re)writing of this book was carried out while I was a postdoctoral fellow in the Department of Political Studies at Queen's University. Susanne Soederberg's supervision and her enthusiastic support for the development of this book were instrumental.

Financial support was provided by the Social Science and Humanities Research Council of Canada through a Joseph Armand Bombardier Canada Graduate Scholarship and a Postdoctoral Fellowship. I also received support from the Ontario Graduate Scholarship programme and from the Department of Political Science at McMaster.

I carried out some of the research represented in this book during a period as a visiting scholar in the Research Department of the ILO. Janet Pennington and Marva Corley-Coulibaly were invaluable in helping me find my way around. This project also would not have been possible without the help of Jacques Rodriguez at the ILO Archives in Geneva and the staff of the South African National Archives in Pretoria and Wits Historical Papers in Johannesburg. Thanks are also due to the people working at the ILO and other organizations who took the time to answer my questions.

The editors at Routledge and at the RIPE Series in Global Political Economy were wonderfully supportive of this book from the beginning. Thanks to James Brassett who managed the review process, and to Robert Sorsby and Claire Maloney at Routledge for helping guide the book through production. Two anonymous reviewers for Routledge, along with the series editors, offered thorough and productive comments which have greatly improved the final product.

Last but not least, I am grateful to my family. My parents, Mark and Sharon Bernards, have supported this project (and most other things I've done, really) in more ways than I care to count. I am most grateful, though, to Laura DeVouge-Bernards for making the years I've spent working on this book a lot happier and a lot more fun than they would have been without her.

Abbreviations

AOF	Afrique Occidentale Française
ARC	African Regional Conference
ASI	Anti-Slavery International
CCTA	Committee on Technical Cooperation in Africa South of the Sahara
CDWA	Colonial Development and Welfare Act [UK]
CGAP	Consultative Group to Assist the Poor
CGT	Confedèration Generale du Travail [France]
CIMA	Conférence Interafricaine des Marchés d'Assurances
CNTS	Confedèration Nationale des Travailleurs du Sénégal
COTU	Central Organization of Trade Unions [Kenya]
CPP	Convention People's Party [Ghana]
DID	Desjardins International Development
ECOSOC	Economic and Social Council of the United Nations
FECECAM	Fédération des Caisses d'Épargne et de Credit Agricole Mutuel [Benin]
FKE	Federation of Kenyan Employers
GB	Governing Body
IAIS	International Association of Insurance Supervisors
IALC	Inter-African Labour Conference
ICFTU	International Confederation of Free Trade Unions
IFC	International Finance Corporation
IGA	Income Generating Activity
ILC	International Labour Conference
ILO	International Labour Organization
ILR	International Labour Review
IPE	International Political Economy
JASPA	Jobs and Skills Programme for Africa
KFL	Kenya Federation of Labour
LNU	League of Nations Union
LUTRENA	Combatting the Trafficking of Children for Labour Exploitation in West and Central Africa
MIF	Microinsurance Innovation Facility
NLC	Native Labour Code

Abbreviations

OATUU	Organization for African Trade Union Unity
OAU	Organization for African Unity
PAC	Pan-African Conference
SAP-FL	Special Action Programme for the Prevention of Forced Labour
STEP	Strategies and Tools against Social Exclusion and Poverty
RPL	Recognition of Prior Learning
RSPC	Simplified Regime for Small Contributors [Senegal]
TAP	Technical Assistance Programme
TIP	Trafficking in Persons Report [US]
TUC	Trades Union Council [Ghana]
UNDP	United Nations Development Programme
UNODC	United Nations Office on Drugs and Crime
USAID	United States Agency for International Development
VETA	Vocational Education and Training Authority [Tanzania]
VVCs	Village Vigilance Committees
WEP	World Employment Programme
WFTU	World Federation of Trade Unions
WTO	World Trade Organization

Introduction

Pierre Bourdieu (1998) insists that 'precarity is everywhere today'. Bourdieu's phrase reflects a widely reported sense that 'standard' employment relationships, with permanent contracts, regular hours, and decent pay, are under assault in contemporary capitalism. Popular and academic debates about the global rise of precarious work are increasingly widespread. Concerns about the possibilities for progressive politics in a context marked by declining union densities and the global growth of temporary, casualized, and 'informal' work are particularly pronounced. A number of authors have suggested that, because precarious workers are faced with a daily struggle to secure their livelihoods, they face a foreshortened 'shadow of the future' that inhibits their political mobilization; or worse, makes them vulnerable to dangerous forms of populism and demagoguery (Standing 2011; Bourdieu 1998). More nuanced perspectives certainly exist (e.g. Harris and Scully 2015; Lambert and Herod 2016), but political possibilities in the context of increasingly precarious work are subject to considerable debate and anxiety.

At the same time, we can point to growing policy and popular concerns about the increase of various forms of informal labour, along with forced labour and so-called 'modern slavery', all of which seem to be multiplying against the backdrop of failed structural adjustment policies and the rise of global production networks. 'Informal' economies occupy an increasingly prominent place in policy debates about labour, poverty, and development (e.g. ILO 2002; 2014a). Forced labour, similarly, has been subject to renewed regulatory attention in the twenty-first century, particularly from the International Labour Organization (ILO). The ILO's conventions on forced labour are among the 'core conventions' identified in the 1998 Declaration on Fundamental Principles and Rights at Work. The ILO established a Special Action Programme for the Prevention of Forced Labour (SAP-FL) and has issued a series of major reports on forced labour in the last fifteen years (ILO 2001; 2005a; 2009a; 2012a; 2014b). This coincides with renewed popular and academic attention to unfree labour and 'modern slavery' in the global economy (e.g. Bales 2008). Several high-profile cases of forced labour have attracted widespread media attention. A number of reports, for instance, have highlighted the brutal (often lethally so) treatment of migrant workers – primarily from East Africa and South Asia – in Qatar's construction industry in the buildup to the country's hosting the World Cup in 2022. Such exploitation is facilitated by a legal framework around immigration that makes 'absconding' from a job a criminal offence subject to financial penalties for migrants and requires workers to obtain 'exit permits' from employers before leaving the country – conditions which activists have argued, not without reason, grant employers an inordinate degree of power over workers and constitute forced labour (e.g. Amnesty International 2013; 2016). A number of recent reports about 'slavery' in South-East Asian fisheries linked to global supply chains have also drawn considerable attention – particularly the exploitation of Rohingya migrants fleeing persecution in Myanmar but lacking legal status in Thailand and Indonesia (e.g. Stoakes et al. 2015).

Against this backdrop of popular, academic, and regulatory attention to the growing crises of precarious work on the one hand and the rise of violent hyper-exploitation on the other, it is easy to lose sight of the simple fact that what are often considered 'standard' employment relations – based on permanent contracts, with regular salaries or wages – have never made up the majority of the world's working population. Neilson and Rossiter are entirely correct in the assertion that 'If we look at capitalism in a wider historical and geographical scope, it is precarity that is the norm and not Fordist economic organization' (2008: 54; see also Breman and van der Linden 2014; Vosko 2010; Harris and Scully 2015). Indeed, this is scarcely a novel observation. Fifty years ago, Ernst Mandel predicted that the welfare states upon which much of our conception of 'traditional' labour relations has come to rest could, 'At most . . . find a momentary success in about twenty countries (the United States, Canada, Australia, New Zealand, Japan, and Western Europe) which account for less than 20 percent of the world's population' (1968: 21). Lamenting the 'loss' of secure, stable livelihoods in the face of growing precarity or informality often reflects a historically narrow and strikingly Eurocentric perspective.

On closer inspection, many forms of 'new slavery' similarly appear to be adaptations of longer-running practices to capitalist property relations, or indeed integral to the origins and reproduction of capitalism on a global scale (see Brass and van der Linden 1997; Brass 2014; Mendiola 2016). Breman's (2010) insightful discussion of 'neo-bondage' in India, for instance, points to the transformation of 'traditional' practices of labour bondage in the context of emerging private property regimes in agrarian regions. Even the historical development of global capitalism in its European heartlands was closely entwined with the development of the transatlantic slave trade. Manchester's textile factories, of course, depended on raw materials produced by chattel slaves in the Americas. By the mid-nineteenth century, as McMichael (1991: 321) notes, plantation slavery in the US was increasingly organized along industrial lines in order to meet growing demand from metropolitan industry, and slave labour thus increasingly 'became a phenomenal form of value producing labour' – different in form, but functionally integrated into global circuits of accumulation in the same way as 'free' labour. The formal abolition of slavery did not end the reliance of metropolitan industry on raw materials produced through violent coercion in peripheral territories either. Nearly half the world's supply of rubber in the decade prior to World War I was derived from brutal forms of forced labour in central Africa, primarily in the Congo

Free State. This irony was not lost on contemporary critics either. Rosa Luxemburg (2003), referring to such colonial abuses, observed in 1913 that 'capitalism in its full maturity also depends in all respects on non-capitalist strata' (2003: 345).

In short, precarity and violent coercion are persistent, *structural* features of life under capitalism. Precarious livelihoods and violent modes of exploitation are emphatically not contemporary aberrations or symptoms of labour market deregulation. The same historical processes that produced 'free' wage labour and the brief, geographically narrow heyday of 'standard' employment relations simultaneously produced a plethora of different kinds of labour regimes, ranging from small-scale self-employment, myriad survivalist activities in 'informal' economies, temporary migration, unemployment, and unstable casualized jobs to chattel slavery, bonded labour, and the emergent range of fraudulent or violent labour recruitment often referred to as the 'new slavery'. Collectively, I refer to this spectrum of forms of work other than free wage labour on formal, long-term contracts as 'irregular labour'.

This will probably strike many readers as a very broad category. It undoubtedly is. The boundary between 'standard' or 'normalized' and 'irregular' forms of work is also without question rather fluid and contingent. 'Normalized' and 'irregular' labour are inherently relative and relational terms – they have little meaning independent of each other and independent of context. The point of making this distinction, though, is precisely to call attention to the fundamentally fraught, contingent, and deeply *political* nature of the ways in which distinctions are drawn between normalized and hence acceptable forms of exploitation and those that are understood as divergent or aberrant (in a word, irregular).

This way of approaching the question is useful precisely because the historically and geographically pervasive character of irregular forms of labour seems too easy to forget. Understandings of precarity, informality, and forced labour often lean heavily on assumptions about the aberrant character of irregular forms of labour. Irregular labour is understood primarily in 'residualist' terms – that is, as a result of exclusions from the 'normal' workings of the market or regulatory protections. These framings have not gone unquestioned. Scholars of international political economy (IPE) and related disciplines have quite compellingly made the argument that precarity, coercion, informality, and the like are integral to the global structure of capitalist production rather than external to it (see e.g. Taylor 2010; Phillips 2011; LeBaron 2014a; Phillips and Mieres 2015). This book seeks to push these previous arguments a step further. The lines between irregular and normal modes of exploitation are indeed blurry at best, and irregular forms of labour are indeed integral to capitalism. But the very practice of drawing such lines – between 'free' and 'forced' labour, 'formal' and 'informal' sectors, 'standard' and 'precarious' employment relations – is historically pervasive and politically significant and thus worthy of analysis in its own right.

The central theses of this book, then, are (1) that the governance of irregular labour across historical contexts has in common the simultaneous normalization of proletarian forms of exploitation and regulatory or discursive insulation of irregular forms of work from the broader workings of capitalist relations of production and accumulation. However, (2) in practice this is often an ambivalent, fraught process which must be carried out through a diversity of political institutions and forms of authority which do not always work coherently. Residualism, in short, is not just problematic theory, it has deep historical roots, it is embedded in regulatory programmes, and it has critically important political effects. All of which begs the question of how these processes of differentiation are carried out in practice and why they vary across time and space in the way that they do.

Theoretically, I frame these arguments by drawing on what might be broadly labelled a non-reductionist historical-materialism. I focus in particular on critical engagements with Marx's discussions of primitive accumulation and Gramscian conceptions of the political relations of force and subalternity. This perspective is outlined in greater detail in the following chapter, but in broad strokes the argument runs as follows: Marx's discussions of primitive accumulation centre on the historical processes through which proletarian 'free' labour is formed. Importantly, Marx points to a number of tensions and undercurrents in this process, two of which are particularly important for present purposes: (1) the ambivalent break between 'free' and 'unfree' labour, and (2) the tendency for capitalist accumulation to produce substantial 'relative surplus populations' not engaged in regular work. In both instances, Marx's notes point to fluid and ambiguous, yet politically highly salient, boundaries between normalized and irregular modes of work. While Marx does usefully point to the political character of these boundaries, however, he does not offer much in the way of a substantive framework for thinking through the patterns of mobilization and contestation through which these processes of differentiation take place. Accordingly, I draw on Gramsci's conception of the political relations of force and the subaltern to highlight the ways in which the regulatory establishment of these boundaries is shaped by complex intersections between a diversity of different social forces and sites of political authority arranged across scales.

The approach developed in this book thus departs from some previous historical materialist analyses in that it prioritizes not so much relations *between* classes as struggles *over* class itself. In short, I treat class, and particularly the making and unmaking of working classes as political agents, as something *to be explained*, rather than an explanatory force. How exactly we understand the linkages between proletarian wage labour and other forms of exploitation is not a question that can be settled in the abstract, but rather is a critical object of political contest. Importantly, the production of class in this sense takes place in no small part through dynamic interplays of relations of production and accumulation with struggles over (among other things) race, gender, colonialism, political organization, and citizenship (see Hart 2006; Hall 1980; McNally 2016). All of this implies a fundamentally historical mode of investigation, concerned with the varied and diverse struggles through which working classes are constituted as political actors in different contexts and across multiple scales.

Empirically, I flesh out this argument by drawing on a historical study of the ILO's efforts to regulate forced labour, labour migration, and informal labour in sub-Saharan Africa from 1919-present. The ILO is certainly not the only example that could be drawn on here. The broader phenomenon in question in this book – the governance of irregular labour – is as pervasive as irregular labour itself. It is embodied in highly diverse national and international regulatory and political frameworks around labour migration, 'informal' economies, forced labour and 'slavery', among other things. Nor is sub-Saharan Africa the only place where these questions might be pertinent. Previous excellent studies of the politics of unfreedom and informality in India and Brazil certainly spring to mind (e.g. Brass 1999; McGrath 2013b; Phillips 2013; Agarwala 2013). That said, the ILO's activities in sub-Saharan Africa do offer us a particularly useful set of examples to consider for at least three reasons.

First, the ILO has been at the centre of many key regulatory debates about irregular labour – particularly around forced labour and informal labour – for close to the entirety of its now nearly hundred-year history. We could note how often contemporary activists make reference to the ILO's definition of forced labour, laid out in 1930 by Convention 29 on Forced Labour (C29), in published reports about 'modern slavery' or 'forced labour' to get a sense of how pivotal and pervasive the ILO's influence on these debates can be – including, for instance, both Amnesty International reports cited above (2013; 2016). Equally suggestive might be the role of the ILO's World Employment Programme in popularizing the concept of 'informal' labour. National and local legislation, white papers, and policy frameworks around both issues, in short, frequently make reference to the ILO's conventions and research. The point, in short, is that the ILO has historically been a hugely important player in the governance of irregular labour, and continues to play a significant role. Africa has, moreover, often been central to the ILO's work on these issues. Debates about the use of legal compulsions to work in colonial Africa, especially the dramatic and brutal violence observed in the Belgian Congo and Portuguese colonies in Southern Africa, drove and shaped the development of C29. Equally, it was a WEP mission in Kenya where the ILO first adopted the concept of 'informal' labour. Africa is certainly not the only place where these debates have played out, but it is a significant terrain on which they have taken place.

A second, related, point is that as a result of this long history of activity, studying the ILO's role in governing irregular labour in Africa gives us a relatively deep and rich archive of material with which to work. This is especially important in light of the emphasis I have placed on the pervasive-yet-variegated character of the governance of irregular labour. The relatively broad sweep covered by this book offers a useful means of both tracing out some recurrent common themes and showing a wide range of variation across time and space. Finally, approaching these questions from the angle of 'global' forms of governance, rather than a particular 'national' case study, is useful insofar as it offers a useful lens on the intersections between actors operating on a number of different scales. The upshot of all of this is that, while I certainly wouldn't make the claim that this book exhausts all of the possible case studies that could be used to examine this problem, it does tackle a number of historically important and currently relevant ones. And indeed, their historical significance is sufficient to enable a reasonable claim to the broader applicability of some of the insights offered up by this analysis.

Irregular labour and residualism

Before digging in to the more specific arguments advanced in this book, I begin with a brief diversion into the ways in which irregular forms of labour have typically been understood. This is a useful step because the kind of non-reductionist historical-materialism advanced in this book is needed in part as a corrective to the poverty of existing debates about irregular labour. Broadly, most conceptions of irregular work understand them as resulting from either regulatory failures or from exclusions from 'normal' labour markets. There are plenty of disagreements and debates here, and different analyses imply very different policy prescriptions. But too much of the discussion around precarity, informality, and forced labour shares a tendency to sideline questions around wider structures of production and accumulation. As a result, it is common to overlook the historically pervasive nature of irregular forms of exploitation, treating them instead as aberrant tendencies in which the 'normal' operations of labour markets break down or as conjunctural consequences of regulatory change. Conventional understandings of irregular labour are, in short, often premised on residualist ideas which explain poverty as the result of 'exclusions' from normal patterns of development, rather than accounting for the forms of exploitation and power relations implicit in the normal operations of capitalism that work to produce poverty.[1]

I map out some more specific ways in which the ILO's approaches to forced labour, migration, and unemployment have reflected such residualist ideas in the empirical chapters below. For the moment, I want to underline how much narratives about 'exclusions', from markets and/or regulatory protections, have tended to colour contemporary debates about irregular labour. In particular, I show briefly in turn how debates about precarious labour, informality, and forced labour have often turned on perspectives emphasizing the dual exclusion of workers from state protection and market opportunities. Different authors and institutions place different emphases and articulate different solutions, and these distinctions are often important, but on a fundamental level their arguments share a common, and critical, shortcoming.

It is common to link the contemporary growth of precarious labour to the rollback of statutory labour protections in the neoliberal era. In perhaps the most widely discussed recent example (if hardly the most sophisticated), Guy Standing (2011) attributes the rise of the 'precariat' to policies enacted during the 'globalization era' between the 1970s and the 2008 crisis, 'a period when the economy was disembedded from society as financiers and neoliberal economists sought to create a global market economy based on competitiveness and individualism' (2011: 26). The hollowing out of regulatory protections as a result of this neoliberal agenda has resulted in 'the creation of a global "precariat", consisting of many millions around the world without an anchor of stability' (2011: 1). Precarious work, it follows from this perspective, is a distinctly contemporary phenomenon produced by the removal or hollowing out of regulatory protections. Precarious workers, meanwhile, are those excluded from regulatory protections at national and international levels. This particular brand of residualism has important effects. In the first instance, it offers us a highly-constrained sense of the political possibilities implicit in irregular labour. Standing worries that

> Some whose social and economic situations place them in the precariat have been politically infantilised. They are so anxious and insecure that they are easily seduced to support populist and authoritarian actions towards those depicted as a threat. Many in the precariat have lost (or fear losing) what little they had and are lashing out because they have no politics of paradise to draw them in better directions.
>
> (2011: 153)

Precarity, hence, is implicitly largely reversible by regulatory reforms, but precarious workers themselves are unlikely to be able to push for them without the assistance of government, and might even be susceptible to decidedly non-progressive nativist politics. There are, it is almost needless to say at this point, a lot of problems with this set of claims.[2] For present purposes, though, the most important issue is that understanding precarity as a result of regulatory roll-backs fails to account for the simple fact that precarious forms of labour were predominant in most of the world long before neoliberal reforms (Munck 2013; Harris and Scully 2015). Neoliberal policy prescriptions *have* in fact often constituted an attack of sorts on established labour protections (Bhattacharya 2014), but the resultant deepening and broadening of precarity is more in keeping with the historical norm than a deviation from it. But as long as we frame precarity as a conjunctural phenomenon, as the by-product of the political agenda of 'financiers and neoliberal economists', we miss its more fundamental, even integral relationship to capitalist relations of production.

Much the same could be said about debates about informality. There are real debates here between perspectives that tend to celebrate the virtues of 'informality', often drawing on the language of 'entrepreneurship' and those that seek to extend regulatory protections to 'informal' work. This debate has taken place, however, against the backdrop of a common residualist understanding of 'informality'. As Roitman notes, 'informal' spheres 'are delineated and analyzed as reactions to state and formal market "failures"'; the concept of 'informal' work thus virtually always describes an *absence* (1990: 679). This residualism manifests itself in different ways, but is a central assumption of most mainstream perspectives on informal labour (see Bernards 2017a). Discussions of the informal economy at the ILO, on one hand, tend to emphasize the exclusion of informal workers from opportunities in the formal economy and more importantly from regulatory protections and social security (see ILO 2002; 2014a). In 2002, for instance, in a report on *Decent Work and the Informal Sector*, the relationship between informal work and 'globalization', is described as follows: 'Where the informal sector is linked to globalization, it is often because a developing country has been excluded from integration into the global economy' (ILO 2002: 34). The ILO suggests that these 'exclusions' from the global economy are compounded by failures in governance. The recent report on 'transitions' to formality is quite explicit on this point:

'Informality is principally a governance issue' (ILO 2014a: 7). The upshot is that the ILO emphasizes the promotion of 'formal' job opportunities:

> A new consensus has emerged around the belief that if economic growth is not associated with formal job creation, a shift towards better employment opportunities in the formal economy and an improvement in the conditions of employment in informal activities, it will continue to generate inequality, poverty and vulnerability.
>
> (ILO 2002: 10)

The main alternative to the ILO's perspective in discussions of informal labour is the brand of institutional economics popularized by Hernando de Soto (2000) and widely adopted by the World Bank. Here 'informality' becomes a form of poor people's empowerment in the face of overregulation by the state, a reflection of entrepreneurial instincts to be encouraged by developing appropriate institutions. Policy initiatives to promote micro-enterprise development, access to credit, skills, and property rights follow logically from this way of thinking about the 'informal'. Here again, though, informality is understood in terms of exclusion from the normal operation of market forces. The World Bank in particular has often promoted policy initiatives along these lines (see Maloney 2004). Breman and van der Linden (2014), indeed, detect in the Bank's initiatives here a wider-reaching 'project of informalization' aimed at extending liberal fantasies about facilitating 'entrepreneurial' drives through the deregulation of labour markets and facilitation of access to credit and property rights.

There is somewhat of a debate here about what kinds of policies are needed to 'formalize' informal labour (although in practice the lines are often rather blurred, see Chapter 6). The ILO's perspective implies a greater emphasis on enforcement of labour regulations and the expansion of social protection, while the de Soto inspired approach is more inclined to celebrate informality and call for better institutions (especially access to credit and training) to bring 'informal' economies into 'formal' markets. Ultimately, though, both are deeply limited insofar as they skirt questions of exploitation, about the relationships between informality and structural changes in the global political economy, and about the fluid boundaries between 'formal' and 'informal' work.

The de Soto-modelled agenda of property rights, credit, and the like has often deepened relations of poverty in practice. Programmes for the privatization or formalization of property rights in informal settlements, where the vast majority of informal businesses are located, have been linked to the exacerbation of inequalities and forms of exploitation within informal economies, particularly by empowering landlords at the expense of tenants (see Desai and Loftus 2013). The extension of commercial credit to 'informal' businesses, in the context of increasingly precarious labour markets, is liable to produce deepening patterns of indebtedness and exploitation – a point well-made in critical commentary on the broader agenda of 'financial inclusion' (e.g. Soederberg 2014). The ILO's 'formalization' agenda is perhaps less prone to such unintended consequences, but still eschews much serious consideration of the roots of urban poverty. Better enforcement of labour standards is a good thing, but does not in itself address the broader patterns of dispossession that lead to the emergence of the kinds of activities that Davis (2006) usefully labels 'survivalist improvisations'.

Much the same could also be said about prevailing conceptions of forced labour. Liberal perspectives on forced labour, of which the most widely cited exponent is probably Kevin Bales (2008), have similarly tended to emphasize the exclusion of 'modern slaves' from the normal operations of the market. Globalization, coupled with rapid population growth in the developing world, for Bales, has resulted in a situation in which 'traditional' ways of life are increasingly displaced by 'modern' markets, and 'the poor have fewer and fewer options. Amid the rapid disruptions of social change, one of those options is slavery' (2008: 13). There are, incidentally, more than minor echoes of interwar colonialism's reformist rhetorics about forced labour, slavery, and modernity here (discussed Chapter 2). Unfreedom, and poverty more generally, is a product of being 'left out' by the advance of modern capitalism. Bales equally puts considerable emphasis on the role of governance failures in allowing 'new slavery' to persist. The decentralization of the state's monopoly of violence, in the form of a 'transfer of the monopoly of violence from central government to localized thugs is essential if the new slavery is to take root and flourish' (2008: 30). Here again, forced labour is understood as a product of exclusions from the 'normal' operations of market economies and from statutory protections. As I argue further in Chapters 2 and 5, these twin dimensions of exclusion have equally been central to the ILO's views on forced labour. Here again, this residualist understanding of unfreedom raises similar kinds of problems as in discussions of precarity or informality. It lends itself to half-solutions – as with informality, it points to 'better enforcement' as a solution – and elides the connections between the dynamics of capitalist production and accumulation and the use of violent coercion in recruitment and labour discipline. In Lerche's (2007) useful phrase, it serves to rhetorically 'cocoon' unfree labour from capitalism.

I am hardly the first to point any of this out. It has been common for critical perspectives to take Standing, de Soto, Bales, and the policy approaches they have often inspired to task because they are inattentive to the production of informal economies, forced labour, unemployment, and migration through capitalist relations of production. Much of the critical literature in IPE and linked disciplines on forced labour (e.g. Phillips and Mieres 2015; Lerche 2007; Rogaly 2008; LeBaron and Ayers 2013; LeBaron 2014a; Phillips 2013) and informal labour (e.g. Meagher 2005; Rizzo 2011; Taylor 2010; Phillips 2011) takes precisely this tack. These arguments aren't new either. Critics of the ILO's (1972) World Employment Programme (WEP) mission to Kenya, for instance, made very similar arguments 30–40 years ago, noting the inattention of the ILO's account of informality to structural forces within and beyond the Kenyan economy that underlaid 'informal' work (e.g. Leys 1973; Sandbrook 1983; see also Chapter 4). These are all compelling critiques. They perform useful services in subjecting the policy ideas produced by the World Bank, ILO, and national governments to critical scrutiny and highlighting the ways in which various irregular forms of labour are linked to the reproduction of global capitalism. It is, without doubt, well worth it to point out that the ILO or the World Bank has a limited, residualist, understanding of 'informal labour' or 'modern slavery'.

But critical analyses too often stop at this point. The actual processes by which residualist understandings of irregular labour have been developed, contested, and translated across time and space – in a word, the *practice* of governing irregular labour – have largely escaped serious critical attention. There is an implicit understanding of governance at work in many of these perspectives that often winds up curtailing the scope of critical work. Governance is seen as something that reacts upon more or less accurate images of the world of production and accumulation. The latter are (often implicitly) understood as ontologically separate from processes of governance. The integral but fraught role of regulatory processes in producing the boundaries between 'normal' and 'irregular' forms of labour, and in securing the reproduction of prevailing modes of accumulation in the process, has not been examined in much theoretical or empirical detail. It is from this point, then, where this book builds on previous critical analysis.

History, scale, and method

A couple of words are perhaps in order about the method adopted in making the argument in this way. First, the historical lens adopted here is at once very broad – covering close to 100 years' worth of developments across an entire continent – and very narrow – zooming in on a series of particular key debates, documents, and policy missions, carried out in particular times and places. The spatial frame of analysis also frequently telescopes between global, national, and local scales of action. The empirical chapters generally move in chronological order, but not according to a strict periodization. There are a number of reasons for this. One is simply empirical – labour regulation in general and the governance of irregular labour in particular are distinctly multi-scalar phenomena. The ILO's activities tend to skip from one place to the next, and move between a 'global' frame of reference and efforts to engage in particular places. Equally, while the ILO itself and its advocates often seek to smooth out the organization's history – as in, say, references to the ILO's 'constant mission' to abolish forced labour (e.g. Maul 2007) – the reality is that this history is somewhat lumpy. Ideas and concerns tend to ebb and flow with broader shifts in global and local political contexts and changing patterns of production. Concerns about forced labour, for instance, were acute in the 1920s and 1930s, briefly in the 1950s (although primarily focused on the Soviet Union), and again in the 2000s. They don't appear much on the ILO's agenda aside from a few isolated incidents in the intervening years. The concept of 'informal' labour was initially coined and popularized in the early 1970s (Hart 1973; ILO 1972), and renewed with gusto (albeit with somewhat different framings with different policy implications) in the 1990s and 2000s. It spoke, however, to a set of concerns about rural-urban migration that had been expressed in different terms since the 1950s. The somewhat mobile and flexible lens adopted here is also useful given the book's emphasis on the persistent-but-variable character of precarity and violence. Efforts to govern irregular labour are at once necessary to the reproduction of capitalism but deeply shaped by the particular political relations of force within which they are rolled out at any given moment, exploring the different manifestations of ILO activity in different places and times is a useful means of exploring these patterns of similarity and difference.

Equally, it is worth underlining why the historical chapters of this book rely on archival and documentary research. Simply put, such sources offer the best window on the day-to-day work of governing irregular labour, and particularly of the ambiguities and controversies bound up in the process. Archival sources and other preparatory documents are useful means of accessing debates that are often airbrushed out or minimized in finished regulatory devices or policy recommendations. If we want to get beyond critiques of the ILO or World Bank's policy frameworks and towards a theoretical and empirical understanding of the real historical *practice* of governing irregular labour, these sources are invaluable.

Beyond the immediate debates and concerns addressed, this book makes a pair of significant contributions to the literature in critical international political economy (IPE) more broadly. Most importantly, the book contributes to a recent (and much needed) revival of interest in the global dimensions of labour issues in IPE. The question of how different forms of labour relations relate to the reproduction of world order was crucial in the development of critical IPE, but has largely been sidelined. It is very much at the core of Robert Cox's seminal (1987) *Production, Power, and World Order*. Indeed, Cox's first use of the concept of 'hegemony' came in an article primarily about the ILO (Cox 1977), and a companion volume to Cox's book focused on the place of 'unprotected' work in the reproduction and transformation of world order (Harrod 1987). But where the concept of 'hegemony' in Cox's work, and more broadly the emphasis on forms of domination and discipline have been widely examined (e.g. Gill 1995), far fewer writers have seriously taken up Cox's attention to work (Moore 2012; Phillips 2016). More recent contributions, discussed above, have examined the dynamics of unfree labour and the expansion of informal work in the context of neoliberalism and globalizing relations of production, along with broader efforts to re-situate labour relations in analyses of development (Selwyn 2014) and world order (Gray 2014). Few attempts, however, have been made to trace out the ways in which irregular forms of work has been regulated over a longer time-frame.

This book also offers a novel perspective on global governance. Where critical perspectives in IPE, from Cox (1987) onwards, have usefully pointed to the role of global governance in securing the reproduction of existing forms of domination and modes of accumulation (e.g. Gill 1995; Cutler 2003), they have not often been sufficiently attentive to the complexities involved in the practice of governance itself. In particular, critical perspectives on global governance have often been too quick to assume that 'global' forms of power exert a kind of disciplinary influence over 'local' actors, without often tracing out the complex struggles through which 'global' frameworks are enacted in 'local' spaces. The Gramscian concepts of the political relations of force and subalternity adapted here are particularly helpful in highlighting the complex range of intersecting political struggles involved in enacting 'global' policy frameworks in particular places.

Plan of the book

The core arguments in this book are fleshed out over the next six chapters. Chapter 1 fleshes out the theoretical framework around which the rest of the book is articulated. As noted above, it does so drawing primarily on Marx and Gramsci to examine the ways in which irregular forms of labour are reproduced within capitalist relations of production and the implications of these processes for governance.

The remaining five empirical chapters are organized (mostly) in chronological order, although the narrative does overlap in a few places. Chapter 2 traces the emergence and evolution of the ILO's conventions on forced labour, focusing on a number of controversies over their application in colonial Africa. The chapter begins by situating the origins of the ILO in the context of broader changes in the structures of world order in the early twentieth century. While the ILO was primarily intended to deal with problems of 'social peace' in Europe in the aftermath of WWI and especially the Russian Revolution in 1917, it also operated in a context in which labour issues in colonial territories were difficult to escape. In particular, I highlight a fundamental tension in colonial labour practices between the reliance on abolitionist discourses highlighting the elimination of indigenous forms of slavery as a crucial ideological justification of imperial rule on one hand and the growing reliance of colonial administrations and private investors on various forms of coercive labour recruitment on the other. The chapter then moves on to consider patterns of contestation around colonial labour practices that emerged at the ILO in the 1920s. The ILO's leadership seized on the issue of forced labour as a means of articulating a limited, reformist agenda for colonial oversight. In particular, by framing 'forced labour' as a temporary expedient that would be gradually eliminated with the further development of colonial economies, and whose worst excesses could be managed by international supervision, the ILO's approach sought to limit the scope of political contestation around colonial labour practices by differentiating certain practices from the 'normal' operations of capitalism. The chapter concludes by tracing out some patterns of contestation around the application of the ILO's standards on forced labour by tracing out a particularly longstanding controversy: whether or not the migrant labour system in South Africa constituted a form of forced labour. Activists in South Africa and Europe sought to mobilize the 1930 convention against forced labour, as well as the process of debating the ILO's second convention on forced labour eventually adopted in 1956, to challenge South African labour practices. While the ILO never conclusively condemned the migrant labour system, these patterns of contestation reveal the fragility of the boundary between 'free' and 'forced' labour, and the ways in which the maintenance of that boundary is bound up with broader patterns of relations of political forces.

Chapter 3 returns to the period during and after WWII. It traces the ILO's role in broader colonial struggles to manage the process of urbanization and the role of rural-urban migrant labour in postwar Africa. It highlights the interplay of workers' mobilization, efforts to preserve fragile colonial authority, and efforts to draw a line between a small segment of recognizably 'working-class' Africans and a larger, ostensibly 'tribal', surplus population. It focuses in particular on debates at the ILO and at a number of linked colonial policy networks, most notably the Inter-African Labour Conference (IALC), over the governance of rural-urban labour migration in the final years of colonial rule. These debates turned on a conflict between colonial authorities who sought to ensure that African workers did not permanently settle in cities, particularly through the implementation of a system of pass laws and migrant labour on the South African model, and those who sought to 'stabilize' a small urban working class through the adoption of 'non-political' trade unionism and the extension of social policy. In no small part, this debate was decided in favour of the stabilizing option (outside the apartheid states in Southern Africa at least) by workers' own actions – most notably a region-wide string of general strikes through the late 1940s and 1950s and the increasingly close (if often conflictual) relations between workers' movements and broader resistance to colonial rule. However, constructions of race and gender had a significant influence on the trajectory of the debate at the ILO and IALC.

Chapter 4 turns to the legacies of these struggles in postcolonial Africa. It begins by briefly tracing how the conflicts outlined in the previous chapters remained unsettled after formal decolonization. In particular, the relationships between the very small contingents of organized labour and the very large surplus populations in most African countries posed significant political challenges in terms of the relationship of organized labour to the state and with other subaltern social forces. The chapter then turns to the diffusion of the concept of 'informal' labour through the work of the ILO's WEP in Kenya. It briefly traces the continuities between the ILO's conception of unemployment in the early 1970s and the colonial discourses analyzed in the previous chapter. The policy prescription implicit in WEP was different – generating more jobs as opposed to stabilizing a segment of the workforce – but the same underlying fears of overly rapid urbanization, dangerous slums, and disorder were always present. This approach was largely at odds with the understandings of development promoted by many African governments, which increasingly emphasized structural impediments to growth in the global economy, but the programme was nonetheless very popular in the region. I argue that this seeming puzzle is best explained with reference to ongoing struggles to organize and discipline irregular labour on one hand and to constrain the political and economic role of organized labour on the other. It then moves on to examine the WEP's landmark mission to Kenya in 1971, which played a major role in popularizing the concept of 'informal' labour (see Bernards 2017a). The concept of 'informal' labour articulated a residualist understanding of unemployment that meshed well with state efforts to restrain the cost of labour and limit the political influence of organized labour. This point is underlined by the highly selective implementation of the recommendations of the WEP report and by a number of controversies relating to this implementation.

14 *Introduction*

The final two chapters both deal with the governance of irregular labour in neoliberal Africa. Chapter 5 examines contemporary interventions dealing with 'informal' work. It shows how efforts to govern irregular labour have been intimately connected to efforts to mitigate what might be called the 'organic crisis of the postcolonial state' in neoliberal Africa. While the ILO's interventions dealing with informal economies and unemployment have remained coloured by residualist ideas, the political dynamics engendered by this organic crisis have often heavily influenced the specific shape of the ILO's interventions in practice. The chapter examines a pair of projects. First, it examines the development of a project on 'Upgrading Informal Apprenticeships' operate by the ILO in Eastern and Southern Africa (see Bernards 2017a). The project originated in Tanzania, which is the main focus of the analysis here. The ILO's project has emphasized the improvement of institutions governing apprenticeships in the informal sector. However, in terms of the actual implementation of follow-up initiatives, many of the concerns raised in the initial report about exploitation and the rules around graduation have largely fallen from view. The much stronger emphasis in Tanzania has been placed on programmes for the 'Recognition of Prior Learning' (RPL) and certification. My analysis situates these dynamics in the context of wider state strategies around the 'formalization' of informal economies and political struggles over the status of 'informal' workers. Second, it traces the development of microinsurance policies in Francophone West Africa (see Bernards 2016), linking the trajectory of this development to broader struggles over the authority of the state engendered by the widespread informalization of labour. I examine the history of ILO efforts to promote alternate forms of social security for informal workers, highlighting the organization's movement in the 1990s towards 'community'-based programmes. I then focus in the latter part of the section on developments relating to microinsurance in Senegal. The Senegalese microinsurance policy involves delegating social protection for informal and agricultural workers primarily to the voluntary sector, but in a way that is actively organized, through a variety of education programmes, subsidies, and regulatory mechanisms, by the state.

The final chapter examines the revival of the ILO's efforts to govern forced labour, focusing in particular on the ways in which residualist understandings of forced labour have remained embedded in the ILO's approach to forced labour. It proceeds by exploring a pair of contemporary projects in West Africa – one dealing with 'traditional' slavery in Niger (see Bernards 2017b) and another set of projects on child trafficking. The chapter opens by situating the revival of forced labour at the ILO in the context of the organization's response to neoliberalism. It highlights the ways in which the erosion of social democratic industrial relations, the declining status of workers' organizations in the 'core', a growing emphasis on securitized approaches to human trafficking and migration, and shifting patterns of unfree labour have combined to shape the ILO's contemporary approach to forced labour. It moves on to briefly outline the ILO's revived agenda on forced labour, particularly in the form of the Special Action Programme on Forced Labour (SAP-FL). This section outlines ways in which residualist assumptions about the relationships between poverty and forced labour are embodied in the

ILO's programming under SAP-FL and related programmes. These programmes work to identify the persistence of forced labour with 'exclusions' from markets and formal governance, and hence articulates a particular vision identifying the interests of subaltern social forces with the extension of capitalism. The remainder of the chapter then traces out the ways in which these assumptions have played out in two different projects. First, it examines a project dealing with 'traditional slavery' in Niger. I show how the reliance of these interventions on the concept of 'traditional slavery' has tended to obscure the linkages between transformations in existing forms of unfree labour and the process of structural adjustment and neoliberalization. But at the same time, the politics of governing forced labour has been rather more complex than this critique implies, with ongoing struggles over the shape of the postcolonial state playing a critical role in shaping and delimiting the practice of ILO interventions. Finally, it traces ILO efforts to govern child trafficking in West Africa, focusing on a major regional project called 'Combatting the Trafficking of Children for Labour Exploitation in West and Central Africa', (referred to by the French acronym LUTRENA) and its successors. It shows how residualist understandings of child trafficking, again emphasizing exclusions from the market and the weaknesses of border enforcement, are embodied in the activities of the programme. Major components of the ILO's interventions have entailed promoting 'income generating activities' in vulnerable communities as well as promoting more effective policing of trafficking through interactions with security forces in the region. Here again, however, residualist conceptions of forced labour are mobilized through more complex configurations of relations of political forces in practice.

Notes

1 On residualism and 'exclusion'-based understandings of poverty, see (among others) Du Toit (2004); Wood (2003); Phillips (2013); and Byrne (1999).
2 Most notable, perhaps, a number of authors have pointed out his conceptually problematic claim that the 'precariat' constitutes a 'new class' (Breman 2013; Wright 2016); his empirically and theoretically questionable assertion that the 'precariat' are a 'dangerous' class especially subject to demagogic or tribalist politics (Munck 2013; Chun 2016), and the Eurocentric focus of his argument (Scully 2016a).

1 Irregular labour in global capitalism

As I noted in the introduction, irregular forms of labour are neither new nor exceptional. If we think in global terms, it is likely that for most of the last few hundred years the majority of the world's workers have been engaged in forms of work other than the kinds of stable, permanent jobs for defined wages that we often consider 'normal' forms of work. Understandings of irregular labour – whether framed in terms of precarity, 'modern slavery', 'informal' labour, or otherwise – have tended to ignore this point. Irregular forms of labour are often understood as aberrant or exceptional, resulting from exclusions from 'normal' labour markets and regulatory protections. Previous critics have, rightly in my view, highlighted the shortcomings of such residualist perspectives. However, previous critical writing has not involved much sustained reflection on the political significance of these residualist ideas themselves, or of the processes by which they have been rolled out in policy frameworks globally and in particular places. In short, the governance of irregular labour – the process of defining and regulating various non-standard forms of work – has often been critiqued, but rarely theorized in its own right.

This chapter, accordingly, outlines a different framework for thinking through the politics of irregular labour. I draw on two main theoretical resources in developing this approach. In the first section below, Marx's discussions of 'primitive accumulation' serve to highlight the ways in which the historical production of 'free' wage labour is an ambiguous and fraught process which depends on the one hand on the production of differentiated forms of coercion and exploitation and on the other on the political 'naturalization' of some of these forms. The governance of irregular labour, in short, is fundamentally entwined with struggles over the differentiation and naturalization of particular forms of exploitation in particular historical circumstances. Marx's notes very usefully suggest (1) a tendency towards the production of irregular forms of work through the dynamics of capitalist accumulation, and (2) the political significance of drawing boundaries between 'normal' and 'irregular' forms of work. However, he does not give us much in the way of theoretical or methodological guidance as to how to analyze the latter. Accordingly, I draw in the second part of the chapter on Gramsci's methodological discussions on the study of subaltern classes, the 'relations of political force', and the international. Central to Gramsci's approach here is an emphasis on the ongoing construction of class through political action. Gramsci takes 'class' in this sense as a fundamentally fluid and *political* category, one whose historical emergence is highly context-dependent and (by extension) inextricably bound up with race, gender, and nationality. Class is made and unmade through the dialectic between shifting patterns of political mobilization, which turn on clashing images of solidarity and constructions of group identity mobilized through the institutions of civil society, and the construction of political authority on the other. Gramsci's notes on internationalism, importantly, suggest that such struggles play out simultaneously across multiple scales, and are bound up in variable ways with broader patterns of political authority within and beyond the state.

Irregular labour and the undercurrents of primitive accumulation

I argue in this section that Marx offers us a number of useful clues through which we can situate the persistence and transformation of irregular labour in the context of the reproduction of capitalist accumulation. The reading of Marx presented here highlights the *political, contingent, and contested* nature of the differentiation of 'normalized' and 'irregular' forms of labour exploitation. In brief, the historical progression of capitalist accumulation tends to produce a variety of different forms of exploitation, of which free wage labour is perhaps theoretically central, sometimes the predominant mode of exploitation in practice, but hardly ever the only. The ways in which particular forms of exploitation are naturalized and differented from the broader matrix of forms of exploitation is thus a crucial axis of political contention.

Of course, on many readings Marx equates the advance of capitalism with the formation of proletarian labour relations. The *Communist Manifesto* certainly seems to suggest as much: 'In proportion as the bourgeoisie, i.e. capital, is developed, in the same proportion is the proletariat, the modern working class developed' (Marx and Engels 2004: 227–228). It is not uncommon for later Marxists to lean on a similar sort of interpretation of the relationship between proletarian working relations and capitalism. Cammack (2004), for instance, locates in the World Bank's 'Post-Washington Consensus' programmes the highest form of a project for the formation of a proletarian working class on a global scale. In the works of 'political Marxists' (e.g. Wood 2002), the bifurcation of politics and economics is the key moment in the origins of capitalism, such that 'extra-economic' forms of coercion are (by definition) 'pre-capitalist'. Yet these formulations of the problem of proletarianization, seem (perhaps ironically) to imply a similar kind of residualism to that implicit in the mainstream perspectives outlined in the introduction: those forms of non-wage or unfree labour that still exist are results of the still incomplete expansion of capitalism. A different reading of Marx, I argue, is more productive for present purposes insofar as it casts capitalist accumulation as a contingent process that tends to reproduce various forms of irregular labour alongside proletarian free labour. A useful starting point here is Marx's writing on 'so-called primitive accumulation'.

Marx's analysis of primitive accumulation does equate of the origins of capitalism with the process of proletarianization – the formation of 'free' labour in the double sense of workers free to contract with employers and 'free' of any non-market means of securing their reproduction. Marx begins his observations on the historic origins of capitalism by suggesting that there is a certain paradox in the fact that capitalist accumulation seems to presuppose itself: 'The accumulation of capital presupposes surplus-value; surplus value presupposes capitalist production; capitalist production presupposes the availability of considerable masses of capital and labour power in the hands of commodity producers' (1990: 873). The 'primitive accumulation' of capital, then, is the process by which the particular historical conditions that make it possible to set this cycle in motion are created. Capital, for Marx, can exist 'only under particular circumstances, which meet together at this point: the confrontation of, and contact between, two very different kinds of commodity owners; on the one hand, the owners of money, means of production, means of subsistence . . . on the other hand, free workers, the sellers of their own labour power' (1990: 874). Fundamentally, then, the process of 'primitive accumulation' is the process by which 'free' labourers are created. Marx's discussion of primitive accumulation could thus be taken to imply a unidirectional movement towards proletarian 'free' labour. There is certainly a tendency in some of Marx's writing on primitive accumulation to consign it to the originary moments of capitalism. This impression is reinforced by the decision to concentrate most of his empirical discussion on England, where Marx thought we could find find the process of primitive accumulation in its most fully developed 'classic form' (1990: 876).

However, if we dig a bit deeper, there are significant complexities to the way that Marx tells this story. In the first instance, as Glassman notes, Marx's heavy emphasis on the proletarianizing dimensions of primitive accumulation was driven to a considerable extent by political rather than analytical concerns:

> In spite of mentioning its multidimensional character . . . Marx's discussion of primitive accumulation focuses largely on proletarianization, since he is pre-eminently concerned with the formation of what he takes to be the most revolutionary subjects and the issues over which they struggle.
>
> (2006: 611)

In practice, 'proletarianization seems much more a contingent outcome of specific class struggles than a predetermined trajectory for capitalist development' (2006: 616). More importantly, we can usefully develop an alternative reading emphasizing the fundamentally *historical*, and hence contingent and inevitably incomplete nature of the process. In introducing the discussion of primitive accumulation, Marx avers that the process of primitive accumulation 'assumes different aspects in different countries, and runs through its various phases in different orders of succession, and at different historical epochs' (1990: 876). Indeed, he hints that proletarianization is reversible: in a footnote, he contrasts the 'classical' form of primitive accumulation in England to the process in Italy, where after the collapse of the commercial supremacy of the northern-Italian city-states in the late fifteenth century 'the urban workers were driven *en masse* into the countryside, and gave a previously unheard-of impulse to small-scale cultivation, carried on in the form of market gardening' (1990: 876, n.1). More substantially, Marx implicitly or explicitly highlights a number of tensions and undercurrents throughout his discussion that are both vitally bound up in the historical processes of primitive accumulation and continually undercut the progress of proletarianization. The point is that the process of 'primitive accumulation' is a continual and partial achievement (see also De Angelis 2004; Read 2002). This understanding of proletarianization as a fraught, contradictory, and inevitably partial process offers us a useful starting place from which to think about the place of irregular labour in capitalist circuits of accumulation. Two dynamics are particularly important: (1) the ambivalent and incomplete nature of the 'freeing' of labour, and (2) the tendency of capitalist accumulation to create 'relative surplus populations'.

The ambivalence of 'free' labour

The first notable point here is that Marx highlights a number of critical ambivalences in the category of 'free' labour as a form of exploitative labour relations and its relationship to capitalist accumulation. Most notably, these include a number of ways in which violently coerced labour contributes to the process of capitalist accumulation, and more fundamentally a number of crucial ambiguities in the distinction between 'free' and other forms of labour.[1] I briefly discuss the latter first, followed by the former.

Marx notes in introducing his discussion of primitive accumulation that 'The starting point of the development that gave rise to both the wage-labourer and the capitalist was the *enslavement* of the worker. The advance made *consisted in a change in the form of this servitude*' (1990: 875, emphasis added). The equation of wage labour to slavery is in fact a rhetorical theme he comes back to often. Elsewhere, he argues that while 'The Roman slave was held by chains; the wage-labourer is bound to his owner by invisible threads. The *appearance of independence* is maintained by a constant change in the individual employer, and by the legal fiction of a contract' (1990: 719, emphasis added). Indeed, even the nominal freedom on offer in the labour market is contrasted with the coercive discipline necessary in the process of production itself: 'In the factory code, the capitalist formulates his autocratic power over his workers like a private legislator, and purely as an emanation of his own will ... The overseer's book replaces the slave-driver's lash' (1990: 549–550).

Of course, these references to slavery are partly polemical flourishes. There are unquestionably significant differences between the types of coercion implicit in 'free' wage labour and those involved in, say, chattel slavery. However, the critical implication here is that the difference consists in the *form* of coercion through which exploitative relations of production are organized, rather than the *existence* of coercion in and of itself. The point here is that, for Marx, the process of proletarianization is not a clear-cut historical progression from 'unfreedom' to 'freedom', nor indeed of 'economic' for 'extra-economic' forms of coercion, but rather a (partial) substitution of more explicit forms of violent compulsion to work for the 'silent compulsion' of the market (see Banaji 2003; Bernards 2017b; Rioux 2013). Further, as Marx's heavy emphasis on the acts of enclosure in England in his historical discussion makes very clear, the very creation of the latter form of indirect or 'economic' coercion was only actually possible on the basis of an ongoing and violent process of expropriation backed by state force. The actual historical 'freeing' of labour is underpinned by violent transformations in the legal and political framework of property relations: 'The expropriation of the agricultural producer . . . from the soil is the basis of the whole process' (1990: 876). Viewed from this perspective, 'free' and 'unfree' labour are better viewed as points on a continuum, rather than discrete categories (LeBaron and Ayers 2013; LeBaron 2014a). Coercion in capitalism is also best understood as multidimensional, involving many different forms of violence (McGrath 2013a). In brief, *all* forms of capitalist labour relations involve some element of coercion. There are few, if any, specific forms of such coercion that could unproblematically be labelled 'forced labour' *a priori*; rather, the definition of both 'free' and 'forced' labour is both fundamentally political and contested.

Moreover, when viewed from the perspective of global circuits of accumulation, even the substitution of the silent compulsion of the market for other forms of coercion itself is hardly ever complete. The process of primitive accumulation in England itself, Marx suggests, was heavily dependent on the use of violently coerced labour elsewhere in the world. Marx notes that the formation of capitalism in Europe coincides with 'the discovery of gold and silver in America, the extirpation, enslavement, and entombment in mines of the indigenous population of that continent, the beginnings of the conquest and plunder of India, and the conversion of Africa into a preserve for the commercial hunting of blackskins' (1990: 915). In short, the historical genesis of capitalist accumulation depended on the incorporation of a variety of different unfree forms of labour (especially chattel slavery). In Marx's words, 'the veiled slavery of the wage-labourers in Europe needed the unqualified slavery of the new world as its pedestal' (1990: 925). We can point to a number of historical examples of these kinds of relationships between industrial capitalism and various forms of violent coercion. Indeed, as noted in the introduction, the integration of plantation slavery into the circuits of British-led industrial capitalism had concrete impacts on the organization of work in American slave economies (McMichael 1991). These arguments are echoed in significant ways by Luxemburg's arguments about the incorporation of 'non-capitalist' forms of exploitation into global processes of capitalist accumulation. Luxemburg notes that 'The process of accumulation . . . requires inevitably free access to ever new areas of raw materials in case of need' (2003: 338). She offers the example of

> The enormous increase in the world consumption of rubber which at present (1912) necessitates a supply of latex to the value of £50,000,000 per annum.

> The economic basis for the production of raw materials is a primitive system of exploitation practised by European capital in the African colonies and in America, where the institutions of slavery and bondage are combined in various forms.
>
> (2003: 339)

In more contemporary terms, a number of authors have noted the incorporation of various forms of coercive exploitation (in recruiting, during the labour process, or both) into global production networks for products as varied as cocoa (Manzo 2005), ethanol fuels (McGrath 2013b), and electronics (Pun and Smith 2007). Phillips (2013) usefully argues in this context that contemporary instances of 'unfree' labour should be understood as so many forms of 'adverse incorporation' into the global economy. Indeed, critically, from the perspective of individual workers, the boundaries between 'free' and 'unfree' forms of exploitation are not so clear cut. Unfree forms of labour draw from the same pools of labour*ers* as 'free' labour – Breman and Guérin note that bonded labourers in India have tended to be drawn from the same social formations as agrarian workers more generally – a 'huge reserve army of labour to be hired and fired according to the need of the moment, in agriculture but increasingly also in other economic sectors' (Breman and Guérin 2009: 3). Various forms of unfreedom, indeed, have also been deployed as disciplinary tactics on workers more broadly under capitalist relations of production. Brass (1999; 2010; 2014) – drawing on studies of bonded labour in India – argues that unfreedom has often served as a mechanism for 'deproletarianization'; in short, as a means of disciplining and cheapening 'free' labour by re-instating violent coercion in place of the 'silent compulsion' of the market.[2]

The point here is that a diversity of different forms of coercion have been deployed in the process of capitalist production and accumulation across a variety of different historical contexts. There is no single form of unfreedom that is integral to capitalist production, nor any single pathway by which unfree labour is bound up in capitalist accumulation, but the substitution of the 'silent compulsion' of the market for more explicit forms of coercion is scarcely ever total (*cf.* de Angelis 2004). Forms of labour exploitation rooted in violent coercion are not incompatible with capitalism and not a result of the 'exclusion' of certain spaces from the world economy. In any event, the boundary between 'free' and 'unfree' or 'forced' labour is blurry at best. All of this has a critically important implication: the binary between 'free' and 'forced' labour, or between 'economic' and 'non-economic' coercion, is fundamentally a historical and *political* one. It is rooted not in any *a priori* or abstract distinction between different phenomenal forms of work organization, but rather in political struggles over which forms of coercion are acceptable and how we understand the linkages between those (normalized) forms of exploitation that are and those (irregularized) forms that are not. The notion of a distinction between 'free' and 'unfree' forms of labour, in short, is in no small part produced through the governance of irregular labour.

Relative surplus populations

The ambivalence of 'freedom' in this sense is significant in terms of how we understand the politics of many forms of irregular labour. But even the operation of the 'silent compulsion' of the market has important tendencies towards the production of irregular work. These are very strongly hinted at in Marx's writing on 'relative surplus populations'. Marx introduces the latter concept in the chapter prior to his discussions on primitive accumulation, dealing with what he calls the 'General Law of Capitalist Accumulation'. These chapters are tightly linked insofar as they stem from a similar preoccupation with the actual historical and dynamic production and reproduction of capitalist social relations, and the respective chapters are extensively cross-referenced. In brief, the concept of 'relative surplus populations' is relevant for present purposes because Marx's discussion here suggests that not only is proletarianization a perpetually incomplete process, but indeed that it often *needs to be so* for the continued reproduction of capitalist accumulation. Marx notes in his discussion of primitive accumulation that as capitalist production develops, 'the constant generation of a relative surplus population keeps the law of supply and demand of labour, and therefore wages, within narrow limits which correspond to capital's valorization requirements' (1990: 899). The 'silent compulsion' of the market *requires* that a considerable portion of working classes at any point in time are in fact not directly employed in capitalist enterprises or cycle in and out of the workforce – or, in contemporary terms, are engaged in forms of work we would deem 'informal' or 'precarious'. In short, Marx usefully suggests that the process of proletarianization is dependent, paradoxically, on the constant construction of non-working populations.[3]

Marx identifies a number of different forces in capitalist accumulation that tend to create relative surplus populations. He introduces the concept by linking it to cyclical patterns of technological innovation and crisis. Marx argues that:

> The path characteristically described by modern industry, which takes the form of a decennial cycle . . . of periods of average activity, production at high pressure, crisis, and stagnation, depends on the constant formation, the greater or less absorption, and the re-formation of the industrial reserve army or surplus population.
>
> (1990: 785)

Significantly, the production of this surplus population is part and parcel of the broader process of primitive accumulation – the accumulation of capital continually coming 'up against a natural barrier in the shape of the exploitable working population; this barrier could only be swept away by . . . violent means' (1990: 785). In any event, though, the 'silent coercion' implicit in processes of proletarianization is fundamentally dependent on the production of non-working populations. This need is particularly acute where the process of proletarianization is more tenuous: Marx notes that in colonial territories, capital 'seeks for artificial means to secure the poverty of the people' (1990: 932) in order to create the conditions for accumulation. Where 'adverse circumstance prevent the creation of an industrial reserve army, and with it the absolute dependence of the working class upon the capitalist class, capital . . . rebels against the "sacred" law of supply and demand, and tries to make up for its inadequacies by force' (1990: 794).

As with his discussion of primitive accumulation, Marx understands the actual formation of relative surplus populations as a highly variegated and fundamentally historical phenomenon. Marx hints at this in his outline of varied 'modes of existence' of surplus populations, divided into three categories: floating, latent, and stagnant. The floating category refers more or less to those workers displaced by industrial cycles: those workers who are 'sometimes repelled, sometimes attracted again in greater masses' (1990: 794) by cycles of accumulation and crisis. Latent surplus populations, by contrast, refer to rural populations displaced by rural dispossession and the mechanization of agriculture and thus drawn to urban areas. Marx suggests that 'part of the agricultural population is . . . constantly on the point of passing over into an urban or manufacturing proletariat, and on the lookout for opportunities to complete this transformation (1990: 796). The stagnant population, finally, consists of those with 'extremely irregular employment' (1990: 796). These forms of surplus population are also further distinguished from a broader 'sphere of pauperism' (1990: 797) encompassing those who are incapable of working. In short, then, surplus populations are produced by a variety of different forces – the relative weight of which varies widely across time and space, and take varying forms which are more or less closely and directly linked to proletarian forms of wage labour.

Three points are worth underlining. First, while Marx points to different conjunctural explanations for the emergence of specific forms of surplus population in particular contexts, fundamentally the formation of relative surplus populations derives from a fundamental tension in the process of primitive accumulation. The 'freeing' of labour is not directly linked to the immediate needs to production, and processes of primitive accumulation thus tend to 'free' more labour than needed. Second, and critically, the boundaries between 'surplus' and working-class populations are always fluid and temporary. In Marx's words: 'every worker belongs to it during the time when he is only partially employed or wholly unemployed' (Marx 1990: 794). Finally, as a result, the precarious nature of labour under capitalism is, on this reading, the historical norm rather than an 'exception' to be explained. Indeed, it is absolutely vital to the creation of 'free' labour itself: 'The relative surplus population is . . . the background against which the law of the demand and supply of labour does its work' (Marx 1990: 792). Like the boundary between 'free' and 'unfree' labour, then, the distinction between surplus populations and 'normal' working classes is fluid and contingent.

The relationship between the production of surplus workers and the process of primitive accumulation, in short, is necessarily not as simple as the 'exclusion' of some from participating in 'free' labour. The ready circulation of workers between working and surplus populations is a necessary condition for 'surplus populations' to have any effect on wage levels. More importantly, the production of surplus populations is given in the processes underlying the ongoing formation of 'free' labour. This discussion is useful for situating the production of unemployment, informality, and labour migration within the broader processes of capitalist accumulation. The operation of 'free' labour based on the silent compulsion of the market is fundamentally dependent on the production of irregular forms of work. As with questions of 'forced' and 'free' labour, moreover, the ways in which we understand the relationships between relatively stable work and more irregular forms of exploitation of workers who might be considered part of the relative surplus population are vitally important political questions.

Politicizing irregular labour

The broader significance of these arguments is that it casts a different light Marx's insistence that the culmination of the process of primitive accumulation comes as 'the advance of capitalist production develops a working class which by education, tradition, and habit looks upon the requirements of that mode of production as the natural order of things' (1990: 899). Capital, Marx notes, 'needs the power of the state, and uses it to "regulate" wages, i.e. to force them into the limits suitable for making a profit, to lengthen the working day, and to keep the worker himself at his normal level of dependence' (1990: 899–900). As De Angelis (2004: 70–71) argues, the implications of this claim are that (1) the 'naturalization' of private property and 'free' labour is the core requirement of the completion of the process of 'primitive accumulation', and (2) that by extension 'primitive accumulation' is necessarily a continual process insofar as this naturalization is almost by definition fragile and subject to contest. In Rioux's apt phrase, 'what Marx's dialectical method reveals is not the purely economic character of capitalist exploitation, but its intrinsic, *politically constituted* nature' (2013: 121). The enclosures by which workers are separated from the means of production and reproduction and thus 'compelled to sell themselves voluntarily' (Marx 1990: 899) are thus a continuous and deeply political process rather than a past event. These observations point, in short, to a fundamental contradiction. The process of primitive accumulation depends politically on the naturalization of particular modes of exploitation, and yet simultaneously and necessarily produces a variety of forms of exploitation other than 'free' wage labour. If the historical formation of 'free' labour is always accompanied by the formation of various forms of irregular labour, then we can start to see how the articulation of proletarian labour forms as the 'natural order of things' is a fraught and difficult process. Practices of governance play a critical role in mediating this contradiction.

This latter point is especially critical for present purposes. In brief, it suggests that the differentiation of 'normal' modes of labour relations – proletarian 'free' labour – from the irregular forms of labour continually thrown up by and entangled with broader processes of capitalist accumulation, is a crucial political dynamic underlying the reproduction of capitalism. Moreover, this 'naturalization' is an ongoing process that is deeply entangled with processes of governance. Indeed, as Steinfeld (2001) has documented in detail in the cases of the US and UK, even in core territories the question of what exactly constituted 'free' labour relations – especially around questions like the use of penal sanctions against breaches of contract by workers – was continually debated throughout much of the nineteenth century. 'Free' labour is not an automatic or *a priori* category.

The point for present purposes is that Marx gives us a solid footing from which we can highlight the significance of struggles to regulate and delineate 'irregular' forms of labour, and situate these regulatory processes within the broader framework of capitalist accumulation. He does not, however, offer a really substantive analytical framework from which to think about the practice of governance itself. Marx seems well aware of the importance of the state, but less so of international governance arrangements (which were just beginning to emerge in their contemporary form around the time he was writing, see Murphy 1994), and equally offers relatively few systematic reflections on the practice of politics. Arguably, this is attributable to a broader methodological shortcoming of Marx's approach. As Hall (2013) notes, the concept of primitive accumulation would seem to imply both violent processes of dispossession and enclosure on one hand and the political processes of institutionalization and naturalization of capitalist property and labour relations on the other – a point certainly underlined in Marx's observations on the 'naturalization' of 'free' labour. However, most applications of the concept (most notably Harvey 2003, but including arguably Marx's own) have tended to concentrate on the former at the expense of the latter.

There is thus a danger of slipping into a problematic kind of functionalism – i.e. of inferring a simple causal relationship between the role of the governance of irregular labour in securing the reproduction of capitalism and its actual shape – if we don't seek to theorize the process and practice of governance in a more substantial sense. To do so would miss out on much of the complexity, and indeed the politics, of these processes in practice – the political delineation of 'free' from 'unfree' labour is vital to the reproduction of capitalism, but it is a contingent and highly variable process. In the following section, accordingly, I turn to a discussion of Gramsci's conceptions of 'subalternity' and the 'political relations of force' in order to develop a set of tools for analyzing the practice of governance.

Political relations of force, the subaltern, and governance

Most Gramscian analysis in IPE has worked by adopting Gramsci's specific concepts to the study of global forms of governance. Early efforts hinged on the concept of 'hegemony' (e.g. Cox 1983; 1987; Murphy 1994); more recently the idea of 'passive revolution' has been perhaps more prominent (e.g. Morton 2007; Moore 2010; Gray 2014). For present purposes, though, I am interested less in these specific conceptual tools and more in what Gramsci's broader methodological approach can offer the present analysis. Gramsci's methodological notes on the political relations of force and on 'subaltern' history, as well as his (admittedly somewhat sparse) reflections on spatiality, problems of scale, and internationalism are particularly helpful. I discuss each in turn.

Political relations of force and subalternity

Gramsci's conception of the 'political relations of force' deepens our understanding of the processes of naturalization and differentiation highlighted by Marx's writing insofar as Gramsci highlights the complex ways in which different conceptions of the 'natural order of things', in Marx's words, are enacted through broader patterns of political organization and authority. For Gramsci, the relations of force present at any given conjuncture can be examined at three overlapping levels: the 'objective' economic sphere or 'structure'; 'military' relations, or prevailing balances of coercive force; and the 'political' sphere of organization and consciousness. The general point is that the analysis of any given situation must take account of all three levels, which are interrelated but not reducible to each other. But it is the category of 'political' relations of force – in Gramsci's words, 'the degree of homogeneity, self-awareness, and organisation attained by the various social classes' (1971: 181) – that is particularly salient as a point of departure for present purposes.

Gramsci differentiates three possible 'moments' in this respect – organization on the basis of common 'economic-corporate' interests, the recognition of 'solidarity of interests among all the members of a social class', and the recognition that the 'present and future development' of a particular class 'can and must become the interests of . . . subordinate groups too' (1971: 181). This latter moment describes Gramsci's more widely cited conception of 'hegemony', but here hegemony is situated as one (relatively rare) possibility among others, established through ongoing political struggles. Where this sequence of 'moments' might be read to imply a teleological movement from the recognition of common economic interests by subordinate classes to their articulation of a broader-based 'hegemony', moreover, Gramsci insists that 'in real history these moments imply each other reciprocally . . . combining and diverging in various ways' (1971: 182). Importantly, these relations of force are arranged simultaneously within and across 'national' territories (1971: 176) – I return to the question of space and scale below, but for the moment it should suffice to note that Gramsci suggests that the political relations of force are articulated across multiple scales at once.

The state and the process of governance are thus fundamentally open-ended, multi-scalar, and contested processes, in which the articulation of different forms of group consciousness (of which, the naturalization of 'free' labour highlighted by Marx would be an important example) is a crucial struggle. As Gramsci notes, 'the life of the state is conceived as a continuous process of formation and superseding of unstable equilibria . . . between the interests of the fundamental group and those of the subordinate groups' (1971: 182). 'Hegemony', then, rather than being a sort of 'master concept' in Gramsci's analysis refers to a particular conjunctural situation in which productive, political, and coercive forces solidify the dominance of one particular social group by securing the consent of subaltern populations. Far more common are situations of 'organic crisis', in which no such balance can be achieved (see 1971: 276). The concept of the political relations of force, then, highlights the dispersed political struggles through which different forms of consciousness and subjective identifications of solidarity are articulated. As Hall suggests, Gramsci's method here is suggestive that 'the "unity" of classes is necessarily complex and has to be produced' (1986: 14). Importantly, Gramsci's approach thus highlights the extent to which the 'naturalization' of any particular mode of labour control is deeply contingent and coloured by complex, multiscalar patterns of political mobilization and contestation.

Gramsci's notes on studying the history of 'subaltern' populations echo many of these broader methodological points and also underline again the significance of such struggles. The 'subaltern' refers in essence to the variable ways in which classes occupying marginal positions in broader structures of production are organized in relation to forms of political order in particular historical contexts. In the context of this book, the 'subaltern' would encompass the full spectrum of normalized and irregular forms of work. Gramsci's crucial contribution here is to highlight the ways in which this range of social forces are articulated politically. This history is closely entwined with what Gramsci calls the 'objective formation' of subaltern classes: 'the developments and transformations occurring in the sphere of economic production; their quantitative diffusion and their origins in pre-existing social groups' (1971: 52). But Gramsci's fundamental focus is on the ways in which the political organization of these subaltern classes is entangled with broader structures of political political relations of force. The history of the subaltern 'is intertwined with that of civil society, and thereby the history of states and of groups of states' (1971: 52). Gramsci's understanding of the 'subaltern', then, refers in a general sense to people occupying subordinate positions in broader structures of production and political power. Crucially, though, this open-ended definition is used to call attention to the *politics* of organizing and mobilizing these populations in particular ways. This argument, importantly, also implies that the ways in which conceptions of 'class' intersect with 'pre-existing social groups' – which might usefully be taken to include race, gender, and coloniality, although Gramsci himself paid more attention to religious and regional differences in the Italian context.

Gramsci differentiates a number of ways in which this engagement of subaltern social forces with existing ruling classes can be structured in particular historical circumstances, which range on a continuum from the incorporation of subaltern classes into the political frameworks of existing dominant classes to autonomous political organization:

> It is necessary to study: 1) The objective formation of the subaltern groups, by the developments and transformations occurring in the sphere of economic production; their quantitative diffusion and their origins in pre-existing social

groups, whose mentality, ideology and aims they preserve for a time; 2) their active or passive affiliation to the dominant political factions, their attempts to influence programmes of these formations in order to press claims of their own, and the consequences of these attempts in determining processes of decomposition, formation, and neo-formation; 3) the birth of new parties of the dominant groups, intended to conserve the assent of the subaltern groups and maintain their control over them; 4) the formations that subaltern groups themselves produce, in order to press claims of a limited and partial character; 5) those new formations which assert the autonomy of the subaltern groups, but within the old framework; 6) those formations that assert the integral autonomy.

(1971: 52)

Importantly, this conception identifies the political organization of the subaltern as a vital hinge on which the reproduction or transcendence of existing ruling classes hangs: if subaltern classes can be persuaded to identify their own interests with the 'corporate interests' of dominant groups, then existing forms of domination are likely to be far more durable. The 'subaltern' thus offers a perspective in which the *political* mobilization of class forces, rather than their rootedness in exploitative relations of production, is the main point of emphasis. Gramsci's open-ended definition of the subaltern is used to call attention to the politics of organizing and mobilizing these populations in particular ways. Gramsci highlights an important degree of indeterminacy in this process: 'The history of subaltern groups is necessarily fragmented and episodic . . . even when they rebel and rise up: only "permanent" victory breaks their subordination, and that not immediately' (1971: 55). The picture that starts to emerge is of governance as a sort of 'tug of war' over the formation of subaltern consciousness, enacted in myriad 'local' spaces, in which 'Every trace of independent initiative on the part of subaltern groups should . . . be of incalculable value for the integral historian' (1971: 55). This implies an analysis of particular regulatory projects, focused on the ways in which they are entwined with ongoing transformations in the relations of production and political struggles over the organization of subaltern populations. These struggles, for Gramsci, are vital because they point to the fundamental political conditions necessary for the reproduction of existing systems of accumulation and associated modes of authority and dominaiton (or their transcendence).

Equally, although Gramsci himself did little to explore these dimensions, this method offers us a useful means of situating the intersections between prevailing conceptions of subaltern social forces in the broader political relations of force with ideas about race and gender in particular. The notion of 'pre-existing' social groups is in some senses problematic. As McNally (2016); Hall (1980); and others have pointed out, class is typically mutually constituted with other forms of social differentiation rather than 'intersecting' with them. Gramsci's broader method remains very useful for these purposes. As Stuart Hall observes, 'Although Gramsci does not write about racism . . . his concepts may still be useful to us in our attempts to think through the adequacy of social theory paradigms in these areas' (1986: 8). Two of Hall's observations on this point are particularly useful for present purposes. First, Gramsci's approach draws attention to the ways in which 'the law of value ... operates through and because of the culturally specific form of labour power, rather than in spite of it' (Hall 1986: 24; cf.McNally 2016). Race and gender have, in particular, 'provided the means for the differentiated forms of exploitation of different sectors of a fractured labour force' (1986: 24). Differential forms of exploitation are constituted, in part, on the terrains of race and gender (Hall 1980: 339). Second, race and gender also play a major role in practice in shaping the extent to which the 'homogeneity, organization, and self-awareness' of class forces is (or is not) actually achieved in practice. Hall notes that racial and ethnic differences in particular can be mobilized 'as a set of economic, political, or ideological antagonisms *within* a class which is subject to roughly similar forms of exploitation' (1986: 25). Ideas about race also frequently serve to depoliticize differential forms of exploitation insofar as they 'dehistoricize – translating historically specific structures into the timeless language of nature' (Hall 1980: 342). The main point, for present purposes, is that the political relations of force through which boundaries between normal and irregular work are articulated in practice are frequently bound up with various other forms of social difference.

There are a number of relevant examples of such dynamics in the empirical chapters that follow. Colonial constructions of race were central to the explicit forced labour regimes in the early twentieth century as well as the slightly more veiled coercion in the migrant labour system that supplied labour to South African gold mines. The close ideological association of 'normal' proletarian labour with European men also troubled efforts to develop stabilized, permanently urban working classes in postwar colonial territories. Postcolonial nationalism was also closely linked to struggles over the boundary between normalized proletarian workers and those in survivalist activities. The ILO's initial articulation of 'informal' work in Kenya was deeply entwined with such struggles over nationality. Contemporary struggles over informality and various forms of forced labour have been strongly coloured by considerations of ethnic and religious identity.

The point here is that Gramsci points us towards the shifting political terrains that we need to take into account if we want to make sense of the ways in which the processes of 'naturalization' and differentiation highlighted by Marx play out in practice. Questions of group identity and solidarity among subaltern classes are frequently co-produced with broader patterns of social difference. They are, moreover, in this sense closely linked with shifting patterns of organizational development on the terrain of civil society and with the practice of government – the 'life of the state' in Gramsci's terms.

Scaling governance

I have so far hinted at Gramci's emphasis on the multi-scalar character of shifting patterns of political relations of force, but have yet to cover the topic in much

Irregular labour in global capitalism 31

detail. A brief comment in closing this section is thus useful, perhaps especially because IPE debates have often interpreted Gramsci's arguments as implying the decisively 'local' character of resistance (as against the 'global' power of capitalist classes and leading states). Robert Cox's assertion that 'The task of changing world order begins with the long, laborious effort to build new historic blocs within national boundaries' (1983: 174) is perhaps a classic example. Gramsci's emphasis on the role of the 'state' has often been used as evidence of the fundamentally 'national' frame of Gramsci's thought (Germain and Kenny 1998). Clearly, for present purposes, any methodologically nationalist or state-centric picture of governance would pose significant problems.

It is perhaps significant, then, that a number of authors have recently started excavating the spatial and geographical dimensions of Gramsci's thought (Ekers *et al.* 2014; Jessop 2005; Morton 2007). There is little space to do justice to these analyses here other than to suggest that they largely agree that in Gramsci's thought, spatiality and scales of political action (including the 'national') are overlapping and historically and socially produced. It is also worth cautioning that Gramsci's reflections on these points are fragmentary and sometimes ambiguous. Ultimately, as Jessop notes, Gramsci 'was a deeply spatial thinker, but he did not explicitly prioritise spatial thinking' (2005: 422). Still, I argue in this section that Gramsci's brief and scattered reflections on internationalism suggest that spatiality is a historical product, and thus must remain an element for strategic consideration in particular contexts rather than a problem to be resolved *a priori*. Equally, the patterns of governance with which struggles over the subaltern are entangled are unlikely to be usefully analyzed if our lens is confined to particular 'national' or 'local' spaces, as these scales of action exist in dynamic interplay with global or international ones.

Gramsci's explicit reflections on the international in the *Prison Notebooks* are limited to a brief reflection on a debate between Stalin and Trotsky on the *praxis* of nationalism and internationalism. Gramsci argues that the construction of an international revolutionary proletarian movement needed to be carried out in particular national contexts, particularly because in order to establish a genuine hegemony the working classes need to enroll peasant and intellectual communities whose outlook is 'national' or even 'local' (1971: 240–241). A better way of reading this assertion, though, would be to argue that in Gramsci's perspective the 'international' is constructed (unevenly) out of myriad more localized forms of action. This point is underlined by Gramsci's passing acknowledgement in his discussion of the political relations of force that 'It is also necessary to take into account the fact that international relations intertwine with these internal relations of nation-state, creating new, unique, and historically concrete combinations' (1971: 182). This point comes out particularly clearly if we situate these passages in the context of Gramsci's broader *oeuvre*.

More importantly, in some of Gramsci's pre-prison writing he develops a view of scale that is more fluid than any rigid division of practices of governance into 'global', 'national', and 'local' would allow. What Gramsci would later call the political relations of force are profoundly multi-scalar, articulated at once within and across 'national' or 'local' sites. Gramsci notes provocatively that

> Nationalism of the French stamp is an anachronistic excrescence in Italian history, proper to people who have their heads turned backwards like the damned in Dante. The 'mission' of the Italian people lies not in the recovery of Roman and medieval cosmopolitanism, but in its most modern and advanced form. Even indeed a proletarian nation . . . proletarian as a nation because it has been the reserve army of foreign capitalism, because together with the Slavic peoples it has given skilled workers to the entire world. For this very reason, it must join the modern front struggling to reorganize also the non-Italian world, which it has helped to create with its labour.
>
> (1985: 247)

Here Gramsci suggests that waves of Italian emigration made possible the expansion of capitalism elsewhere. Moreover, in such practices of transnational labour mobility Gramsci locates the possibility of a kind of subaltern internationalism – Italian labour migration gives 'Italy' a profound stake in the reorganization of the 'non-Italian' world. Indeed, Gramsci suggests that the intimate connection of Italian labour to the expansion of global capitalism makes 'nationalism' anachronistic and dangerous. Further, as Featherstone notes, Gramsci's focus on labour migration here 'signals the productiveness of diverse trajectories and articulations in shaping internationalist practices' (2014: 75).

Similarly, Gramsci argues that international political action made possible the emergence of communism in Russia by blurring 'national' histories:

> Socialist propaganda put the Russian people in contact with the experience of other proletariats. Socialist propaganda could bring the history of the proletariat dramatically to life in a moment: its struggles against capitalism, the lengthy series of efforts to emancipate it completely from the chains of servility that made it so subject and to allow it to forge a new consciousness.
>
> (1977: 36)

International *praxis*, in short, for Gramsci made possible a kind of warping of 'national' space-time in Russia. He echoes this argument again in attributing the spread of liberalism in the wake of the French revolution to the prior dissemination of 'enlightenment' ideas through mundane practices:

> Each new comedy by Voltaire, each new pamphlet moved like a spark along the lines that were already stretched between state and state, between region and region, and found the same supporters and the same opponents everywhere and every time. The bayonets of Napoleon's armies found their road already smoothed by an invisible army of books and pamphlets that had swarmed out of Paris from the first half of the eighteenth century.
>
> (1977: 12)

In all these cases, 'international' action (leading to the fundamental transformation of both 'global' and 'national' political economies) consists of very mundane, minute everyday practices carried out by a wide range of actors. As a number of previous authors have noted, Gramsci's reflections on 'passive revolution' suggest much the same of the constitution of the state – 'national' states are fundamentally historical creations, produced in part through patterns of uneven development on an international or global scale (see Morton 2007; Gray 2014).

It would be difficult to argue that these statements represent anything like a concrete and fully elaborated theory of space or globality. Nonetheless, the broader point is that implicit in some of these reflections is a rejection of the naturalization of particular scales of action – i.e. either the 'national' or the 'international' – as fixed, pre-given terrains for action. 'National' and 'international' scales of action are historical products themselves rather than ontological givens. Gramsci's method would thus seem to compel us to investigate the uneven and variable production of scale – how 'international' or 'global' actors and structures are created at the intersection of multiple relations of force – rather than taking the 'international' or the 'global' as a discrete sphere to which concepts can be 'applied'. Equally, rather than assuming, as has often been the case in critical IPE, that 'local' spaces are disciplined by the exercise of 'global' forms of governance (e.g. Gill 1995; Cutler 2003), we ought to pay attention to the complexities involved in enacting 'global' policy frameworks in 'local' spaces. This kind of multi-scalar analysis is particularly pressing in the case of governing irregular work. Of interest, in short, are the ways in which 'global' frameworks are circulated into local spaces, and the ways in which they intersect with localized struggles over the political relations of force, particularly over the articulation of subaltern populations.

Taken together, these aspects of Gramsci's method offer us a useful framework for analyzing the practice of governing irregular work. Two points are particularly key. First, the governance of irregular work is bound up with broader political struggles to mobilize subaltern social forces in particular ways. It is particularly important to analyze irregular labour in the context of struggles over the political organization of subordinate classes more broadly, especially in their relation to the state. Second, we should expect that these struggles will not be confined to particular 'national' contexts, but rather arrayed across scales in uneven ways. The Marxian approach to irregular labour outlined above highlights the importance of differentiating proletarian forms of exploitation from the other forms of work that are continually produced in the process of primitive accumulation; this Gramscian method offers us a more fully-fleshed out means of analyzing *how* these struggles take place and *why* they vary across time and space in the ways that they do.

Conclusion

The approach outlined in this chapter contrasts in important ways to more conventional readings of irregular labour – which tend to emphasize the twin exclusions of various forms of irregular work from the market and from effective regulatory protection. These approaches are problematic insofar as they imply that irregular work is a novel and aberrant phenomenon, and one that could be eliminated (relatively) easily by better enforcement of laws, stronger rules, or the removal of barriers preventing access to markets (through e.g. better provision of credit or skills training), without more explicitly challenging processes of primitive accumulation. While previous critical perspectives have done very well to point out many of these shortcomings, however, they have not done enough to analyze the ways in which these limited conceptions of irregular labour are enacted through actual practices of governance.

This chapter thus drew on readings of Marx and Gramsci to suggest that the process of proletarianization is inherently contested, political, and incomplete. Importantly, the 'naturalization' of 'normal' working-class forms of labour relations is thus a politically fraught and complex process in which the governance of irregular labour is often a key axis of contention. The differentiation of irregular forms of labour from 'free' wage labour, and the discursive separation or 'cocooning' of various unfree, informal, unpaid, or transitory forms of work from the broader workings of capitalist production and accumulation, are important sites of political struggle. Categories like 'free' and 'forced', 'formal' and 'informal', 'stable' and 'precarious' labour are as much artefacts of historical practices of governance as they are analytic categories that can be applied in the abstract. This suggests the need for analyses of the processes of governance through which this differentiation is carried out. In the latter part of the chapter, I elaborated a more substantive framework for analyzing these processes by drawing on Gramsci's conceptions of the 'subaltern' and the 'political relations of force' and his thoughts on the construction of scale. Taken together, these arguments imply a method of analysis that traces out the variable ways in which irregular forms of labour have been governed across time and space, and the ways in which these regulatory patterns are entangled with wider struggles over political order and the mobilization of subaltern social forces.

Notes

1 A version of this argument is presented in Bernards (2017b).
2 Bonded labour relationships are perhaps historically most common amongst agrarian labourers in South Asia (see Breman and Guérin 2009; Lerche 2007), but are certainly not unheard of elsewhere, particularly amongst migrant labourers (cf. LeBaron 2014b). Indeed, the issue of payment of transport costs for migrant workers out of future wages was discussed extensively in ILO debates about whether or not the migrant labour system in twentieth-century South Africa constituted a form of forced labour (see Chapter 2).
3 There is a growing literature drawing on the concept of 'relative surplus populations', much of which draws on conceptions of 'biopolitics' derived from Foucault and Agamben to study the creation and regulation of populations of 'disposable' workers 'surplus' to the demands of capital – particularly as a means of tracing the racialized politics of mass unemployment and dispossession in contemporary capitalism (e.g. McIntyre and Nast 2011; Li 2009; Tyner 2016). Soederberg (2014; 2017) has emphasized the

ways in which the governance of surplus populations is bound up with wider patterns of capitalist accumulation, including through the articulation of new forms of 'secondary exploitation' outside the labour process, primarily through relations of indebtedness. The present approach is closer in emphasis to the latter, but still somewhat different insofar as it emphasizes the historically pervasive character of the tendency to create surplus populations and the vital importance of the fluidity of boundaries between working and 'surplus' populations.

2 The governance of forced labour and the antinomies of colonialism

The ILO's first engagements with irregular work in sub-Saharan Africa date to debates about the governance of forced labour in colonial territories in the first decade of the organization's operations. The ILO's approach to these questions was quite fundamentally residualist. Convention 29 on Forced Labour (C29) prohibited the use of coercion in cases where the worker had not 'offered himself voluntarily' – a definition deeply rooted in liberal notions of contract and consent that framed the 'silent compulsion' of the market as acceptable (see Banaji 2003; Rioux 2013). Indeed, the ILO implicitly (and at times explicitly) approved of practices that were meant to force colonized workers into 'free' wage labour so long as the worst abuses were avoided. Forcible recruitment for public works projects was also generally tolerated. Insofar as 'forced labour' was defined in terms of coercive recruitment directly backed by state power in 'backwards' territories, and as a temporary expedient that would be eliminated as such spaces were more thoroughly incorporated into world markets, the ILO's interventions helped to discursively 'cocoon' persistent practices of forced labour from the broader workings of capitalism in ways that are again echoed in the organization's contemporary interventions (see Lerche 2007), albeit in significantly different forms. Putting these understandings into practice was a good deal more complicated than we might expect – and in fact opened up a series of debates about where the boundaries between 'free' and 'forced' labour actually lay. These were nowhere more acute than in the case of South Africa's emerging migrant labour system for gold mining.

In tracing through these controversies, the chapter underlines two arguments critical to the book as a whole. First, the normalization of particular forms of exploitation is dependent on a fraught and contested process of differentiation. The understanding of forced labour adopted by the ILO explicitly framed coercive recruitment practices as a temporary expedient necessary for certain purposes in underdeveloped territories, and confined itself to 'non-economic' forms of coercion. Such understandings of forced labour were explicitly contested by the widespread idea among radical movements at the time, both in Europe and in colonial territories, that both forced labour and imperial rule were the products of capitalist relations of production. Moreover, as the latter parts of the chapter on debates about the pass law systems in Southern Africa illustrate, the boundary between forced and free labour continued to be contested. The ILO never actually accepted any arguments that the complex of pass laws, vagrancy laws, and land reserves that made up the migrant labour systems in Southern African settler territories constituted forced labour. Still, various actors within and beyond South Africa continued to push arguments that the pass laws constituted a system of 'forced labour'. The sheer persistence of these arguments, I argue, is indicative of just how fraught and politically determined the boundary between 'free' and 'forced' labour could be.

Second, if we want to understand the specific trajectory of these struggles, we need to understand how these contests over the boundary between normal and irregular forms of labour were bound up in broader patterns of political relations of force on global and more local levels. The fact that the ILO would be discussing forced labour in colonial territories by 1927 at all might have been surprising to negotiators at Versailles only a few years earlier. Against the backdrop of the Russian Revolution and increasingly powerful radical working-class movements, the establishment of the ILO was centered on fears that the immiseration of workers in industrial economies would result in the overthrow of capitalist relations of production. Craig Murphy (1994: 200) usefully argues that the organization became a kind of 'midwife of the welfare state', or a space in which the alliance between capital, the state, and conservative elements of the labour movement – under construction already in the nineteenth century – could be solidified. The contradictions implicit in colonial labour relations, however, were mobilized effectively by a broad range of activists in Europe and in colonial territories, to the point where they threatened the legitimacy of the colonial project as a whole. The particular matrix of political relations of force on a global level, within Europe and in African colonial territories, into or out of which the ILO was born played a critical role both in pushing the organization towards engaging with forced labour and in shaping the regulatory agenda that eventually emerged. In short, we need to understand the complex and contradictory landscape of colonial world order to make sense of the emergence of forced labour regulations. The abolition of indigenous forms of slavery played a crucial role in the legitimization of colonial rule to European and American audiences. Yet in territories where the enclosure of land was partial at most, the 'silent compulsion' underlying free labour was difficult to establish. Colonial authorities and capitalist firms seeking to mobilize 'natives' for the commercial production of agricultural goods, mining, and public infrastructure projects often relied on legal compulsions to work or outright violence to solve what was commonly referred to as the problem of 'labour shortage'. The hypocrisy implicit here was not lost either on activists in Europe or in colonial territories, who after the formation of the League of Nations increasingly targeted protests to international organizations, including the ILO. The ILO itself was closely linked to colonial governments, and its conceptions of African labourers were profoundly shaped by colonial understandings of African labour. However, calls for the regulation of forced labour, including in some instances those directed at the ILO, were at times entwined with broader resistance to colonial rule. The ILO's position in the broader colonial world order of the interwar period, then, played a major role in driving the adoption of C29 and shaping its subsequent trajectory.

These arguments are taken up in four steps. The first two sections situate the establishment of the ILO in the context of the broader context of the colonial world order of the early twentieth century, and the problem of forced labour in the context of processes of primitive accumulation in colonial Africa. The third section explores specific debates within and beyond the ILO about forced labour in the 1920s, and the ways in which these created pressures on the ILO to adopt some form of forced labour governance on the one hand and shaped the actual convention that was adopted on the other. The final section considers the fraught nature of the focus on 'non-economic coercion' implicit in the ILO's approach. It focuses in particular on one example where conflicts around these questions were particularly chronic: pass laws and other migration controls in Southern Africa.

Colonial world order and the origins of the ILO

The idea of international labour standards was closely linked to the naturalization of proletarian forms of exploitation in nineteenth-century Europe. Proposals for international labour standards date to Robert Owen in the 1830s, but the idea began to be taken more seriously with the growth of trade unions, the expansion of the franchise, and the rise of socialist parties in the latter part of the nineteenth century. As Robert Cox (1996) has noted, the promotion of international labour standards was closely linked to the nationalization, depoliticization, and de-radicalization of socialist parties and labour movements in Europe, and gained support in part as a conservative response to perceived revolutionary pressures. A number of international treaties dealing with various aspects of labour standards were signed after 1890, and an 'International Labour Office' was established in Brussels in 1905. This first 'ILO' primarily played an information-sharing role – tracking changes in industrial legislation across Europe. These developments were disrupted by the outbreak of WWI. However, European and US trade unions and socialist parties had started to press for some expanded forms of international labour regulation to be incorporated into the postwar international order already in a series of conferences held between 1916 and 1918.

This conservative lineage was reflected in the debates in 1919 at Versailles that led to the formation of the ILO, a tendency that was given extra impetus by the Russian Revolution in 1917. Cox once described the establishment of the ILO as 'Versailles' answer to Bolshevism' (1973: 102). James T. Shotwell, a member of the American delegation at Versailles, similarly recalled that:

> The Governments of Europe were nervous in the face of a rising industrial unrest, with unknown Bolshevist possibilities, with menacing fires of revolution in Germany, and with at least one or two of the governments represented at Paris in daily danger of being overthrown.
>
> (1933: 18)

Fears about communism also unquestionably shaped the early operations of the ILO. Most notably, they amplified the depoliticizing character of the ILO's activities. While the ILO's conventions have typically attracted the most attention, perhaps the biggest difference between the postwar ILO and its precursors was that ILO aimed to fill this purpose through the application of technical knowledge as much as through the promulgation of standards. Indeed, well over half the organization's staff and budget even in its early years were devoted to research activities (Haan 1933).

Nonetheless, despite its primary concern with 'social peace' in Europe, the ILO operated in a world order that was unavoidably colonial in character. Most importantly, the very deeply racialized understandings of proletarian labour tied up in the naturalization of 'free' labour in Europe raised some fraught questions about the limits of international labour standards. This point is made especially clear in the ways in which colonized populations were discussed (albeit briefly) in wartime debates about how the new international labour regime should address migration. The French *Confedération Generale du Travail* (CGT) raised the spectre of competition from imported colonial labour in its proposals to the Leeds Conference in 1916 (reprinted Shotwell 1934: 19–21). The poor treatment of migrant labour was linked to the degradation of labour conditions for European workers: 'In every country capitalism has caused the importation of foreign labour to become a fighting weapon against national labour'. The CGT anticipated greatly expanded migration from the colonies in response to the loss of labour supply due to the War, coupled with expanded demand for labour across Europe as industrial progress continued: 'Search . . . will be made, and has already commenced, for labour among the populations at a still lower standard of living, among the natives of our colonies of Africa and Asia, among the Hindus, Chinese, or Japanese'. In order to prevent the erosion of wages and working standards, the CGT argued it was essential to guarantee the same standards to immigrant workers from colonial territories as to European citizens. The resolutions of the Leeds Conference included provisions on immigrant labour, reflecting agreement that 'Should the need arise to employ coloured labor, the recruiting must proceed under the same conditions as apply to European workmen' (reprinted Shotwell 1934: 24). The proposal was contested. The President of the International Federation of Trade Unions suggested in comments on the Leeds programme that it was impossible to grant the same standards to colonial workers as to Europeans: 'The Zulus and the Cingalese know no more of trade union organization than the Chinese coolies do' (reprinted Shotwell 1934: 33). The Berne Conference of International Trade Unions in 1917 abandoned the demand for immigrant labour to be guaranteed the same conditions as European workers. This particular footnote to the broader debates about international labour standards in the postwar settlement is significant for present purposes because it demonstrates how far the process of naturalization of proletarian forms of work hinged on ideas about race. The concerns about the possibility of treating non-white workers in the same ways as Europeans reflected deeper-lying concerns about whether colonial subjects could in fact be 'compelled to sell themselves voluntarily'. This particular set of assumptions would have far-reaching consequences for the governance of labour in Africa and globally.

African labour and the antinomies of colonialism

The abolition of indigenous forms of slavery was an important legitimizing device in the early extension of colonial rule in Africa. Indeed, eradicating the slave trade was a critical motivation of many of the first European 'explorers' of the African interior, especially missionaries. The Berlin Conference in 1884–1885 saw European colonial powers lay down some commitments to abolish slavery, and in 1889 a conference explicitly devoted to the abolition of slavery in Africa was held in Brussels. British and French administrations across Africa in the early twentieth century passed decrees abolishing slavery. Yet, colonial administrations across Africa increasingly relied on various forms of forced labour. The most famous example is probably the horrific system of rubber harvesting under King Leopold II's Congo Independent State (which, as noted in the introduction, accounted for more than half of the world's rubber production in the early twentieth century). Portuguese and Belgian colonies, as will be seen below, were especially heavily targeted by activists. The British and French, however, also practiced similar forms of forced labour (see Fall 1993; Mamdani 1996).

The use of forced labour was intimately linked to the trajectories of primitive accumulation carried out in colonial territories. Colonial projects depended to some extent on the mobilization of African labour in mines, large-scale plantations, and for the construction of roads, railways, and the like through which primary products could be exported. Actually mobilizing workers for such work, however, was easier said than done. Colonial states, in Cooper's (1994) apt terms, exercised 'arterial' modes of power – very strong in major cities and around key infrastructural nodes, and practically non-existent anywhere else. The kinds of enclosures and rural dispossession that had underpinned the process of primitive accumulation in Europe were not carried out in colonial territories in the same way (with the partial exception of South Africa, and even then not until somewhat later, see below). Colonized populations retained considerable access to non-wage sources of subsistence, particularly as long as land remained (whether *de jure* or *de facto*) largely outside the realm of private property. As Mamdani aptly notes, 'to the extent that peasant households remained in customary possession of land, without the right to alienate it, the sway of market forces was limited' (1996: 52).

As a result, the perceived problem of 'labour shortage' in colonial Africa was widespread. The *Journal of the Royal African Society* published an entirely straight-faced article in 1902 discussing the potential use of elephants as a solution to the labour shortage for railway construction in South Africa (Stopford 1902). The 'shortage' was not a problem of underpopulation. In one authoritative estimate from the late 1920s, the proportion of Africans in wage employment was lowest in Nigeria, at 0.4 percent of the total population and 2.1 percent of adult males, and highest in the Transkei in South Africa at 8.2 percent of the total population and 41 percent of adult males (Buell 1928a; 1928b).[1] 'Labour shortage', then, was fundamentally a problem of *recruitment* in a context where labour was not yet 'freed' from non-wage means of reproduction. Racialized and gendered constructions of 'normal' working classes played a significant role in compounding these difficulties.

One obvious solution to the relatively limited power of the silent coercion of the market might have been to simply offer better pay and working conditions as means of enticing workers away from subsistence activities. Some employers did so. Indeed, two major factors in the eventual elimination of state-backed forced labour in Afrique Occidentale Française (AOF) (in the 1940s) were the fact that indigenous elites relying on voluntary labour, especially in Côte d'Ivoire, were able to demonstrate that they were more productive than French plantation owners still reliant on forced labour (see Cooper 1996a) and ongoing patterns of migration by Africans from French and Portuguese territories into British and South African ones where they expected better wages and working conditions (although did not necessarily find them). But often the assumption that African workers were fundamentally different from white proletarian workers and could not be motivated by wages made for a kind of self-fulfilling prophecy. It could, indeed, serve explicitly as a means of lowering wages (perhaps paradigmatically in the migrant labour system in South Africa). If it could be assumed that male workers relied on family and community subsistence activities to secure their reproduction, wages could be kept well-below subsistence levels. The most common solution was to resort to various coercive recruitment regimes. Outside of the migrant labour regime in Southern Africa, recruitment was often organized through local 'chiefs', who would be asked to provide a certain number of workers for particular projects, this was often supplemented by legal requirements to work a certain number of days per year on public works, or simply through threats of violence and corporal punishments administered by military officials (for more detailed histories, see Fall 1993; Mamdani 1996; Cooper 1996a). Marx's argument that capital 'makes up for its deficiencies by force' in areas where the conditions for the formation of a sufficiently large relative surplus population available to capitalist production (discussed in Chapter 1) seems apt in these cases.

But the abolition of slavery remained key to the legitimization of colonial rule. The point, in brief, is that colonial labour relations raised a potentially loaded set of political problems, both in Europe and in Africa. The tension between the legitimizing discourse of abolition and the practical reality of forcible recruitment was politically significant because it meant that colonial labour practices threatened to undermine the basic legitimating claims of colonial authority. A pamphlet written in 1900 by the secretary of the Aborigines Protection Society in London, for instance, after detailing abuses in the Congo Free State, argued that 'If there is any honesty in our professed desire to put an end to slavery in Africa, we must condemn and abandon all the systems of forced labour, and all the devices for procuring it, which are now tolerated by the Governments of

Great Britain, France, Germany, and other European nations, as well as by the Congo Free State' (Fox-Bourne 1900: 14). While the 'freeing' of labour was a critical means by which colonial authorities sought to justify the expansion of colonial rule, colonial infrastructure and economic projects could often only proceed by force – at least, barring a major realignment of fiscal and administrative structures, understandings of proletarian labour, and rural political economies. Even if the ILO's mandate was centered on the problems of 'social peace' in Europe, colonial labour politics were at the very least a problem lurking in the background.

The ILO and 'Native Labour', c. 1919–1930

Questions around the viability of 'free' labour in colonized Africa, and of the scale of abuses to which irregular workers in Africa were subjected, quickly became more politically salient for the ILO in the decade after its establishment. This set of concerns was largely pushed on to the ILO's agenda from outside. A pair of points are worth underlining here. First, the debates that led to the development of C29 reflect the ambivalence of the free/forced binary very clearly, as well as the strongly racialized contents of the processes through which the exploitation of 'free' labour was naturalized at the time. Second, the entanglements of these debates with broader struggles over the political relations of force underpinning colonial rule – both in Europe and in colonized territories – played a major role in shaping the trajectory of debates. The ILO's approach to forced labour studiously marginalized arguments, prevalent on the radical left at the time, that linked questions about 'forced labour' to both the broader workings of capitalist accumulation and the legitimacy of the colonial project more broadly. The regulatory embodiment of a rigid binary between acceptable 'economic' forms of coercion and unacceptable extra-economic ones, and the subsequent differentiation of unregulated abuses from legitimate uses of the latter in the short term, did much to depoliticize these debates.

The earliest archived correspondence with the ILO regarding colonial labour is a letter from W.E.B du Bois sent on behalf of the Second Pan-African Congress (PAC) in London in 1921.[2] The conference itself had included representatives from Nigeria, Sierra Leone, the Gold Coast, Senegal, the French Congo, Belgian Congo, Madagascar, Angola and Mozambique, Ethiopia, and Liberia, along with several representatives from the Caribbean, African-Americans, and Africans living in Europe. Du Bois's letter asked for the establishment of a permanent section of the ILO devoted to 'native' labour, 'especially that of Negroes'. He gave four reasons why this was needed: (1) unprotected and unorganized native labour formed a growing proportion of world labour; (2) machinery and transport were increasing levels of competition between white and native labour; (3) labour problems in colonized territories could not be resolved by 'ignoring native labour, helping to enslave it, or by attempting to climb to power on its back'; and (4) the need for regular research and public awareness-raising of 'the real costs of Congo and East African slavery'. Du Bois also visited the ILO in Geneva shortly afterwards. Du

Bois' letter and visit seem to have been partly responsible for the establishment of a native labour section of the ILO. Thomas exchanged letters with several officials referring to du Bois' visit and discussing suitable candidates to head a native labour section or research project, in which it is fairly clear that there were no serious plans to do so before the interaction with du Bois.[3]

Similar engagements with a variety of groups outside the ILO carried on through the 1920s. A member of the League of Nations Union (LNU) in Britain, a non-partisan group counting a considerable portion of Britain's political elite as members, cabled Thomas in January of 1925 to call attention to a debate in the House of Lords where it had been suggested that the ILO prepare a charter dealing with 'certain forms of coloured labour'.[4] This suggestion bore some resemblance to the PAC's insofar as it suggested that the ILO should set up a more comprehensive programme to deal with 'native' labour. But the LNU did not connect international regulation of African labour relations to either any anti-imperial agenda or any appeal to the interdependence of African and European workers. It was, nonetheless, still further than the ILO's officials thought it prudent to push in the immediate term. The ILO's response to the LNU suggested that it would be better to work on an issue-by-issue basis, rather than adopt a 'charter' *per se* right away.[5] The problem of forced labour, highlighted in a series of reports on colonial labour situations in the mid-1920s, provided a useful starting place.

Networks of academics and activists, primarily in Europe and the US, began publishing evidence of forced labour in colonial Africa in the mid-1920s. The report with probably the greatest impact was submitted to the Temporary Slavery Commission of the League of Nations in 1925 by E. A. Ross, a sociologist at Columbia. Ross interviewed African workers in Angola and Mozambique over several weeks in 1924. His report described the system of labour recruitment in Portuguese Africa as 'virtually state serfdom' (1925: 9). Books targeted at the general public also played an important role in heightening the emphasis on forced labour. French author André Gide's travel diaries of a trip through French Equatorial Africa and the Belgian Congo in 1925 and 1926 are among the most important examples (Gide 1927). Gide describes a series of punishments handed out by French administrators to villages that refused to participate in the rubber harvest for concessionary companies in French Equatorial Africa, including imprisonment and corporal punishments. Gide's book was not written for the ILO or the League specifically, but had enough influence on the broader perception of colonial violence that it made an impact on the organization. Indeed, Gide's book was explicitly referenced by at least one delegate in the debates about forced labour at the ILO's annual International Labour Conference (ILC) (ILO 1929: 409).[6]

Much of the discussion tended to centre on reforming colonial practice in order to live up to the promise of the 'civilizing mission'. The LNU, for instance, was not necessarily opposed to forced labour. The Union convened a conference on colonial forced labour ahead of the ILC in 1929 – Wilfred Benson, an ILO official in the Native Labour section, was present (JRAS 1929: 287). Much of the discussion was about Britain's record on the issue. The Parliamentary undersecretary of state for the colonies noted that the use of forced labour was on the decline, and that

> the main use today of . . . various forms of compulsory labour, whether for native governments or for the Protectorate Government, is in connection with roads . . . In almost all our administrations in tropical Africa some recourse is had to compulsory labour for road purposes, though this is steadily diminishing.
>
> (JRAS 1929: 284)

Forced labour, then, was framed as a temporary expedient that would be gradually eliminated. The point of international regulation, then, would be to prevent the worst excesses.

Ross, Gide, and the participants in LNU meetings – and ILO officials like Benson and Thomas – typically framed their arguments in terms of promoting a more humane imperialism. Such discussions of colonial labour practices, though, because they turned on such a central practical and ideological tension in the colonial project, always risked opening up the possibility of fundamental challenges to colonial authority. By the 1920s, the brutality of colonial forced labour was emerging as a common theme in communist propaganda, an argument that was pushed especially heavily by French-educated colonial subjects. Lamine Senghor, a Senegalese radical living in France, and founder of the *Comité de Défense de la Race Nègre*, gave a speech in Brussels in 1927 centering on forced labour in AOF:

> We have to work ten hours of forced labour a day under the hot African sun, to earn nothing but two francs! Women and children work the same hours as men, yet we're told that slavery has been abolished, that negroes are free, that all men are equal, etc.
>
> (Senghor 2012: 60)

On its own, this is a rather more colourful description of colonial forced labour, but not incompatible with the assertion of the British parliamentary undersecretary of state that 'some recourse is had to compulsory labour for road purposes'. The key here is that Senghor explicitly connected these and other abuses to capitalist imperialism, rather than dismissing them as a temporary expedient. Senghor suggested that coercive labour practices were inherent in the structure of colonialism, and thus identified the solution to colonial labour abuses with the overthrow of capitalist relations of production (2012: 63). There could be no gradual elimination of coercive labour practices, or restriction of the worst excesses, if the brutal exploitation of colonial subjects were central to the operations of capitalism itself. Senghor, in this respect, echoed arguments that had been circulating in radical circles for at least ten years – the passages from Luxemburg (2003) on forced labour in colonial territories, cited in the previous chapter, are notable examples.

Antonio Gramsci (1977) and future Vietnamese communist leader Nguyen Tat Thahn (see Daughton 2013), among others, would also publish similar arguments at around this time.

This highlights a number of the arguments raised above. In the first instance, international debates about forced labour in colonial territories, especially in sub-Saharan Africa, were driven by the need to mitigate the political threat to the colonial system posed by the reliance of colonial authorities and capitalists on forced labour recruitment on the one hand and the perceived incapacity of Africans to work for wages on the other. 'Cocooning' colonial practices from the wider operations of capitalist accumulation was politically critical. Yet, the political and material structures within which colonial labour was mobilized made it difficult to 'cocoon' colonial labour or to frame it decisively as a 'temporary' expedient. The ILO's efforts to regulate forced labour, in short, always risked becoming more deeply entangled in a kind of radical or anti-colonial politics that ran very much counter to the organization's rather conservative roots. Relatedly, a very wide range of different agencies were implicit in the debate about forced labour. By the mid-1920s, tensions between anti-slavery discourses and the use of forced labour, and over the position of African labour more broadly, were being highlighted by networks of European, American, and African activists, researchers, and politicians. These were increasingly articulated around the ILO, and so the organization was becoming increasingly entangled in colonial politics through the actions of a loose set of actors in Africa, the US, and Europe. Some colonized subjects and European leftists also sought to make more radical claims against the basic legitimacy of colonial rule. While labour relations had been at least a latent political problem for colonial authority for decades, by the 1920s, in part because of the new availability of international spaces and networks built up around the League of Nations and the ILO, colonial powers faced growing pressure. The leadership of the ILO, in this context, seized on forced labour as a means of articulating a limited agenda of colonial reform.

Regulating forced labour

The Director General's report to the 1927 ILC included a discussion of labour conditions in colonial territories, with a particular emphasis on efforts to eradicate slavery and the regulation of forced labour (ILO 1927a). An Indian workers' delegate moved a resolution calling on the Governing Body to place the topic on the agenda at a future ILC in 1927 (ILO 1927b: 334). Action against forced labour was debated at the ILC in 1929. Following the standard procedure for ILO conventions, the problem was referred to committee, to draw up a questionnaire to be sent to governments on a draft convention to be voted on the following year. Outright opposition was rare. At the ILC it came only from the Portuguese (ILO 1929: 44). Some informal letters opposing the convention were also sent to ILO officials.[7] In any event, by 1929 there was near-consensus on the need for an international convention on forced labour; the disagreements among speakers in the main session of the conference and in the committee in 1929 were about its contents. The most problematic questions were whether the ILO's convention should call for the outright abolition of forced labour or set minimum standards to limit abuses, and how broadly 'forced labour' should be interpreted. There was broad agreement that forced recruitment for private enterprises should be prohibited, but not about how recruitment for public works should be handled. One ILO official summarized these latter debates as follows in an article for the International Labour Review (ILR – the ILO's in-house journal):

> With reference to forced labour for general public purposes . . . it seems that certain broad principles are generally accepted by the colonial powers: authorization of forced labour in cases of emergency . . . ; efforts to abolish porterage whenever possible, and until this can be achieved strict regulation of forced porterage; admission of compulsory cultivation . . . only as a protection against famine and on condition that the food so produced remains the property of the natives themselves. There remain the large scale public works on which it appears difficult at first sight to reach agreement, since the developmental work of various colonies is at various stages of progress. It is to be expected, however, that the Governments . . . will not object to agreeing that it should be subject to strict regulation and that a maximum should be fixed for the duration of the forced labour of each individual, if the existence of situation that are closely analogous to slavery are to be expected.
> (Goudal 1929: 632–633)

The committee on forced labour at the ILC in 1929 still failed to reach a consensus on the basic question of whether the convention should aim to regulate or abolish forced labour. The committee report and draft questionnaire emphasized regulating the abuse of forced labour, and a relatively narrow definition based on the use of coercive violence (ILO 1929: 388–389). The workers' delegates on the committee prepared a minority report, complaining that the questionnaire 'would embody, besides vague and insufficient solutions, so many exceptions that the abuses to be suppressed could be perpetuated' (ILO 1930: 46). In the end, Article 1 of the convention avoided addressing the issue directly. It did establish the goal 'to suppress the use of forced or compulsory labour in all its forms within the shortest possible period', but then went on to qualify this by stating that 'recourse to forced or compulsory labour may be had, during the *transitional period*, for public purposes only and as an exceptional measure' (emphasis added). The Governing Body was vaguely committed to reviewing whether or not the transitional period could be declared over after five years. (In fact, it was not formally ended until the passage of a Protocol to the Forced Labour Convention in 2014!)

Notably, while the role of 'indirect compulsion' to work was debated at the ILC, it was not incorporated into C29. The convention also passed a non-binding recommendation (R035) suggesting that authorities refrain from 'indirect means of artificially increasing the economic pressure upon populations to seek employment', notably through taxation, restrictions on land use rights, abuse of vagrancy laws, and the manipulation of pass laws. The latter, which we might usefully describe as colonial processes of primitive accumulation – in Marx's phrase, as capital's creating the laws of supply and demand by force where they did not otherwise exist – were explicitly differentiated from 'direct' forms of compulsion. They were also not outright prohibited, with R035 instead insisting that they be carried out with an eye to their potential negative effects on indigenous communities.

In short, the thrust of the ILO's efforts was an effort to manage the worst abuses of colonial authority while still enabling the introduction of 'progressive' forces to 'backwards' areas – including, if need be, by certain forms of coercive force. The *intent* of the forced labour convention was thus expressly depoliticizing: 'The continuity of the work of the Office is a new guarantee to the native races that there will be a steady and wise pressure by the international society to secure better conditions for them.' (Chamberlain 1933: 85). More generally, Harold Grimshaw, the head of the ILO's Native Labour Section, put the problem as follows in a lecture in 1929: 'One certain result of continued contact between ourselves and the primitive systems of society found in colonial areas is the destruction of the latter'. The most important force behind this destruction, for Grimshaw, was the colonial demand for labour. The point, then, was that the role of the ILO, particularly with respect to the forced labour conventions, was understood in terms of managing the destruction that would necessarily accompany the development of a new society (Grimshaw 1928: 131). The ILO's regulation of forced labour, in short, was intimately connected to an idealized vision of progressive, compassionate imperialism. In this sense the rigid differentiation of 'free' from 'forced' labour – rooted in an emphasis on the 'voluntary' offer of labour – did the job well. But, in practice this binary was rather harder to implement.

The Witwatersrand gold fields and the limits of freedom

C29 was weakly effective, at best, in eliminating the forms of forced labour that it targeted in colonial Africa. Fall (1993) credits the debates in Geneva with focusing public attention on the problem and increasing pressure for the abolition of forced labour. Cooper (1996a: 30), however, has shown that C29 had little impact on the day-to-day practice of colonial rule, and not much more on the ways in which administrators sought to manage and understand labour issues. Moreover, the ILO's supervision could be applied only where the convention had been ratified. Among colonial powers, only the British ratified C29 immediately. The French government initially passed its own decree calling for the gradual elimination of forced labour in 1930, reporting to the ILO that 'Some Articles of the Convention infringe our sovereign rights (that is the case with the Article which covers the employment of the second military contingent) or are in obvious contradiction with the present situation in some or other of our dependencies' (qtd. ILO 1937a: 36). Most notably, the French government did not want to do away with the use of military conscripts in road construction. They did eventually ratify C29 in 1937, though. Belgium took until 1944. While the Portuguese, like the French, passed their own decree almost immediately after the passage of C29, they did not ratify the convention until 1956. South Africa, the other notable colonial power in the region, did not ratify the convention until the country was re-instated to the ILO in the 1990s. Of course, even ratification did not mean very much. Reports from the ILO on the application of the convention typically documented only legislation related to forced labour (see e.g. ILO 1937a), which was often not all that reflective of actual practice. Regulations were often as much means of obscuring the actual practice of colonial labour recruitment as they were means of regulating it. The Governor General in AOF wrote to the Ministry of Colonies in 1937 saying that 'we lie in Geneva and at the International Labour Organization when, regulations and circulars in hand, we speak of the organization of public work in the colonies' (qtd. Fall 2002: 12). Prohibitions on forced labour could usefully 'cocoon' the practice of forced labour from the accumulation of capital, but were unlikely to be actually enforced as long as unfreedom continued to serve the needs of accumulation.[8] The result of all of this is that the ILO's efforts did very little to actually reduce the use of forced labour or to curb abuses – indeed, the use of forced labour increased dramatically in many parts of Africa during WWII. All of this would seem to call into question the usefulness of the ILO's reliance on moral suasion and 'shaming' (Weisband 2000) to ensure the implementation of its standards, and of the central focus of its supervisory mechanisms on legislative change.

Notwithstanding the weak enforcement of the convention, for present purposes the consequences of the fundamentally fraught differentiation between 'free' and 'forced' labour in terms of the later application of the convention are more relevant. This dynamic is probably most visible in longstanding struggles over the application of C29 and extension of subsequent conventions to the migrant labour regimes emerging in the settler territories in Southern Africa.

Some context might be useful here. The migrant labour system emerged around the specific demands of gold mining in South Africa at a time when gold dominated the country's economy. A number of historians of labour in South African mining have noted that, for much of the twentieth century, the internationally fixed price of gold ensured that profits in gold mining could only be made by constantly forcing down costs and increasing productivity – in both cases the most readily available means of doing so was by intensifying the exploitation of labour, especially African labour (see Perrings 1977). This was largely carried out in the South African case by the implementation of a heavily racialized 'migrant labour system'. The processes of primitive accumulation were strongly shaped by the presence of a racially organized state. The state actively promoted the formation of a large relative surplus population through a series of policies confining 'native' populations to ever-shrinking 'reserves' of poor agricultural land. This was accompanied by the implementation of a policy of controlled, temporary migration to urban areas and mining operations managed through legal restrictions on length of contract, pass laws and vagrancy regulations that prohibited permanent settlement in urban areas, and criminal sanctions for breaches of contract by employees (see Wolpe 1972; O'Meara 1975; Jeeves 1975). Labour recruitment was largely carried out by two agencies closely linked to the Chamber of Mines – the Witwatersrand Native Labour Association, which primarily operated in Mozambique; and the Native Recruiting Corporation, which operated within South Africa and in other British territories. The importation of labour from elsewhere in Southern Africa (especially Mozambique) was often used as a means of further eroding wage costs. Workers were primarily responsible for their own transport costs, since few workers could afford to cover these costs outright it was common for these to be covered by recruiting agencies as advances against wages. Employers often also withheld workers' wages until the end of their contracts. These systems were also widely copied in other settler territories in Southern Africa. Recruiting agencies outside South Africa did not have the same reach and were largely out of business by the 1930s, but pass law systems persisted. While the most obvious forms of forced labour (like, for instance, the brutal corporal punishments handed out for refusing to participate in the rubber harvest in the Congo) were absent, the migrant labour system could nonetheless easily be interpreted as contributing to the formation of an unfree workforce. Viable options aside from work in the mines or on settler farms were systematically and deliberately dismantled. Once recruited, moreover, workers were subject to a range of public and private policies that deeply restricted their opportunities to exit, including debts incurred for transport costs and criminal penalties including imprisonment for breaches of contract. In short, if it did not necessarily violate C29, the migrant labour regime undoubtedly ran counter to the R035 on indirect compulsions to labour.

These ambiguities around the coercive character of the migrant labour system in South Africa were mostly overlooked in initial debates about forced labour at the ILO in the late 1920s, but became increasingly fraught for the organization in the next decade. The ILO's efforts to expand the scope of its convention on forced labour to incorporate a broader set of standards for labour recruitment in colonized territories – referred to as the 'Native Labour Code' (NLC) – proved especially problematic in this respect. The ILO published a key report on labour recruitment in colonial territories in 1935, with an eye to establishing a subsequent convention. To some extent, the move to develop a broader regulatory framework around recruitment stemmed from a recognition of the limits of C29's narrow focus on coercion: 'It was already realised in 1929 by the Committee appointed . . . to discuss the question of forced labour that the problem of eliminating compulsion in the employment of Native labour would not be disposed of by the proposed decisions on forced or compulsory labour alone' (ILO 1935a: 1). The final recommendations of the report, indeed, recognized that the continued need for recruiting agencies seemed to fly in the face of the principle of labour 'offered voluntarily': 'the final object to be attained is the obtaining of workers by the spontaneous offer of labour', hence the committee hoped 'the recruiting of labour will be rendered progressively unnecessary by such measures as the improvement of conditions of labour . . . and the creation of public institutions ... for facilitating and if necessary controlling the voluntary movement of labour to areas where it is in demand' (ILO 1935a: 255). In the meantime, the committee sought, as in debates about forced labour, to minimize the worst abuses, particularly through the licensing of recruiters and by maintaining health and safety standards for recruited workers in transit. Questions around transport costs and advances against wages (both, incidentally, especially widespread in South Africa) were particularly central to these debates. South African practices were discussed extensively in the 1935 report. The report itself avoids any direct criticism of South African labour recruiting, but did suggest (over South African dissent) that the ILC should discuss the merits of some general principles which would require a change in practices in South Africa – most notably that the employer should bear the cost of transport to and from the region of work, rather than the worker (ILO 1935a: 197). In discussions of the report at the ILC, South African employers' and government representatives objected to suggested provisions that would require employers to provide for the housing of workers' families near worksites (ILO 1935b: 14), and to the payment of travelling expenses by employers (1935b: 25), with the employers noting with respect to the latter that

> a system was in place whereby any native wishing to reach the Rand could offer himself at one of the offices of the Native Recruiting Corporation where, if proved fit, he was sent to Johannesburg with the help of the Corporation, subject to his undertaking to offer himself for employment and to repay his travelling expenses from his wages.
>
> (1935b: 25)

In any event, among colonial powers only the UK ratified the subsequent convention (C50) on labour recruitment.

A similar debate took place two years after around standards for contracts for 'Native' workers, in which the use of penal sanctions for violations of contracts was particularly contentious. Here again, South African practices proved difficult to square with the ILO's broader objectives – especially in debates about transport costs (this time for repatriation at the conclusion of a contract, ILO 1937b: 221), and more importantly about penal sanctions for breaches of contract (which, again, were widespread in South Africa).[9] The latter issue would subsequently be elevated to a separate convention – a move to which South Africa objected (ILO 1939: 41). The proposed convention was (once again) fairly minimal, instead of calling for the abolition of penal sanctions, it proposed the progressive reduction of their use. In any event, the convention on penal sanctions was again ratified only by the UK among colonial powers.

The point here is that the migrant labour system in South Africa occupied an increasingly awkward position with respect to efforts to promote 'free' labour. It did not, for the most part, incorporate 'direct' coercion of the sort prohibited by C29, but still fell well short of the 'fully voluntary' recruitment of labour sought by the ILO. It is perhaps not surprising in this context that South African officials had developed a reputation among ILO officials for their tendency 'bitterly to resent the mildest criticism of [their] native administration' even in the 1920s.[10] More significantly, it was precisely the most overtly coercive features of the migrant labour system – the uses of advances against withheld wages to pay for transport, and criminal penalties (including hard labour) for violations of contracts – which were most controversial and which South African authorities sought to defend.

This ambivalence is significant for two reasons. In the first instance, it shows particularly clearly how difficult to negotiate the binary between 'free' and 'unfree' labour could actually be. Equally, the naturalization of irregular forms of labour recruitment – and a racialized regime of precaritization and temporary work based around state-backed patterns of dispossession certainly conformed ambiguously at best to normal forms of 'free' wage labour – in South Africa was a fraught process resting in large part on the racialization of irregular work. Second, the debate about whether or not the migrant labour system constituted a form of forced labour or incorporated forms of forced labour was never merely an abstract or academic question. It was a deeply political one that was actively contested and had significant implications for the wider legitimacy not only of the structures of accumulation that were emerging around gold mining and agriculture in Southern Africa, but also for the settler state and colonial project more broadly.

Contestation around the coercive dynamics implicit in the migrant labour system was neither new in the 1930s nor necessarily engendered by the ILO's debates. In fact, debates about the coercive character of labour recruitment for mining in South Africa predated the ILO. A pamphlet published by the Aborigines Protection Society in 1903 titled *Forced Labour in British South Africa*, for instance, highlighted the shortage of voluntary labour for mining in the face of the 'stinginess' of mining houses who had agreed that pay would not exceed 50 shillings a month per head (Fox-Bourne 1903: 9). The pamphlet raised concerns that the response on the part of the British administration in South Africa, in the aftermath of the Boer War, would be to implement a steep increase in domiciliary taxes as an inducement to find waged work – a policy that would

> deprive those natives of all that is valuable in their rights and liberties, and subject them to a thraldom more degrading and more oppressive – seeing how different work in the mines is from work in the fields – to that from which we claim to have delivered a million or so of them by putting an end to the Boer republics.
>
> (1903: 20)

The implication here is that the introduction of increased taxes as an inducement to seek wage work – especially in a context where it would not fund an appropriate level of public services and where the policy was being promoted by mining capitalists as an explicit alternative to raising wages enough to recruit voluntarily – constituted a form of coercive labour recruitment.

The debates at the ILO about forced labour and about colonial labour recruitment more generally did, however, open up new fronts in these struggles. Given that South Africa never ratified any of the conventions making up the NLC, however, this did not take place through the ILO's normal supervisory mechanisms (on which see Weisband 2000), but rather mostly informal contacts. British leftists affiliated with the anti-colonial wing of the Independent Labour Party or the union movement – many of whom moved between England and South Africa fairly regularly (see Bush 1999) – were especially prominent in this respect. For instance, in 1934 the 'Friends of Africa', a committee of British and South African leftists devoted to the formation of cooperatives in South African native reserves, led by British expatriates William and Margaret Ballinger (both significant, if somewhat problematic, figures in the development of both non-racial unionism and in efforts to radicalize the Liberal party in South Africa), appealed for support from the ILO by pointing to a systematic process in which 'the land . . . has been gradually enclosed until a large proportion of the population can no longer live on it and is forced to seek employment under European capital', and standards of work were further undercut by frequent resort to 'the use of convict labour and indentured labour from the Reserves, Protectorates, and Portuguese East Africa'.[11] This language echoed arguments about the 'indentured' or 'indirect[ly] forced' character of migrant labour on the Witwatersrand and on white-owned farms that Ballinger and others affiliated with the Industrial and Commercial Workers Union in South Africa had frequently raised in the late 1920s and early 1930s.[12]

The ILO took very little action, it does not appear that these allegations were ever investigated closely. Such arguments were, however, raised again in the 1950s as the UN and the ILO launched a new series of committees and reports on forced labour. The committees themselves were distinctly Cold War phenomena – they responded to a 1947 request from the American Federation of Labour–Congress of Industrial Organizations that the ILO and Economic and Social Council of the UN (ECOSOC) investigate allegations of forced labour in the Soviet bloc.[13] ECOSOC and the ILO set up a joint 'Ad-hoc Committee on Forced Labour' in 1951, which worked primarily on the basis of a series of meetings held by ECOSOC to discuss allegations of forced labour. On the basis of the Ad-hoc Committee's report, the ILO established its own committee on forced labour in 1955 to draw up a new convention on forced labour. Both committees, and the ILO's eventual convention (C105, passed in 1956), concentrated primarily on uses of forced labour in Soviet territories. While a good deal of evidence of labour abuses in colonial territories was submitted, these were typically downplayed by both committees, in contrast to unambiguous findings about abuses in Soviet-controlled territories (see UN/ILO 1953; ILO 1956).

The committees were notable, however, because they provided an opportunity to press claims about forced labour in a number of territories, including South Africa, that had not ratified any of the conventions making up the NLC. A number of British and South African activists did, indeed, seek to press arguments about forced labour in South Africa to both committees. The Ad-hoc Committee, for the most part, hedged on the question of whether the migrant labour system as a whole constituted a form of forced labour, but did conclude that the widespread use of convict labour on farms constituted a form of forced labour. When the South African government objected to these findings, the Movement for Colonial Freedom (another group affiliated to the anti-colonial wing of the British Labour Party) wrote to the ILO and the UN in 1954 protesting the widespread use of prison labour in South Africa – 'it can hardly be argued held that the choice of working on a farm or remaining in prison is a free one, and the payment of the inadequate wages of 9d. a day (withheld from the worker until the end of his sentence) shows the worker to be under compulsion'.[14] The Movement for Colonial Freedom was keen to point out that this practice was particularly problematic not just because of the use of penal labour, but because the majority of prisoners turned over to farmers in this context had been arrested either for breaches of contract or for pass law violations – both of which already constituted systematic means of forcing Africans to work in mines and farms.The Anti-Slavery Society similarly wrote to note that the practice of 'convicting Africans and sentencing them to terms of imprisonment with hard labour and then hiring them out to private enterprises' violated a number of international conventions.[15]

Neither the ILO nor any other UN body ever took any substantive action against South Africa for the use of 'forced labour', indeed as long as the country refused to ratify C29 (or later C105), there was little of substance for the ILO to do. All the same, the point here is that the very persistence of such debates shows that the boundary between 'coercive' and 'voluntary' recruitment at the core of C29 and the NLC more broadly was hard to maintain in practice. In the context of capitalist relations of production, (1) a good deal of ambiguity inevitably persisted around the extent to which wage work could be 'voluntary', and (2) various forms of unfreedom were intimately bound up in various regimes of accumulation. These ambiguities were especially clearly reflected in the case of South Africa in the first half of the twentieth century because the migrant labour regime depended on a variety of liminal forms of coercion that were neither purely 'free' labour in the liberal sense (see Banaji 2003; Steinfeld 2001), nor marked by the direct application of violence in the recruitment process. South African labour practices were subject to various forms of active contestation both within the ILO's own debates in preparatory committee work and at the ILC about expanding the NLC and by various forms of pressure mobilized by outside actors.

Conclusion

For present purposes, two points are worth underlining. First, the ILO's conventions on forced labour draw a binary between free labour based on regulated, voluntarily-entered contracts and coercive recruitment backed by state violence. In doing so, they serve to 'cocoon' the operations of colonial labour regimes from the 'normal' operations of capitalist production and accumulation. Of course, this binary was troublesome to maintain as long as colonial labour regimes ranging from the naked violence on display in the Congo rubber harvests to the less directly violent but no less systematic coercion implicit in the migrant labour system in South African gold mining *were* implicated in global circuits of accumulation. This point, incidentally, was hardly lost on contemporary radicals – including well-known intellectual figures like Gramsci and Luxemburg as well as colonial political activists like Senghor or Thahn in the 1920s, and the arguments raised by the anti-colonial wing of the British Independent Labour Party about South Africa between the 1930s and 1950s. The free/forced binary was even more problematic where regimes like that in South Africa so ambiguously straddled the boundaries between 'free' and 'forced' labour even according to the lines drawn by the ILO. Here the reading of Marx's notes on primitive accumulation as a fundamentally incomplete process dependent on the naturalization of 'acceptable' forms of coercion is very useful.

Second, however, we cannot explain the actual development and application of the ILO's regulatory framework on forced labour and labour recruitment in colonial territories more broadly without reference to the patterns of multi-scalar political mobilization and organizational development highlighted by the Gramscian methodological devices introduced in the latter part of the last chapter. The intersections of political contestation over the organization of subaltern populations with the structures of political authority at global and national or territorial levels do much to explain the actual timing, colouration, and contents of the regulatory frameworks developed by the ILO. The effort to govern the use of forced labour in colonial territories stemmed from the political tensions underlying the colonial abolition of slavery, and was driven by the growing political attention to forced labour from a diversity of political organizations in the 1920s. While the boundary between 'forced' and 'voluntary' labour served to depoliticize the question of forced labour, it also opened room for ongoing indirect challenges to colonial labour practices – perhaps most vividly in the case of South Africa discussed in the latter part of this chapter. All the same, Gramsci's attention to the specific organizational and institutional forms through which these particular understandings of race, class, and irregular labour were advanced should probably encourage some caution about these challenges to colonial labour practices. They were primarily advanced by European activists and the relatively narrow strata of colonial subjects with European education. The activities of African workers themselves certainly mattered – flight, migration, and foot dragging, as Fall (1993) documents in vivid detail across AOF, were widespread if dispersed forms of resistance to forced labour. But they did not constitute anything approaching what Gramsci might call an 'integral' consciousness on the part of subaltern classes.

The centrality of the political relations of force to the actual practice of governing irregular labour is also perhaps illustrated by the decline in salience of 'forced labour' as a means of governing irregular labour in the latter part of the twentieth century. Already by the 1940s, as discussed in the next chapter, the question of 'free' and 'forced' labour was being superseded by concerns about 'development'. There was a brief flurry of activity in the early 1960s – formal complaints by newly independent Ghana against Portugal that the labour recruitment systems in its Southern African territories violated C29 and C105, and a largely retaliatory complaint by the latter against the former, were subject to official investigations by the ILO's Governing Body; there was also a heated debate about the widespread adoption of Youth Labour Services in Africa at the ILC in 1962 (on which see Maul 2007). But forced labour in Africa fell almost entirely off the ILO's map in subsequent decades. To some extent, this reflected the more or less complete elimination of overt, state-backed coercion directly targeted by C29 and C105 as the structure of colonial and postcolonial political economies increasingly shifted towards the problem of surplus labour rather than that of labour 'shortage'. The ILO's role was certainly not diminished by this shift, but it did require new means of drawing boundaries between normalized and irregular workers that went beyond the simple racialized binaries on which the NLC rested. Forced labour has indeed been forcefully revived (albeit in dramatically different form) as a concern for the ILO in the last two decades – a development to which I return in Chapter 6. As I show in the following two chapters, however, concerns about abuses of forced recruitment were increasingly superseded by worries about overly rapid urbanization and the destabilizing potential of widespread casual and precarious labour.

Notes

1 Although in both cases, and particularly in South Africa, regulatory measures aimed at ensuring the temporary character of Africans' wage work probably contributed to deflating these numbers. It is not clear from Buell's estimates what kind of time-frame is under consideration (i.e. workers currently in wage work or who had worked for wages over the preceding month, year, etc.).
2 W.E.B. du Bois to Albert Thomas, 15 September 1921, ILOA N 206/1/01/3. N.B., citations to unpublished archival materials are given as endnotes, and not included in the reference list.
3 See especially Royal Meeker minute to the Director, 7 October 1921, and reply, 10 October 1921, ILOA N 206/1/01/3.
4 Gilbert Murray cable to Albert Thomas, 15 January 1925, ILOA N 206/0/2.
5 Harold B. Butler to Gilbert Murray, 9 February 1925, ILOA N 206/0/2.
6 The ILC is the ILO's annual tripartite 'parliament'. Each member country is represented by two government delegates, and one representative each of organized labour and organized business. The ILC passes all of the organization's conventions and recommendations. The specific details of these processes are not of primary interest here. For concise descriptions of the mechanics of standard-setting activities at the ILO, see Hughes and Haworth (2011) and Weisband (2000).
7 Albert Thomas to Louis Franck, 11 December 1929, ILOA N 206/1/01/5.
8 Brass (2010) makes a similar observation about India in the latter parts of the twentieth century, and similar dynamics are in evidence in the cases reported in Chapter 5.
9 It is perhaps worth noting here that the question of whether penal sanctions for breaches of contract by workers could be consistent with the principle of 'free' labour was hotly contested across most of the nineteenth century in the US and UK (see Steinfeld 2001).
10 Minute, Mr. Phelan to Mr. Ayusawa, 12 September 1927, ILOA N 206/1/01/3.
11 Julius Sewin to Wilfred Benson, 16 November 1934, ILOA N 206/1/01/12.

12 e.g. William Ballinger, n.d., 'Native Workers of South Africa: Indirect Forced Labour', Wits Historical Papers, Johannesburg (WHP), Industrial and Commercial Workers' Union Records 1925–1947, A924 A4.2.5; see also Bush (1999: 147–148).
13 A detailed history of these committees is beyond the scope of the present argument, but see Haas (1964: 221–225) and Maul (2007: 483–488; 2012: 202–211).
14 Douglas G. Rogers to The Secretary, International Labour Organization, 15 October 1954, ILOA FLA 1–65.
15 C.W.W. Greenidge, 'Memorandum addressed by the Anti-Slavery Society (UK) to the United Nations and to the International Labour Organization commenting on the comments of the government of the Union of South Africa (UN Doc. E/2815/Add. 6) of the 9th May 1956 on Forced Labour', 10 July 1956, ILOA 1–25–0.

3 Urbanization, colonial crisis, and social policy

This chapter examines how debates about the governance of labour migration and social policy were entwined with broader patterns of resistance to colonial rule between WWII and the end of formal colonial rule in the 1960s. This history is important in the context of this book because it is particularly revealing of the political nature of the differentiation of proletarian forms of labour from irregular labour – particularly insofar as colonial debates about labour migration explicitly turned on the question of who could be a 'worker' in the normalized mould of European proletarians. In short, these debates are particularly indicative of the significant role of race and gender, and of broader shifts in the political relations of force in shaping these political struggles.

As noted in Chapter 2, the ILO's initial approach to colonial labour consisted of regulating the worst excesses of forcible labour recruitment. This made sense only in a context in which it was understood that workers in Africa were fundamentally 'different', and not suitable for the same standards of work and livelihoods as European working classes (i.e. not subject(able) to the 'silent compulsion' of the market). However, these boundaries were always fraught and often overtly contested. During the pre-war and interwar periods, colonial authorities largely refused to consider African workers as proletarian working classes – which continued to be understood as an implicitly European phenomenon. This crudely racialized mode of differentiating standard from irregular work, however, came under increasing pressure as African workers were increasingly *de facto* permanently employed in wage work, especially in mines and transport, and (more importantly) began to challenge colonial understandings of labour relations. Strikes and riots were particularly important developments in this respect. Significantly, such protests often drew in broader communities and casualized workers alongside permanent wage workers. From the early 1940s onwards, we can trace a series of colonial debates about social policy and migration which turned on the question of how to maintain the boundary between proletarian workers and 'tribal' surplus populations. These debates often hinged on assumptions about race and gender – both in the sense of recurrent concerns about the suitability of African workers for normalized forms of wage labour, and in ideas about gender roles and household structures often embodied in social and wage policy frameworks. They were also constantly animated by the actions of African workers and anti-colonial activists.

This chapter traces out these developments in two broad steps. The first section traces out the context in which the ILO and colonial authorities were forced to rethink the straightforward racially based differentiation of 'normal' European workers from 'irregular' African ones implicit in the NLC. Workers' protests, compounded by a broader crisis of colonial authority driven by the Great Depression and the advent of WWII, called into question the idea that African workers could not be organized in proletarian forms. The shift towards ideas about 'development' during the War was an explicit reaction to these dynamics. The second section shows how debates about normal and irregular labour, particularly in the context of accelerating urbanization, continued to shape the implementation of this agenda from the late 1940s. Debates about the management of rural-urban labour migration, productivity, and social policy all turned on the troublesome question of who should count as a 'worker' and where the line between permanently urban wage workers and irregular forms of labour should be drawn.

War, depression, and colonial crisis

One of the most important early catalysts for the rethinking of colonial labour, especially in terms of its impact for the ILO, was a series of strikes and riots in British colonies beginning in the Copperbelt region of Northern Rhodesia in 1935. Subsequent strikes in Gold Coast, at the port in Mombasa, and once again on the Copperbelt in 1939 reinforced the sense of disorder. Labour action in sub-Saharan Africa, moreover, also coincided with unrest in the British Caribbean and Gandhi's civil disobedience campaigns in India.

Debates about these 'disturbances' show a gradual fraying of the ideas about African workers underpinning colonial labour regimes. The report of the commission invited by the Colonial Office to examine the 1935 Copperbelt strike, for instance, noted that 'tribal' authority in the Copperbelt was weak, and unable to either represent workers' grievances or to 'succeed in any way in controlling the disturbances when they had arisen' (Russell *et al*. 1935: 40). The commission concluded that, as a result, 'the choice lies between the establishment of native authority, together with frequent repatriation of natives to their villages; or alternatively, the acceptance of definite detribalisation and industrialisation of the mining population under European control' (Russell *et al*. 1935: 40). Notably, though, nowhere does the commission's report mention either trade unions or social security for mine workers. This hesitance to create a regularized proletarian working class underlines the theoretical argument made in Chapter 1 that the distinction between normal and irregular labour is contingent and fundamentally contested. Equally, the central role of race and coloniality in the differentiation of diverse modes of exploitation is clearly visible here – ideas about the 'African-ness' of Copperbelt workers played a critical role in shaping subsequent debates.

A second wave of strikes on the Copperbelt in 1940 was followed by another commission. A review of its report was published in the ILR. The review made note of the second commission's similarly uneasy stance on unionism among African workers. The ILR report also noted the dilemmas posed by urbanization and the need for policy choices around migration and settlement of African workers:

> Of these problems the primary is that of the choice, where choice is possible, between the creation of an urbanised permanent wage earning population and that of the maintenance of the labour supply through migrant labour, the natural destiny of which will be to return to African agriculture in the intervals between contracts of employment.
>
> (ILR 1942: 546)

This is a debate to a considerable extent about how to draw the line between limited processes of proletarianization and persistent irregular labour. Implicit here is the fact that it was no longer possible to do so on purely racial terms in the face of growing urbanization and continued demand for labour in mining. Put in slightly different terms, the debate revolves around how to articulate the boundary between workers and surplus populations. Preventing the formation of any regular working class through the maintenance of temporary systems of labour migration, underpinned by an alliance of 'traditional' authorities in the countryside and colonial authorities in the cities, remained one widely considered option. However, efforts to forestall the eruption of further disruptive labour action by more clearly delineating a regularized working class from the broader rural surplus population were now being seriously considered. Yet to do so would mean potentially tinkering with the bases of colonial rule, which continued to rest on delegation to 'tribal' authority and a clear separation between European colonial authorities and settler citizens on the one hand and tribal 'subjects' on the other (Mamdani 1996). These debates would remain unsettled for much of the period in question in this chapter, in no small part because of the complex and multi-scalar array of political forces through which they were mobilized in practice.

The ILO, for its part, was closely entangled in these colonial debates, and would play an increasingly important role after WWII. Wilfred Benson, the official most responsible for the research and policy documents that made up the ILO's early postwar development agenda, had close links to British colonial policy circles.[1] Indeed, Benson was relocated to London during WWII, while most of the rest of the organization was moved to Montreal (see Maul 2012). Developments in British colonial policy were thus highly influential for the ILO. The Colonial Development and Welfare Act (CDWA), passed in 1940, was a crucial part of the British effort to restore colonial authority. The act identified four 'pillars' of the new 'development' agenda: education, cooperatives, local government reform, and trade unionism (Lee 1967: 147–148). The CDWA also did away with the longstanding requirement that colonies be self-financing. It committed the British government to invest treasury resources in the development of infrastructure and social institutions in colonial territories. This was unquestionably seen as a means of preserving the British empire – a contemporary commentator described the CDWA as 'a testimony surely of almost heroic faith in the future of Britain and

62 *Colonial crisis and social policy*

her empire at a time when her fortunes seemed to be at their lowest ebb' (Jeffries 1943: 7). In practice, the funds disbursed to the colonies (aside from the Caribbean territories) were limited at best, particularly as mobilizing colonies in support of the 'war effort' took increased priority. Nonetheless, the move to 'development' in Britain spilled over into the ILO's work on 'Native Labour'. Benson provided a positive commentary on the CDWA to the Colonial Office in the name of the ILO shortly after the CDWA was passed (Maul 2012: 37). Subsequent commentaries on the progress in implementing the CDWA were also published in the ILR (ILR 1941a; 1941b). All of these documents express a general approval of the principles underlying the CDWA on the part of the ILO, while advocating for more rigorous implementation.

This new approach was further institutionalized at the ILO with the growing emphasis on development issues after WWII. The Philadelphia Conference of 1944 – where the ILO issued the widely repeated declaration that 'poverty anywhere is a threat to prosperity everywhere' – was a key event in this respect. The ILO's preparations for the Philadelphia programme involved an unprecedented exercise in information gathering on health, population, education, and labour issues in 'underdeveloped' territories, most of which was carried out from London by Benson. Much of this research went into a discussion paper drawn up for the Philadelphia conference (ILO 1944). A subsequent report similarly argued that:

> The modern world is beginning to recognise the dangers resulting from the poverty of underdeveloped areas and to realise that the supply of cheap raw materials from these areas is less important than the expansion of their purchasing power . . . Modern policy cannot return to slavery. The alternative is the development of measures for better health, housing, education etc.
>
> (ILO 1945: 16)

The report assigned considerable scope for colonial officials in adapting social policies to the diversity of circumstances prevailing in colonized territories. The Philadelphia conference passed a recommendation on 'Social Policy in non-Metropolitan Territories', reflecting most of the same concerns and prescriptions, which was later promoted to a convention in 1947. While the 1944 report – in line with the CDWA – highlighted a role for (non-radical, non-political) trade unions and cooperatives in ordering and representing the interests of colonized populations, it also noted that 'In some territories and among some workers the current possibilities of effective organization are not so great'. In such cases, 'it might be of value for the administrations to appoint . . . persons with appropriate experience to defend the interests of workers and to encourage their closer association' (ILO 1944: 11). Perhaps even more importantly, the report argued against raising living standards too quickly:

> social welfare, defined solely by material standards, may lead to a desire to impose particular forms of material welfare; *it would not be psychologically*

sound to enforce conditions, however admirable in themselves, which are likely to provoke resistance among the people they are designed to benefit.

(ILO 1944: 16, emphasis added)

This hesitance to promote regularized working-class forms was a critical and persistent dynamic throughout the early development of the ILO's ideas on development. Such views were common within the organization as well. For instance, in response to an inquiry from the head of the ILO Section on Non-Metropolitan Territories, asking about the possibility of formulating a recommendation about social security for underdeveloped or colonial territories, the head of the Social Insurance Section replied that the main stumbling block would be that 'no one yet knows whether or how social insurance will work when applied to an illiterate population having no acquaintance with the insurance principle'.[2] A draft statement for a meeting planning the ILO's contribution to the UN's postwar technical assistance programme (TAP) even suggests that in the immediate term there would be some policy areas – especially working conditions and health and safety – for which 'dependent' territories were not yet sufficiently equipped to receive assistance.[3]

Here the importance of understandings of race and coloniality in shaping the normalization of particular forms of labour and the ways in which subaltern social forces were mobilized is particularly clear. The hesitance of colonial authorities in promoting more regularized modes of labour relations stemmed in no small part from concerns about the suitability of Africans for 'normal' forms of work. Proletarian wage labour was delineated from other forms of labour relations in part by a set of cultural assumptions linking normalized forms of exploitation with white male workers in Europe. The centrality of racial ideas to the structure of colonial authority was also critical. In the face of growing political challenges to this vision, it continued to limit the responses of the ILO and of colonial officials. It also, as the debates about labour migration discussed in the following section show particularly clearly, continued to have real impacts on colonial structures of accumulation, particularly in terms of the ways in which the relations between surplus populations and urban wage work were articulated in practice.

Migration and productivity, 1948–1960

In the early 1950s, only independent countries were involved directly in ILO technical assistance programme. In sub-Saharan Africa this meant that the ILO's direct involvement in technical cooperation projects was limited to Liberia and Ethiopia. However, the ILO was involved in ongoing colonial efforts to link labour issues to the emerging 'development' agenda. This section maps out some debates among ILO experts and colonial administrators about how to approach African labour in the 1940s and 1950s. The most prominent recurrent conversation involved how to deal with labour migration. While everyone involved more or less agreed that managing the flow of migrants into urban areas and increasing the productivity of African workers were the most important goals of 'development' programming insofar as labour issues were concerned, there were considerable disagreements over how to go about meeting these ends. These debates, notably, turned in significant ways on the interplay of political struggles over colonial authority, constructions of race and gender, and shifting patterns of production and reproduction increasingly reliant on permanent urban settlement. The first subsection below lays out the contours of debates about migration; the second examines debates at the ILO and Inter-African Labour Conference (IALC).

The politics of labour migration after WWII

Debate about migration in the 1940s and 1950s revolved around the two options that had been laid out in debates about the Copperbelt (see above; Cooper 1996a: 252–256). The first was to try to 'stabilize' a limited set of 'working-class' Africans living in urban settings by various measures aimed at creating permanent communities and higher living standards. The other option was to restrict the movement of 'native' populations using passes and limits on urban settlement (the latter approach was epitomized by the migrant labour systems in Southern Africa, discussed in Chapter 2). The stated objectives of either approach were to control the flow of migrants to urban areas, to protect 'traditional' society in the countryside, and manage the perceived strain on resources and threat of social unrest in the cities created by processes of urbanization on the one hand, while still managing to supply sufficient labour for mines, plantations, and transport infrastructures on the other. In either case, in short, the stabilizing and restrictive options offered different means of delineating regularized 'free' labour from the majority of irregular workers living in colonized territories. They differed on two main points. First, the stabilizing option required seeing at least a small segment of the African population as normalized, permanently urban workers, while the restrictive option held more strongly to the idea that all Africans were essentially rural and 'tribal' and could be wage workers only temporarily. Second, the stabilizing option made a small segment of African labour potentially much more expensive. This was in part because it required admitting that workers were no longer able to subsidize their wages with subsistence agriculture in their 'home' areas. Indeed, recognizing this shift in the bases for workers' social reproduction from rural households to wage work in a context in which 'workers' were assumed to all be male implied the reverse – that wages would need to cover the subsistence costs of whole families. Also, and for colonial officials more concerningly, it even opened the possibility that Africans might demand to be paid the same and hold the same political rights as Europeans doing similar jobs in territories governed by Fordist compacts. However, both options were responses to the same perceived underlying dilemma – how to manage the 'detribalization' of African workers involved in colonial labour systems. Moreover, in both cases 'social policy' practices were (explicitly) intended to ensure the preservation of colonial authority and (somewhat less explicitly) the preservation of large 'surplus' populations of non-proletarian labour.

The actions of African workers themselves were largely responsible for the eventual emphasis the ILO and IALC placed on policies for stabilization. In the

Colonial crisis and social policy 65

first instance, urbanization proceeded apace in most territories. African workers continued to move to urban areas in search of work, and indeed to settle there permanently, in numbers that were hard to ignore. Moreover, by the late 1940s miners, dockworkers, and railway workers – workers directly involved in the infrastructure of colonial export economies – were organized into trade unions capable of disruptive strikes, had begun to establish links to metropolitan union confederations, and were pressing for labour law reforms and social security programmes. General strikes in major cities or even across whole territories occurred in Nigeria in 1945, Dakar in 1946, Dar es Salaam, Mombasa, Sudan and Tunisia in 1947, and Zanzibar in 1948; railway strikes took place in *Afrique Occidentale Française* (AOF) in 1947–1948, and in Ghana and Southern Rhodesia in 1947; urban protests involving unionized workers also took place in Douala in 1945 and Ghana in 1948 (see Oberst 1988).

Critically, many of these strikes drew in a broad selection of normalized and irregular workers. Among the most notable of these was the AOF railway strike, in which a little under 20 000 striking workers virtually shut down the entire railway network across the AOF territories for more than five months.[4] Following a reform undertaken shortly after WWII, the railways themselves were operated by a parastatal company – the *Régie des Chemins de Fer de l'Afrique Occidentale Française* – which was run by a tripartite board and received no budgetary support. To control its labour costs, the *Régie* split its labour force into a small number of permanent workers (of which higher ranks were mostly made up of Europeans and lower ranks were predominantly African) and a much larger population of irregular 'auxiliaries' who were not provided permanent contracts, housing, or other benefits (despite the fact that many worked on the railways for years). In 1946, the *Régie* employed just over 2 000 permanent workers, against more than 15 000 auxiliaries (Cooper 1996b: 89–90). The strike effectively revolved around a demand on the part of African workers for the organization of a single pay-scale – a *cadre unique* – which would do away with the distinction between permanent and auxiliary employees. Moreover, the longevity of the strike was made possible in large part because of the ways in which striking workers were able to draw on family and community resources to ensure their ongoing reproduction. While the strikers' demands were eventually only met in part, the strike itself played a significant role in nudging French authorities towards stabilizing policies.

Another key event, the general strike in Mombasa in 1947, turned on similar issues. Mombasa was a critical port in East Africa, and the strike was thus similarly disruptive to the British East African colonial economy. The strike itself, which included roughly 15 000 workers, seemed to confirm for officials that African labour was indeed permanently urbanized. The considerable role played by Mombasa's dockworkers, who were largely employed on a casual basis – at the time, roughly 70 percent worked less than fifteen days a month (Cooper 1996a: 236) – equally highlighted the problem of delineating normal from irregular forms of labour. Although the primary demands of the strikers were for higher wages rather than an end to casual labour, *per se*, the official response to the strike emphasized the political dangers of casual labour and endorsed the need to promote the formation of a regularized working class. The policies through which this was to be implemented – a substantial pay rise for existing workers, combined with policies to restrict migration into Mombasa and to expel 'vagrants' and surplus labour – equally clearly turned on the explicitly articulated objective of differentiating normalized from irregular labour in order to stabilize the colonial order. This response to the strike, notably, was harshly criticized by the African Workers' Federation (which had been formed during the strike) precisely because it introduced new 'distinctions within a working class that the federation wished to unite' (Cooper 1996a: 238). In short, for all that the resolutions to the strike, as with the AOF railway strike, were ambiguous (see Cooper 1996a; 1996b), they represented a fundamental challenge to pre-war modes of differentiating (European) normalized proletarian and (African) irregular migrant workers on the basis of race alone.

African workers also increasingly established and drew upon links to the international labour movement in order to press for reforms to colonial labour policies. In 1948, the World Federation of Trade Unions (WFTU) sponsored a 'Pan-African Conference' in Dakar.[5] CGT-sponsored unions from AOF dominated proceedings, but territorial confederations from Nigeria, Sierra Leone, and the Gambia were present, along with some unions from South Africa, the Belgian Congo, French Equatorial Africa, Madagascar, and North Africa. The AOF delegates called for a revised *Code de Travail* based on metropolitan standards, and the conference resolved in favour of trade union rights, better pay, and social security (Cooper 1996a: 224). Indeed, the CGT and the Communist party in Paris supported a colonial campaign for the *Code* that would take place over the next few years. The International Confederation of Free Trade Unions (ICFTU), for its part, supported by US trade unions in particular, focused on interactions with 'moderate' unionists in Anglophone Africa. Kenyan unionists were prime targets. While the ICFTU put a strong emphasis on supporting anti-communist unionism, it appealed to African workers in no small part through anti-colonial rhetoric, and reinforced a process of de-radicalization that was already well underway in Kenya in the early 1950s and in which African unionists were significant actors in their own right (see Zeleza 1987). This process was also certainly contested within the labour movement.[6] Colonial governments, and the ILO for that matter, may well have been rather ambivalent about the stabilizing option, but they were under increasing pressure to move that way anyways. Here the shifting political relations of force, in short, help a good deal in understanding why the particular understandings of regular and irregular labour that were eventually adopted played out the way they did.

The similarities and differences between these cases and South Africa, the most prominent case where the maintenance of a regime based on temporary migrant labour was ultimately upheld, increasingly by military force after the establishment of the apartheid system, help to underline this point (see Cooper 2006). The early-twentieth-century system of reserves and pass laws, discussed in greater detail in the previous chapter, certainly had much in common with systems of labour recruitment based on controlled temporary migration and the preservation of 'traditional' authority in rural areas elsewhere in the region (Mamdani 1996). The South African system was also under similar strains by the 1940s, as urbanization proceeded rapidly despite the intentions of the government. These tensions, indeed, were amplified in South Africa for two reasons (see Wolpe 1972; O'Meara 1975). First, under pressure from white farmers, the reserves were confined to a small and shrinking proportion of the country's agricultural land and thus increasingly unable to provide for subsistence needs. Second, the sheer scope of wage labour in South Africa, particularly in gold and diamond mining, far outstripped anything else in the region. Neither was South Africa immune from the wider wave of strikes in the region in the mid-to-late 1940s. Most notably, in August of 1946, black workers organized by the African Mine Workers' Union on the Witwatersrand gold fields went on strike. Estimates of the actual number of striking workers vary considerably, but its scale was undoubtedly massive compared even to the general strikes carried out elsewhere. The Johannesburg Star's figure was roughly 50 000, official statistics count precisely 62 091, and the Chamber of Mines estimated 76 000, while the Communist Party triumphantly pegged the number of striking workers at over 100 000 (see O'Meara 1975: 160). Migrant workers shut down mining operations for a week and provoked a violent police response. Both the principal demands of the strikers – for better pay, food, and housing – and the longer-run causes of the strike itself – which hinged on the growing contradiction between the assumption of circular migration of African workers underlying the migrant labour system and the reality of an increasingly permanently urbanized and organized working class whose workplaces remained organized on a highly irregular basis (see O'Meara 1975) – were similar to the dynamics on view elsewhere in the region. The South African government, much like colonial administrations elsewhere, was also very much split on how to respond (see Mamdani 1996: 98–100; Chanock 2001). Two separate commissions on 'Native Law' issued reports in 1948. The Fagan Report recognized the 'inevitability' of African urbanization, driven by the demand for wage labour; the Sauer Report called for an active reversal of urbanization through the forcible removal of 'surplus' urban-dwellers and the intensification of control over migration. The National Party's election in 1948 came on the strength of a manifesto largely based on the Sauer Report, although as Posel (1992) shows in considerable detail, in practice the demand for labour in mining and increasingly in industry underpinned a number of persistent ambivalences.

Internal divisions over social policy for 'natives' in South Africa, which were themselves proxies for a broader ambivalence within the white ruling faction about a system of maintaining surplus populations that was increasingly threatened both by overt protest and by the weight of everyday choices by African workers, were reflected before the institution of apartheid in a considerable ambivalence about the ILO and its reformist tendencies. Of course, the debates at the ILO in the latter half of 1930s about South Africa's labour recruitment systems in relation to questions of free and forced labour compounded these suspicions even if they led to very little substantial regulation. Benson's report to the Philadelphia Conference in 1944 approvingly described General Smuts' efforts at reforming social policy:

> In the Union of South Africa . . . General Smuts has advocated, in amplification of the principles of trusteeship, wide measures of social reform, and far

reaching recommendations have been made by government commissions with a view to the improvement of the position of the low-income groups among the population of the Union.

(ILO 1944: 3)

Even prior to the institution of apartheid, though, the ILO's role was viewed in South Africa with some suspicion. A government memo on the postwar role of the ILO circulated in 1945, for instance, suggested several broad principles related to the reform of the ILO, including (notably) increased flexibility in the requirements of conventions and recommendations. It concluded that these options for reform 'should be carefully considered in South Africa in the light of their affect [sic] on local conditions and the general interest which appears to exist concerning the peculiar problems of this country'.[7] In any case, however, the fact that it is in South Africa that policies seeking to maintain a circulating population of (African) irregular labour, against a minimal 'normalized' class of (white) skilled workers, were ultimately maintained, despite the fact that the South African economy unquestionably had the largest demand for wage labour in capitalist enterprises, underscores the importance of political struggle and of racial dynamics in shaping these outcomes particularly strongly.

The broader point is that the articulation of proletarian working classes with rural surplus populations was contested across the region and these conflicts came to a head in the mid-to-late 1940s under increasing pressure from a widespread wave of strikes and the continued movement of African workers into urban areas. Previous means of delineating proletarian work from 'irregular' labour, which, as described in the previous chapter, rested largely on colonial imaginaries of difference between 'African' and 'European' workers, were increasingly inadequate. The postwar wave of strikes and the regulatory debates that they drove also thus had strong racial and colonial undertones. The struggles of colonial officials to come to grips with this problem were reflected particularly clearly in a series of international 'expert' meetings over the course of the late 1940s and the first half of the 1950s – to which I turn in the following section.

The troubled progress of stabilization policies at the ILO and IALC

Existing patterns of political relations of force go a long way towards explaining the difficulty in re-articulating the boundaries between proletarian and irregular work after WWII. It proved difficult, in short, to reformulate the boundary between proletarian and irregular work without undermining the whole edifice of colonial rule. The ILO played a significant role in international institutional mechanisms in which colonial administrators sought to manage labour relations within the new framework of 'development'. A set of overlapping international agencies for the management of colonial labour relations were established in the late 1940s. The ILO established a Committee of Experts on Social Policy in Non-Metropolitan Territories in 1947. After a string of international meetings, starting in 1946, of 'expert' delegations from the colonial powers on various 'technical' facets of development, European officials established a 'Committee on Technical Cooperation in Africa South of the Sahara' (CCTA) in 1949. An 'Inter-African Labour Conference' (IALC) was convened in Jos, Nigeria, in 1948, and afterwards brought under the rubric of the CCTA and held at regular intervals. These networks to some extent represented competing projects. South Africa in particular explicitly promoted the IALC and CCTA as means of forestalling the development of ILO field projects.[8] In practice, though, the ILO was usually represented at the meetings of the IALC, many of the same people participated in both the IALC and the Committee of Experts, and they typically dealt with the same issues. Managing the flow of migrants from rural to urban areas was perhaps the predominant topic of discussion in both settings.

Misgivings about the suitability of Africans for 'modern' labour relations played a major role in shaping international debates. They led to a number of surprising or contradictory outcomes. These concerns were reflected in the first key meeting of the Committee of Experts, in 1947 in London. There was some debate over how the ILO should approach the issue of migration. The South African employers' representative endorsed the system of restricted migration adopted in the Witwatersrand gold mines, in which workers' stays in urban areas were temporary, limited to the length of their contract term, and they were required to save money to remit to their 'home' areas. Some other committee members variously argued for protections of migrant workers on the jobsite, especially from poor wages, or that migration was necessary given the 'uneven distribution of labour' in African territories (ILO 1947: 8–10). Notably, though – and surprisingly given the rather fraught questions about coercion in South African recruiting systems discussed in the previous chapter – the final text advocated something that looked a good deal like the Witwatersrand system. It recommended mandatory remittances, contract term limits, and the allowance (or requirement) of 'visits' to home areas (ILO 1947: esp. 19–25). The first IALC in Jos the following year nonetheless came out in favour of the stabilizing option. They recommended the establishment of trade union rights, along with social security 'to assist the wage earner in meeting his immediate family obligations' and pension programmes 'where tribal organisation has ceased to be effective' (qtd. Cooper 1996a: 222). Given South Africa's preference for working through the IALC rather than the ILO, this is perhaps ironic – but also reflective of the relatively similar composition of both panels. It is also notable that the question of 'free' and 'unfree' labour was largely sidelined in these debates.

By 1950, the IALC at Elizabethville had concluded (over South African objections) that 'It must be acknowledged in a general manner that the stabilization of workers at the site of employment constitutes a goal to be achieved' (ILO 1950a: 13). Solutions emphasized raising levels of productivity, and providing better training and education for a small core of proletarian workers. Training and education were framed not only as a means of making workers more productive, but also as issues of dignity, which were intimately connected to political questions of stability: 'Technical training has the effect of raising the esteem of the worker in his own eyes. It also has the effect of raising his esteem in the eyes of others, which is very important for African workers' (ILO 1950b: 5). The twin issues of productivity and stabilization were also intimately connected to various policies for social security – family allowances, housing, and healthcare were mentioned particularly frequently (ILO 1950b). The last lines of the same report are telling: 'In matters of stabilization, like in matters of training, [colonial] governments can and should take the initiative . . . The future of the indigenous population depends largely on their foresight' (ILO 1950b: 10). Here the careful delineation of a small subset of proletarian workers, organized into nuclear families, from a broader latent surplus population was a deliberate political strategy aimed at securing the continued stability of the colonial order – the interplay between these struggles over the normalization of certain forms of exploitation and the broader political relations of force is particularly clear here. Housing, social security, and training were seen as mechanisms for the normalization of proletarian modes of labour – and, more broadly, 'modern' nuclear family structures oriented around male wage-working breadwinners – for a small subset of African workers. This was seen as a mechanism for the maintenance of colonial authority in the face of continued strike activity.

Yet, these solutions were scarcely ever implemented in full or with much enthusiasm. The Committee of Experts met again in Geneva in 1951, and largely followed in the same vein as the Elizabethville meeting. It did reach more substantive conclusions with respect to social protection. The Committee's recommendations included family wages; adequate housing; education and training; improved healthcare; cooperatives, especially for food marketing; social security, including old age and disability insurance; and trade union education (ILO 1952: 108–113). But the report still cautioned that growth of productivity would always need to be balanced against the possible disruption of existing patterns of life:

> The social and political structure of African territories has its roots in an economy based on small-scale individual exploitation, often in the context of a communal property regime. In such regions, over-hasty introduction of mechanization or large-scale agriculture in search of higher productivity will raise technical and social problems that will not be easily resolved.
> (ILO 1952: 40)

In the early 1950s, then, 'development' solutions to the political problems posed by challenges to existing systems of labour migration remained hamstrung by the difficulty in identifying African workers with implicitly European cultural images of proletarian workers.

These political challenges were compounded by the broader fragility of colonial economic structures and the resistance of employers or colonial administrations to substantially increasing their spending on wages or social security. Pension policies in particular were effectively hamstrung by these issues. The campaign for the *Code de Travail* in AOF made demands for pensions and social security, but the *Code* did not ultimately make mention of pensions. Even the British, who were outwardly the most supportive among the colonial powers of social security and stabilization, pleaded that fully implementing the provisions of the 1947 convention was 'unrealistic' in the short term in their reports to the ILO (see Cooper 1996a: 362). Ironically, these British arguments were echoed quite closely by officials in the Native Affairs Secretariat in South Africa, commenting on the inapplicability of proposed ILO conventions on social security to the 'Native' population:

> The Union is in a difficult position as regards the inclusion in social security measures of its native population on account, mainly, of the difference in the cultural background and mode of life of purely tribal natives and those persons who, having severed all ties with tribal traditions, have become urbanised and therefore accustomed to a standard of living approximating that of the European section.[9]

For 'natives' in 'tribal' areas, care for the poor was left to the community, 'and it is certainly not desirable that the state should seek to destroy this practice by providing a comprehensive scheme of social security'. Moreover, given the widespread poverty of native populations, their ability to contribute to social insurance schemes was relatively limited, and 'in fact it is largely for this reason that it has not yet been found practicable to provide for benefits for natives in the form of pensions, as opposed to lump-sum grants'.[10] The Secretary for Labour would repeat most of these arguments verbatim in a letter to the ILO explaining why South Africa would not ratify the proposed convention.[11] International arguments about pensions and stabilization then, remained ambiguous and unsettled enough in the early 1950s that officials representing the paradigmatic repressive system of labour migration and the most outwardly vocal supporters of stabilization could make closely parallel arguments.

That the issue was never entirely down to cost, however, can be seen in the trajectory of debates about other aspects of social policy in subsequent years. While the debate about pensions stalled, vocational training, employment services, and housing policies were primary objects of discussion. In these areas too, ambivalent views about the suitability of Africans for urbanization continued to hamper both the ILO and colonial experts. The Committee of Experts met in Lisbon in 1953. The bulk of the discussion in Lisbon focused on housing. Housing policies went to the root of the debate about migration and stabilizing. The ILO prepared a report giving estimates of the magnitude and causes of shortages of workers' housing in colonial territories, then proposing a range of solutions from workers' cooperative organizations and employer provided housing through to various policy options for governments including housing and zoning legislation, resettlement schemes, and financial aid. The report suggested that it would be ideal in the long run if workers were to own separate family homes, but 'until workers can be encouraged to become owner-occupiers the provision of rental housing for workers, especially for those in the low-income groups, must be regarded as a social service' (ILO 1953a: 113). This implied a primary responsibility for government in the provision of housing. Discussion of the report in Committee was still bedevilled, however, by concerns about order and overly rapid urbanization:

> Reference was made to the danger of permitting towns to expand beyond a certain limit; then they became unwieldy to administer and control. Under such circumstances, everything should be done to encourage the erection and development of satellite towns with suitable and cheap transport facilities for workers to get to and from their places of work.
>
> (ILO 1953b: 7)

The committee did agree on a number of conclusions. These included the responsibility of governments for the provision of housing, and the general principle in favour of home ownership 'in order to assure respect for human dignity, to give maximum freedom and security and as incentives for stability and better living' (ILO 1953b: 23). Nonetheless, these debates remained marked by the ambivalence between the perceived need to normalize a subset of proletarian workers and the expectation that this would be difficult to do because those workers were 'Africans'. Critically, these debates about housing also show the importance of shifting patterns of household formation and gender relations to the governance of 'stabilization' particularly clearly. The normalization of 'standard employment relationships' in Europe and North America, ongoing at the same time, was heavily rooted in specific patterns of household formation based on nuclear households oriented around a male sole breadwinner (see Vosko 2010). 'Stabilization' debates, as clearly evidenced here, rested on the assumption that urbanization would be accompanied by similar forms of gender relations and household formation.

The Committee of Experts met again in Dakar in 1955. Here the Committee gave more explicit consideration to social security proper. Debates continued to reflect concerns about the feasibility of social security in colonial territories. The Committee identified a number of features of colonized populations that posed difficulties for the introduction of social security programmes – the persistence of 'collective responsibility' for welfare in 'tribal' communities; the relative weight of unskilled agricultural employment; the absence of adequate registries of birth, marriage, and death, and illiteracy among workers. Meanwhile, the introduction of development programmes and industrialization 'had changed certain traditional features of social life so that some sections of the population had become permanent wage earners and no longer formed part of the communal pattern' (ILR 1956: 627). These 'classes of wage earners who . . . could no longer rely on the solidarity engendered by the family or tribal community . . . were consequently vulnerable to the ordinary risks of life and to the fluctuations of employment' (ILR 1956: 628).

Yet it was still not easy to nail down exactly who was 'stabilized' enough to need these social security measures. The 1957 IALC in Lusaka dealt explicitly with the

Colonial crisis and social policy 73

issues raised by the differentiation of 'stabilized' from 'tribal' populations. This was noted in discussions of old-age pensions:

> The committee considered various technical aspects of old age pensions. In respect of the field of application it gave special consideration to criteria for the definition of a stabilised worker. In certain countries the only criterion is the period of residence, whilst elsewhere other criteria apply, such as technical qualifications, a minimum period of service, and the period of residence in non-tribal areas. In these circumstances the choice should be left to the initiative of the individual Governments, who could usefully be guided by solutions already adopted.[12]

The conclusions of the report clearly suggest that this delineation of 'stabilized' workers depended on the exercise of government control: 'The necessary steps should be taken to establish the identity of workers and their entitlement to benefits, these measures being subject to control by the competent authorities'. Further, 'Where contributions are payable, these should be paid to Government organisations, or where collected by private organisations to a management committee on which employers and employees should, as far as possible, be represented subject to government control'.[13] Social security, and the stabilization of an urban workforce more broadly, were intimately interlinked with the expansion of state control.

The role of the ILO across these debates is worth unpacking. The ILO played an indirect role in shaping and refining the practices through which colonial governments sought to 'stabilize' African workers, and its workshops and the production of reports were important practices through which the ILO sought to influence colonial policy. The institutional set-up of the IALC and the Committee nonetheless prevented the emergence of technical assistance schemes directly operated by the ILO. This was not for lack of interest on the part of the ILO. The Committee of Experts concluded in 1951 that the newfound emphasis of the UN system on technical assistance to underdeveloped areas 'would fully justify' the application of the ILO's TAP facilities in colonial territories.[14] Wilfred Jenks, a long tenured Deputy Director General at the ILO, suggested to the Committee of Experts in 1953 that 'all . . . subjects on the agenda for this session . . . concern fields of activity from which administrations might well derive benefit from the international programme of technical assistance of the United Nations and the Specialized Agencies' (ILO 1953c). Two years later in Dakar, Jenks would express frustration that so little technical cooperation under ILO auspices was happening in sub-Saharan Africa, in spite of the apparent success of the ILO in 'development' programming elsewhere.[15] The importance of the resistance of the colonial powers in limiting the role of the ILO is perhaps most clearly illustrated by the speed with which technical assistance funds to Africa and expanded after 1960 (see Chapter 4). In any event, even in the 1950s, the ILO's participation in these debates – as with the forced labour commissions taking place around the same time (Chapter 2) – did mark out the ILO as a space in which conflicts over postcolonial social order could be pursued.

Another significant point for the purposes of this study is that workers themselves articulated crucial challenges to the ways in which colonial authorities sought to delineate standard and irregular workers. The colonial debates that the ILO contributed to producing constantly ran up against the material trajectory of urbanization and the growth of a politically influential 'working class'. The effort to articulate a clear line between a small class of regularized proletarian workers and a large population of various forms of irregular labour, then, did not in fact prevent challenges to colonial order. 'Stabilizing' policies in practice contributed to creating more formally organized bases for resistance to colonial rule. Cooper notes that the significance of unions in the process of decolonization stemmed from two factors. First, as noted above, in relatively narrow colonial export economies, workers situated at strategic nodes (mines, plantations, railways, or ports) were able to exert a profoundly disruptive influence with work stoppages. Second, and at least as importantly, 'the discourse that labour movements employed in the postwar era – putting claims to resources in the terms in which imperial rule was now asserting its justification – made them hard to combat without calling into question the modernizing project on which France and Britain had staked so much' (2005: 205). Proletarianized workers were able to redeploy the ideas about stabilization circulating at the IALC and the Committee of Experts in order to make claims for greater pay and higher standards of living. In the process, they undermined the imagination of difference upon which the colonial project rested. They also stretched the material limits of colonial rule – administrations could not really argue with workers' claims, but were unwilling to actually shoulder the cost of wage increases and social security (see Cooper 1996a; 2005). Yet, this mobilization of 'development' discourses against the colonial state also opened up a complex matrix of problems surrounding the relationship between labour and nationalist movements. Workers' successes in gaining higher wages and increased social protections may have helped undercut colonial authority, but also widened gaps between unionized workers and the broader population.

Conclusion

This trajectory is significant in the context of the broader set of arguments presented in this book for three reasons. In the first instance, it underlines the political character of the differentiation of proletarian forms of exploitation from irregular labour. The exact location of the boundary between proletarian labour forms and irregular migrant labour was variable, embodied in regulatory debates at national and international levels, and remained contested and controversial throughout the period in question. Efforts to delineate a small, regularized working class in territories outside of the apartheid states in Southern Africa emerged out of a complex dialectic between workers' mobilizations and colonial efforts to contain them. Second, the role of race and gender in these political struggles is equally revealed particularly clearly in these debates. While the suitability of colonized populations for 'normal' modes of exploitation was the subject of debates in the early twentieth century – as noted in the previous chapter – the difficulty in maintaining the boundary between 'normal' and irregular work on a racial basis became particularly acute in the debates about migration in the 1950s. These debates overlapped with struggles around gender roles and family structures.

Third, in moving into the discussion of employment policies and the development of strategies targeting the 'informal' sector in the next chapter, it is worth underlining that the salience of broader patterns of political relations of force in shaping the trajectory of these debates is particularly clear. The continued mobilization of African workers, particularly in making claims for higher wages, housing, and social security, drove these debates to a considerable extent. The increasing efforts to tie workers' organizations into broader anti-colonial struggles also had significant implications for the ways in which formal decolonization impacted on these struggles. The unsettled relationship of organized labour to the broader surplus population equally remained politically problematic after the formal end of colonial rule. These relations remained bound up in struggles over the political mobilization of subaltern social forces and the tenuous hegemonic project of postcolonial states for much of the 1960s and 1970s.

Notes

1 Benson is sometimes even credited with pioneering the contemporary meaning of 'development'. This is inaccurate, but it does speak to the significance of Benson's activity both within and beyond the ILO in wartime and postwar debates about colonial agendas.
2 Stack to Blelloch, 4 August 1947, International Labour Organization Archives (ILOA) O/200/15
3 'Technical Assistance: ILO Programme, Notes for Opening Statement' ILOA Z 6/1/7/1, p. 6. The date and author are unclear, but most likely this was a statement delivered by Morse for an internal meeting.
4 The strike's retrospective significance has been enhanced by Ousmane Sembene's (1960) novel *God's Bits of Wood*, which dramatized the strike and played a significant part in memorializing it as a kind of proto-nationalist movement against colonial rule. As Cooper (1996b) has argued convincingly, more immediate concerns over wages and working conditions, tied to the delineation of normal from irregular labour, played a far more important role in shaping the strike than this narrative admits.
5 The WFTU and ICFTU were rival 'international' trade union federations. The former was dominated by trade unions with links to communist parties, and heavily influenced by the direction of the Soviet Union – although the French CGT remained a significant Western European member and had an outsized influence on the WFTU's policy towards colonial workers. The ICFTU was explicitly anti-communist and dominated by British and Western European members.
6 The broad outlines of these struggles and their consequences are traced further in the discussion of the ILO's policy on unemployment in Kenya in the following chapter.
7 F. C. Williams, 'The International Labour Office in its Relation to World Social Structure: A Report on the Probable Future of the International Labour Office with Special Reference to Constitutional Amendment', December 1945. NASA HEN 477/1/20/3.
8 The fullest statement to this effect comes from an undated aide memoire for the South African Minister of External Affairs, '11th Session of CCTA: ILO Expert Committee on Social Policy in Non-Metropolitan Territories', in National Archives of South Africa, Pretoria (NASA) BTS 8/26/5 Vol. 1.

Colonial crisis and social policy

9 Secretary for Native Affairs to the Secretary for Labour, 'International Labour Conference, 1951: Objectives and Minimum Standards of Social Security', 27 October 1950, NASA NTS 207/280 (2).
10 *Ibid.*
11 Arthur D. Lee, Secretary for Labour, to The Director General, International Labour Organization, 10 December 1951, copy in NASA NTS 207/280 (2).
12 'Inter African Labour Conference, Fifth Session: Final Report', n.d., NASA NTS 703/280.
13 *Ibid.*
14 'Committee of Experts on Social Policy in Non-Metropolitan Territories, Second Session, Geneva, 26 November – 8 December 1951: Draft Report', copy in NASA BTS 8/25/6 Vol. 1A.
15 Wilfred Jenks, 'The ILO in Africa', annexed to letter from Secretary of Labour to Secretary for External Affairs, 21 December 1955, NASA BTS 8/26/5 Vol. 1A.

4 Irregular work in the postcolonial social order
The World Employment Programme discovers the 'informal'

The concept of 'informal' labour, as noted elsewhere in this book, has become rather pervasive, both in the ILO's activity and in academic debates about irregular forms of labour. The contemporary governance of irregular labour is shaped in no small part around the concept. We can point to major policy initiatives at the ILO (see next chapter), and increasingly the World Bank and states in the global south as well. The 'informal' is also, as noted in the introduction to this book, a deeply problematic concept insofar as it tends to lump together what is in fact a vastly differentiated range of different forms of work, and obscure the linkages between these irregular forms of work and the workings of capitalist production and accumulation on the basis of a binary between 'formal' and 'informal' activity. This latter argument has been well-made by a number of critics (e.g. Roitman 1990; Taylor 2010; Phillips 2011).

However, as I have insisted throughout this book, it is worthwhile taking seriously the politics involved in actually producing, circulating, and applying a concept like 'informal' labour in governing persistent forms of irregular labour. The concept does much of the same work of cocooning 'irregular' forms of exploitation and normalizing others (in this case, the 'formal' sector) that the concept of 'forced labour' does. It does political work by reifying fluid boundaries between what we might call, in the Marxian terms introduced in Chapter 1, relative surplus populations and normalized working classes. At the same time, the actual contents, ideological colouration, and political impacts of its development and rolling out in particular places have been profoundly shaped by wider political relations of force. This chapter, accordingly, takes up the historical origins of the ILO's attention to 'informal' labour in the context of the organization's flagship World Employment Programme in the late 1960s and early 1970s, focusing in particular on the policy mission to Kenya in 1972 that is widely credited with popularizing the concept of the 'informal' sector.

It is at this point that the discussion of 'informal' labour plugs in to the broader historical narrative sketched over the two previous chapters. In the first instance, while the 'informal' was in many ways a conceptual innovation, it also very plainly drew on older ideas about 'modern' and 'traditional' sectors that were crucial to the colonial interventions discussed above and remained very much at the core of thinking in development economics (e.g. Lewis 1954). Second, moreover, the ways in which the concept was rolled out and the wider employment policy framework developed by the ILO's mission were actually applied in Kenya were profoundly shaped by ongoing struggles over the relationship between normalized and irregular work, highlighted in the previous chapter, that carried over into postcolonial political economies.

This early history of the 'informal' as a regulatory tool is important in the context of the broader arguments presented in this book for two reasons. First, as noted above, the concept of 'informal' work, particularly in the way it was deployed by the ILO, rests on the dynamics of naturalization and differentiation highlighted in Chapter 1. The ILO highlighted the need to create productive 'linkages' between formal and informal economies as a means of fostering inclusive economic growth (most notably in ILO 1972). This approach 'cocooned' the irregular forms of labour in which most African workers were engaged insofar as it framed 'informal' workers in terms of their exclusion from formal markets. Notably, these policy frameworks around informal labour did not reflect some of the more nuanced uses of the concept of 'informal' work that emerged at around the same time. Keith Hart's (1973) analysis of 'informal' economies in Accra, for instance – likely the first use of the concept – situates the growth of the informal sector in the context of growing rural-urban migration coupled with rising unemployment and falling real wages since the 1950s. Hart notes the increasing prevalence of 'moonlighting' by formally employed workers in 'informal' jobs, as well as the growing turn, particularly by rural-urban migrant workers, to illegal or unregulated livelihoods in a context where earnings in formal jobs were being eroded. Hart's arguments are not especially critical – they are cast in largely Weberian terms, and emphasize the consequences for planning of the persistence of 'informal' activity – but do point to more complex patterns of inter-linkage between 'formal' and 'informal' economies than the ILO's perspective did. As several contemporary critics were keen to point out (e.g. Leys 1973; Sandbrook 1983), the ILO's understanding of 'informal' work tended to occlude the structural factors underlying the persistence of unemployment and 'informality'.

Second, in order to understand the specific shape of the ILO's efforts to govern 'informal' economies, it is useful to highlight how these processes were shaped by prevailing patterns of political relations of force. The process of decolonization did not eliminate the challenges noted at the end of the previous chapter, and in the 1960s in particular these posed significant problems for the ILO's efforts to expand the scope of its activities in the region. The expanded scope of ILO activity in Africa – and the relative smoothness with which they were able to carry out projects 'on the ground' – going into the 1970s was reflective, in part, of the tenuous solidification of what Bayart (2009) has usefully called the 'postcolonial historic bloc'. Importantly, these developments rested to a considerable extent on the organizational differentiation of normal and irregular modes of labour relations. As is perhaps especially clear in the Kenyan example discussed in greater detail below, by the early 1970s trade unions and other elements of civil society were largely brought under the control of governing parties, with dissident factions increasingly marginalized or expelled.

Critically, this process often rested on the increasingly rigid differentiation of normalized and irregular workers.

These arguments are presented in three broad steps. The first section below outlines the political challenges posed by the relationships between nationalist parties and organized labour in the period after decolonization. The next section moves on to the broader context of WEP's activity in the early 1970s. It situates the turn to WEP in the context of the ILO's activity in response to the growing crisis of Fordist 'standard employment relations' in the global north (see Cox 1977) on the one hand and the continuation of colonial regulatory ideas on the other, and outlines in broad terms the shifting patterns of relations of force in sub-Saharan Africa. The final section examines the ways in which these dynamics played out in one particular case: Kenya. It shows how the WEP mission's findings dovetailed with broader struggles for control over the boundaries of trade union political action, but the substantive implementation of the ILO's recommendations remained relatively constrained.

The antinomies of decolonization

Decolonization marks an important departure for present purposes because it presented an opening for the ILO to expand its technical assistance activities in the region beyond the relatively narrow limits of participation in the IALC and Committee of Experts, but also brought into the open latent conflicts about the relations between labour and postcolonial regimes. ILO technical assistance activities expanded rapidly after 1960. In 1952, only 2.7 per cent of spending on technical cooperation had gone to African projects, the proportion reached 27.2 per cent in 1962, and 33 per cent by 1964 (ILO 1966: 14). But ILO officials often found it hard to implement projects in practice in the context of ongoing political struggles, particularly over the relationships between unionized workers and governing parties (see Bernards 2017c). The ways in which the fragile articulation of the distinction between proletarianized workers and other irregular workers had been cemented in the late-colonial period posed a number of political challenges. These were especially acute around the problem of the political role of unionized workers in postcolonial Africa. These latter tensions are worth exploring briefly because they are suggestive of the fraught and politicized nature of the differentiation of proletarian workers from irregular labour.[1]

Here it is worth briefly laying out in broad strokes – at the risk of some oversimplification – the context of the relationship between labour and the state that was taking shape at the time of decolonization. The ability to control trade unions took on increased political salience as many postcolonial governments settled into a neocolonial developmental and political model predicated on control over export production and trade with core countries, which Bayart (2009) has usefully labelled a 'strategy of extraversion'. Railways and ports remained crucial choke points on export economies that were central to the survival of postcolonial regimes. To use Wright's (2000) terms, although organized workers in postcolonial Africa often had limited 'associational' power insofar as they represented a small segment of the workforce and the population more generally, they exercised a considerable degree of 'structural' power because they occupied key nodes in export economies. The cooptation or suppression of trade union activity, especially in transport and mining, took on an enhanced significance in this context, as indeed it had in the colonial period. This control was, however, by no means assured. The decade following decolonization was characterized in many African countries by ongoing struggles over the scope and limits of state power, the shape of national development, and the boundaries of political contestation.

These unsettled dynamics are particularly visible in conflicts around the relationships of trade unions and nationalist parties. To a considerable degree, these struggles turned on the character of the relationship between the small core of proletarian workers represented in the trade unions and the broader population. For present purposes, it is worth outlining that these were widespread struggles. Some postcolonial regimes recognized the value in claiming that unionized workers were part of a wider 'nation'. Tanzania's Julius Nyerere, in a pamphlet released in 1961, very clearly articulated the arguments that many leaders would make for subordinating labour to the nationalist party. He compares Tanzania to Britain – the Labour Party, he argues had emerged had emerged out of union struggles against capital and the state, while in colonial Tanganyika Nyerere suggests that:

> Our development has been the other way around. When . . . we established our nationalist movement, its first aim was political – independence from colonialism. Within this nationalist movement, and very much a part of it, one of our objectives was to help the growth of a trade union movement . . . Once firmly established, the trade-union movement was, and is, part and parcel of the whole nationalist movement.
>
> (1969: 282)

Factually, Nyerere's claim is questionable – trade unionism developed around the transport infrastructure of Tanganyika prior to and largely independent of the organized nationalist movement (see Illife 1975). The politics of the argument, however, are very clear. It suggests that national struggles for independence from colonialism ought to take priority over other interests for workers. Nyerere's effort at assimilating all pre-independence political activity into the rubric of the 'nationalist movement' is a powerful political tactic. Yet the fact that he felt a need to articulate this view in the first place is itself indicative of a recognition that workers did not all see things the same way. Nyerere survived an army mutiny supported by the labour movement in 1964 before bringing trade unions more directly under the control of the Tanganyika African National Union, either imprisoning or giving ambassadorships to the former leadership of the trade unions (Bienefield 1975).

Similar patterns were visible in Ghana. Ghanaian trade unions had played an important part in the struggle against colonialism, but even prior to the country's independence from Britain there were considerable divisions within the workers' movement over how closely they should be linked to the Convention People's Party (CPP). Broadly speaking, the leadership of the national confederation, the Trades Union Congress (TUC), were closely linked to the CPP, but rank and file unionists – especially in certain sectoral unions, most notably the Railway Union – continued to press for greater autonomy from the government. In short, the relations of political force were marked by particularly unsettled group formation, both within the trade union movement and in terms of the CPP's ability to claim authority over the 'nation' as a whole. This fragile political balance had potential material implications, especially for the ruling party. The fragility of the CPP's position was highlighted particularly clearly by an illegal seventeen-day strike by the railway and harbour workers in Sekondi-Takoradi in September of 1961. The demands of the strikers were put in terms of relatively minor economic issues – the July budget had included a compulsory savings scheme and a property tax on larger than average houses which were unpopular among skilled workers likely to suffer somewhat from these measures. However, the strike was widely supported by unskilled workers, market women, and even some of the unemployed in the area. These actors would not have been especially affected by these measures, instead their support for the strikers was driven largely by 'the wider significance these economic issues assumed in the context of the politics of the national labour movement, and of widespread popular opposition to the direction of development of the CPP regime' (Jeffries 1975: 263). This support was crucial for the union, which was able to arrange to have food supplied to the strikers by market women. The broader mass support for the strike also heightened its political salience. There were wider debates at play about the relation between the TUC and CPP – the Railway Union in particular advocated for a role for the TUC as a check on the power of the CPP, whereas the TUC leadership and CPP sought to maintain closer control over the workers' movement. For marginal urban workers to support the strikers meant an explicit challenge to the CPP's efforts to articulate a 'national' consciousness centered on the party.

For Kwame Nkrumah, emphasizing the subordination of the labour movement to nationalist, anti-colonial ends was a critical means of trying to mitigate some of these conflicts. He noted in a speech to parliament that 'Creating our own African international trade union organizations, we cannot individually opt to associate with other international unions, for this will do exactly what we must guard against' (Nkrumah 1961: 8). If these concerns undoubtedly reflected Nkrumah's famous concerns about neo-colonialism and pan-African solidarity, they also have to be read in the context of the CPP's political struggle to control the labour movement. It is worth noting in this respect that the TUC leadership – fragile though their position in Ghanaian union politics was – were among the leaders of the movement pressing for a 'pan-Africa' trade union confederation made up of unions under the control of 'nationalist' parties, and saw the ICFTU as a potential threat to their own position to the extent that it might provide support for breakaway factions like those in the Railway.[2]

Elsewhere, the delineation of organized labour from the broader population could be mobilized as a means of disciplining organized labour. In Kenya, for instance, the government frequently claimed that the trade unions represented a relatively privileged segment of the population, and thus had limited claim to political legitimacy or to make demands about pay or working conditions. Tom Mboya, a former union leader and key figure in the country's independence movement who served as Minister of Economic Planning and Development until his assassination in 1969, gave a lecture to the ILO's International Institute for Labour Studies in 1967 in which he contrasted organized workers with 'the "have nots" in society [who] are not normally well organized and *must rely on the government or political parties* to represent their interests' (Mboya 1967: 5, emphasis added).

Such political strategies varied widely, as did responses from trade unions. The point for present purposes is that the delineation of proletarian labour from irregular work remained unsettled, but politically vital, well after decolonization. The ways in which struggles around this problem played out varied widely, as will become especially apparent in the following chapter. We can trace the fundamental problem, though, to the troubled negotiation of the boundary between proletarian and surplus populations in the last decades of colonial rule. These struggles were driven by the interplay between workers' actions, especially the successive waves of general strikes in the 1930s and 1940s, and efforts to re-establish bases for colonial authority. At no point were colonial authorities, linked to the ILO's emerging 'development' agenda, entirely successful in doing so. This unsettled character of the relationship between organized labour and the much larger surplus population played a considerable role in shaping struggles over unemployment and 'informal' labour in the following decades, and profoundly shaped the operation of WEP in practice.

WEP and the 'discovery' of employment

WEP was probably the ILO's defining programme in the late 1960s and early 1970s. The project was started with a considerable degree of fanfare in 1968, as one of David Morse's final acts as Director General before retirement (the Pope even attended the ceremony to launch the programme). The program would contribute to several major ideational developments in the governance of poverty in the 1970s – not only the concept of the 'informal', but also 'basic needs' and 'redistribution from growth' which were highly influential at the time (see Saith 2005; Bangasser 2000).

Many insider histories produced by the ILO and former officials locate the genesis of WEP in the 'discovery' that without widespread employment, economic growth did not necessarily lead to 'development' in the sense of greater human wellbeing (see Saith 2005: 1168). In contrast to conventional approaches to development at the time, emphasizing economic growth and capital formation, the ILO sought to place 'employment generation into the center of the national planning and development efforts as an explicit policy objective in its own right, instead of leaving it as a residual and eventual consequence of "successful" development efforts' (Bangasser 2000: 5). Importantly, employment was seen in this context as a means to increasing human wellbeing rather than an end in itself. In explaining the purpose of the WEP, outgoing Director General Morse would argue that:

> Productive employment by itself is very much an economic concept. But it leads ... to a wider sharing of the fruits of development ... Where poverty is widespread, these elementary gains are the first and almost the only meaning of social progress.
>
> (1968: 519–520)

The 'discovery' narrative in many of these accounts overstates the unique-ness of the ILO in this respect. Similar 'discoveries' of the social were certainly taking place across the complex of organizations involved in global development governance at the time – the shift to 'human development' approaches under Robert McNamara at the World Bank is particularly notable here (see Rojas 2015; Best 2013).

Moreover, in significant ways, WEP continued within the general *problematique* that had been laid out in the stabilizing debate in the 1940s and 1950s. One official, introducing an early event on WEP in 1971, framed the problem of employment in terms that would not have looked out of place in a report from the IALC: 'People are moving from the rural areas much faster than the small modern sector that attracts them can absorb them. If this continues, large numbers of unemployed people will be living in slums by the end of the decade'.[3] The first project document for the African regional component of the WEP – the Jobs and Skills Programme for Africa (JASPA) – written in late 1972, similarly notes that 'The concentration in the cities of large and growing numbers of dissatisfied young people had potentially a politically explosive character; it creates a social climate where delinquency flourishes; it affects, therefore, the very fabric of society'.[4] The policy prescription was different – generating more jobs as opposed to stabilizing a segment of the workforce or restricting rural-urban migration – but the same underlying fears linking irregular forms of work to dangerous slums and disorder were always present.

WEP also reflected institutional pressures on the ILO that were emerging because tripartite corporatism was coming under pressure in Europe and North America. More critical histories of the WEP have tended to focus on this dimension. Robert Cox discusses WEP in the context of the constraints posed on innovation at the ILO by the context of American hegemony (1977: 417–422). Standing (2008: 363), somewhat similarly, describes the turn to employment, including the growing attention paid to the informal sector, as a strategic blunder that served as a distraction from the broader crisis of tripartite corporatism facing the ILO. That the crisis of Fordism, particularly in the US, helped drive the ILO's emphasis on the WEP is hard to argue. In particular, as relations with the US became increasingly strained, and the US refused to pay its contribution to the ILO's budget in 1970 after the appointment of a Soviet citizen as Assistant Secretary General, the WEP was increasingly relied on as a means of raising funds from the UNDP and from Northern European development agencies.

84   *Irregular work in the postcolonial order*

Indeed, in the context of the deepening funding constraints facing the ILO in the early 1970s, WEP and JASPA were prioritized over other policy areas. The UNDP informed the ILO in 1972 that its funds for new international development projects were limited and that funds for JASPA would have to come in part by reallocating resources from other areas.[5] The response on the part of the African section of the ILO, after it became clear that this 'restrictive' stand on the part of the UNDP would not change, was that JASPA should 'obtain first priority on the envisaged agenda'.[6]

WEP involved five operational tracks in practice: devoting more field resources to employment issues; sending 'high-level missions' to particular countries to advise on employment issues; running regional meetings of policy-makers to call attention to employment issues; sending 'minor' missions on request to governments; and developing a research programme on employment problems.[7] In practice, 'reinforcing the field structure' in the context of budget constraints meant approaching the UNDP for money to appoint 'employment' specialists to field offices – the African Regional Office in Addis Ababa and the field offices elsewhere in the region being the most relevant here.[8] JASPA was established at the ILO's African Regional Conference (ARC) in 1969. The relationship between JASPA and WEP was initially somewhat uncertain. Generally speaking, JASPA was the component of WEP which involved permanent staff working at field offices in Africa. Some national missions, especially in the early 1970s, were carried out under the rubric of the WEP with minimal involvement from the field offices. This disjuncture was in part a result of the fact that the field structure for JASPA was still being established in the early 1970s, but the ILO saw a need to have concrete missions to show for its efforts as early as possible.[9] The ILO started to assemble multi-disciplinary 'Comprehensive Employment Missions' to report on a broad range of policies related to employment and unemployment. The first of these went to Colombia in 1969. The Comprehensive Mission approach, however, was rather expensive and time consuming, and in practice more limited missions to deal with particular issue areas ('manpower training' or employment statistics were particularly common) or sectors very quickly became more common.[10] Even in 1972, while one 'comprehensive' mission was launched (the 'pioneer' mission to Kenya), projects dealing with 'manpower planning' and employment service organizations were sent to Burundi, Chad, Egypt, Ethiopia, Libya, Malawi, Sierra Leone, Somalia, Tanzania, Uganda, Zaire and Zambia; rural employment projects were sent to Chad, Congo Brazzaville, Egypt, Kenya, Nigeria, Rwanda, and Tanzania; and missions dealing with small-scale industries or handicrafts were sent to Dahomey, Ethiopia, Madagascar, Mauritania, Nigeria, Swaziland, and Upper Volta.[11]

The scope of activity carried out under WEP and JASPA poses something of a puzzle. The objectives of the ILO and of national governments in sub-Saharan Africa were scarcely ever a good fit. Indeed, dozens of WEP/JASPA missions had very little to show in terms of actual changes to national policy. Yet, the missions not only received enormous emphasis at the ILO, but continued to be invited by African governments on a regular basis, and generated volumes of research and policy recommendations. The reports themselves had plenty of shortcomings – many of which were pointed out by contemporary critics. The limited implementation of recommended reforms would seem to point to a certain weakness on the part of the ILO with respect to its authority over national governments – yet none of the missions took place without the invitation of the governments involved. Indeed, often they were solicited by African governments.

In order to understand these dynamics, it is important to understand that both WEP and JASPA were rolled out against the backdrop of some significant changes in the political relations of force at play in postcolonial territories, which had particular consequences for the politics of irregular labour. These might be summarized (at the risk of some oversimplification) as the solidification of what Bayart has called the 'postcolonial historic bloc' in sub-Saharan Africa. Leaderships of strategically important groups were increasingly brought into networks of patronage centered on governing party/state complexes in a process of passive revolution (2009: 180–192). As I have noted previously in this book, organized labour was one such strategically important segment of society – among others like students, professionals, and intellectuals. At the regional level, this meant the establishment of a regional confederation committed to a nationalist, 'non-political' form of unionism. Single party or military governments were widely consolidated in the late 1960s and early 1970s. A growing number of African countries were adopting bans on international union affiliation, and after 1973 most banned affiliation to confederations other than the nationalist-dominated Organization for African Trade Union Unity (OATUU), which was set up by the Organization for African Unity (OAU) (see Bernards 2017c). This movement towards 'non-political' unionism, notably, came along with a growing emphasis on delineating unionized 'normal' workers from all others, and restricting their activities to the direct representation of union members in industrial relations. Ironically, postcolonial regimes in the late 1960s and 1970s started to construct the kinds of union movements that colonial authorities had sought to carve out in stabilizing debates. The significance of WEP, in short, is usefully explained by the ways in which political struggles over the relationships between normalized and irregular labour were bound up with struggles over the re-shaping of the state and the wider political relations of force in postcolonial Africa.

These shifts had serious implications for the ILO's work under WEP. To a certain extent, the ostensibly 'technical' focus of WEP reinforced state claims to greater control over economic policy and the 'non-political' character of policy for irregular workers. This was visible even in internal controversies among ILO officials about who should participate in setting priorities for the programme. After the ARC in 1969, the ILO began planning regional seminars for policy-makers to discuss the role of employment in development strategy in Africa. The first of these was held in Dakar in December of 1970. Workers' and employers' participation in the Dakar meeting were discussed. At an early meeting with an external consultant it was suggested that workers' and employers' organizations might be invited to Dakar. The ILO official reporting on the meeting immediately noted that 'this might create a problem regarding the number of participants'.[12] At a later meeting it was pointed out that 'there might be some long-term political advantage, especially vis-à-vis the Governing Body, if some form of employers' and workers' representation were devised' – it was suggested that logistical problems might be avoided if the workers' and employers' groups of the GB were invited to nominate a candidate for participation.[13] The debate, in effect, revolved around whether the political cost in the tripartite GB could be minimized enough that excluding workers would be worthwhile. Eventually workers' participation was rejected. The reasoning was that, since the purpose of the meetings was to 'focus the attention of those people who effectively shape and implement development policies' on employment, and workers' and employers' associations did not fit that bill, it would not be worth the cost to invite workers and employers.[14] A reflection on the Dakar seminar equally noted that the exclusion of workers' and employers' organizations had been beneficial for discussions of national-level policy because 'we could expect that the involvement of particular interest groups . . . in a seminar of this type could take debates towards an impasse because they would tend to situate themselves according to their particular interests and not the general interest'.[15] This approach seems to have been carried forward with little further debate; I found no mention of workers' and employers' organizations in any of the planning materials for the second JASPA seminar in Kericho.[16]

State objectives dovetailed well here with the ILO's continued concerns about the politicization of development activity. Indeed, these fears were substantive enough that at least one official even suggested that the decision on the participation of workers' and employers' organizations at Dakar should not even be referred to the tripartite GB, 'where the normal reflex actions could be expected'.[17] Escaping politics, of course, remained impossible in practice.

In the first instance the idea that limiting participation to government officials would prevent the politicization of the programme depended on a problematic identification of governments as dispassionate representatives of the 'general interest'. Even some ILO officials had misgivings about whether or not this was the case: there were reservations expressed as early as the planning for the Dakar seminar that the ILO's approach was 'too academic and [did] not concentrate sufficiently on what is politically feasible'.[18] Deliberately or not, the 'technical' emphasis of the ILO put the focus of development assistance squarely on the state and on policy reform, and tended to marginalize the active role of organized labour in the development process. It depended on the idea that governments were autonomous actors solely concerned with achieving the greater wellbeing of society as a whole, and particularly of those not participating in 'normal' labour markets – through technical adjustments to policy. A number of critics would later remark, quite rightly, that this view was politically naïve (e.g. Leys 1973). It did also frequently lead to policy proposals in the name of promoting 'employment' that sought to discipline organized labour – including, very often, through proposals for wage restraint.

More broadly, the 'technocratic' approach of the ILO under WEP virtually always bumped up against the political situation within which the ILO operated. This was at times true even at the very basic level of planning missions. In early

1970, for instance, the Ethiopian government contacted the ILO to request that the first JASPA mission be sent to Ethiopia, pointing out that they had recently conducted a preliminary survey of underemployment and set up an inter-ministerial committee on employment issues.[19] Wilfred Jenks, at the time an Assistant Director General, apparently assigned considerable importance to maintaining close links with Ethiopia, and saw the WEP mission as a useful means in this respect.[20] Other officials worried that Ethiopia was 'so different from all other African countries, especially the more advanced ones which have serious employment problems, that we can learn very little from a mission to such a country'.[21] These concerns were enough to prevent the 'pioneer' mission being sent to Ethiopia, but when the Ethiopian government raised the issue with Jenks again in 1972,[22] Jenks quickly committed the ILO to sending a mission to Ethiopia as soon as possible.[23]

The inevitably politicized nature of the missions shows up even in internal discussions of recommendations. Indeed, echoing complaints that the Dakar meeting failed to pay enough attention to the political feasibility of recommendations (discussed in the previous section), the 'technical' focus of individual WEP missions sometimes proved controversial even within the ILO. This was also the case with Ethiopia – a brief memo regarding the mission report and policy recommendations from the head of the Workers' Relations department is worth quoting in full:

> The WEP report on Ethiopia illustrates once again the danger of looking at employment from a scientific point of view.
>
> Presumably this report will not be shown to the Workers' Group of the Governing Body, but if they should see it their future support for WEP would be gravely endangered.
>
> I therefore suggest that the present draft be reviewed from a social point of view, with special reference to the following points:
>
> 1) The argument that wages and salaries in urban employment and the public service are too high, and should be reduced.
> 2) The suggestion that present Ethiopian laws and regulations on minimum wages, hours of work, and safety and health are contrary to economic growth, and should be rescinded.[24]

The memo echoed conflicts over the report that were raised in Ethiopia as well. The recommendation on freezing wages in urban employment and the civil service was contested by the Confederation of Ethiopian Labour Unions in a national workshop where the Ethiopian government had invited workers' and employers' organizations to comment on a draft of the report.[25] The recommendation, albeit in somewhat watered down form, nonetheless found its way into the final version of the report (ILO 1973: 29). The 'technical' focus of the WEP, in short, sometimes only very thinly obscured political conflicts – over the role of states and labour in the promotion of development, over the distribution of resources, and more broadly over the position of the ILO in the region – both within the ILO itself and among different actors in 'national' contexts. It is also worth noting here, at least in passing, that the debate about wage freezes, a recurrent theme in a number of WEP missions, shows particularly clearly how debates about irregular labour (in this case un- and underemployment) could both discipline and normalize 'standard' forms of work too.

Informality, the state, and the politics of poverty in Kenya[26]

Of more immediate importance, for present purposes, is the way in which these dynamics helped to drive the circulation of the concept of 'informal' labour. The Kenyan mission, while not necessarily typical of JASPA's activities even at the time given its 'comprehensive' character, held tremendous significance for the ILO, and was widely debated within and beyond the ILO in the 1970s. In particular, the concept of the 'informal' sector is almost universally cited as a chief innovation of the ILO under WEP, and continues to inspire a good deal of research and practical work within and beyond the ILO (on which see Chapter 5). The Kenya mission thus had probably the farthest-reaching impact of any of WEP's work in Africa. It is, accordingly, worth discussing in greater detail. Kenya seemed to exemplify very clearly the problem of 'employment' that WEP had identified. Kenya had managed to achieve rapid rates of growth in the ten years following its independence from Britain, but it was not at all clear that the benefits of this growth were reaching the vast majority of the population. This problem of inequality was clearly identified in the preparatory work for the mission:

> Perhaps more important than all the rest, there seems to exist, in Kenya, a very notorious dualism between the prosperous basis of certain aspects of the economic picture, highly productive farm units, relatively good infrastructure, sophisticated financial services, high-quality education, by European standards, in some schools, and the majority of the population. A striking proportion of economic resources seems to be directed towards the needs of a small proportion of the population ... while the large majority stagnates. *This perhaps would explain unemployment as much as any other factor.*[27]

The problem of employment, then, was fundamentally conceived in residualist terms. The poor were simply those 'excluded' from the 'modern' parts of Kenyan society.

Yet the mission also took place in a context where the state sought increasing control over economic decision-making and where the ILO sought to avoid 'politicizing' the issue of employment. This point may be underlined by tracing in more detail the ways in which the report fit into debates in Kenya about labour and development. The government was making significant moves to establish greater control over the trade unions by the early 1970s. Kenya's Central Organization of Trade Unions (COTU) had been formed in 1965 after the government dissolved the Kenya Federation of Labour (KFL) and the rival Kenyan African Workers' Congress. The KFL had split over a combination of personal disagreements among the leadership of the KFL and interlinked questions of international affiliation and the 'political' independence of trade unions. Amsden, writing in 1971, noted that 'it is clear that Kenya's trade union movement is no longer free to participate in opposition politics. With this avenue of activity blocked, COTU's new administration has taken the path of least resistance' (1971: 118). This approach often put the position of rank and file workers at risk. Trade unions, indeed, were identified as a major source of unemployment in the 1970 report of the Parliamentary Select Committee on Unemployment in 1970 – high levels of wage disparity between urban and rural areas, partly 'as a result of the trade union activities' were blamed for excessive rural-urban migration and the resort of capital to labour-saving technologies (Republic of Kenya 1970: 3). The report accordingly recommended wage-restraint policies in urban areas (1970: 8). The broader point, though, is that the basic problem facing the WEP mission was how to frame the governance of irregular labour in a 'non-political' manner, relying on policy reforms managed by the state rather than driven by trade unions or other independent political organizations.

This 'non-political' character of the then-newly-formed COTU in fact contributed to making Kenya an appealing target for the WEP mission.[28] The Worker Relations Department was asked to report on the trade union situation in Kenya in terms of how it might impact the mission. The report concluded: 'Relations with the ILO are excellent. The General Secretary and President of COTU have both attended the International Labour Conference and are very well-disposed towards the ILO. They can be expected to give their full cooperation to the mission and will appreciate a request to cooperate'.[29] A similar report on employers' organizations noted approvingly that 'Both the [Federation of Kenyan Employers (FKE)] and the COTU . . . co-operate fully with the government, and in particular the Labour Ministry, mainly through the labour advisory board which is composed almost entirely of FKE and COTU representatives'.[30] It was acknowledged that because of this proximity of the labour movement to the government 'certain traditional trade union freedoms have been curtailed in the whole process of labour evolution that still continues',[31] but this did not temper the generally positive assessment of the possibility for the ILO to work in Kenya.

The concept of the 'informal', as adapted by the ILO mission, was brilliantly suited to this matrix of political relations of force. The Kenyan mission did not invent the term. It had in fact first been used by Keith Hart in a paper, discussed elsewhere in the introduction to this chapter, based on doctoral research in Ghana. The paper had been presented to a conference at the Institute for Development Studies at Sussex (where the leaders of the ILO mission worked) in 1971 (see Hart 1973). A footnote in the ILO report, indeed, credits the Kenyan academics participating in the mission with advancing the concept (ILO 1972: 6, fn.1).

The ILO employment policy report cast its discussion of the 'informal' in residualist terms – in fact, in the report the 'formal/informal' binary maps quite closely onto the older 'modern/traditional' conception of inequality, noted above. Of course, Kenya is different from Ghana, but Hart's basic picture of the 'informal' as a highly diverse range of livelihood strategies that were often packaged with formal employment, financial techniques, and communal social protections by individuals likely applied equally there are well. The mission's employment plan for Kenya nonetheless highlighted the 'exclusion' of most of the population from the 'modern' economy (now recast as the 'formal sector') and put its primary emphasis on 'linking' the formal and informal sectors:

> Our strategy of a redistribution from growth aims at *establishing links that are at present absent* between the formal and informal sectors ... The various policies which we recommend ... are intended to reduce risk and uncertainty on the part of those employed in the informal sector and to ensure a dynamic growth of this large segment of the Kenyan economy.
>
> (ILO 1972: 7, emphasis added)

The concept of the 'informal' did break rather decisively from the ILO's traditional focus on 'industrial relations' and tripartism (see Cox 1977: 417–421). In so doing, it unquestionably also made possible the explicit consideration of unorganized, politically marginal forms of work as crucial components of the development process. However, engineering 'dynamic growth' in the informal sector through appropriate policies reinforced a politics that situated labour as the passive object of 'development' interventions. Moreover, the 'informal' as it was conceived in the Kenya report to a considerable extent reinforced residualist understandings of poverty. Importantly, then, the image of separate 'formal' and 'informal' sectors obscured power relations and linkages between the 'formal' capitalist economy and the 'informal' that already existed. As Colin Leys (1973: 426) noted in a perceptive critique:

> Smallholders provide cheap food crops, pastoralists provide cheap beef, petty traders provide cheap distribution, 'subsistence' transporters provide cheap communications, the makers of shoes out of old tyres and the bicycle repairers and the charcoal burners and sellers provide cheap goods and services designed for the poverty life-style of those whose work makes the 'formal sector' profitable, and which enable them to live on their wages.

In short, the 'informal' was already intimately connected to the 'formal', particularly by ensuring the reproduction of relative surplus populations which were precariously employed or worked at poverty wages. Emphasizing the 'creation' of linkages 'that are at present absent' obscured these relational aspects of poverty and the power dynamics involved. The idea that the 'informal' was central to the creation of employment also closed down the active role allotted to workers in the development process. Indeed, while the report did briefly discuss the role of trade unions in agriculture (ILO 1972: 259) it had little or nothing to say about the possibility of organizing workers in the informal economy to have any kind of voice in policy-making, whether into existing union structures or independently. WEP and JASPA, then, not only depoliticized urban poverty, but also contributed to the marginalization of labour as an oppositional political voice in articulating the relationships between normalized and irregular forms of labour in the way that they did through the concept of informality.

Irregular work in the postcolonial order 91

COTU contested these dimensions of WEP's work to some extent. Indeed, the organization had sought to carve out a greater role even before the mission was launched. In 1970, the OAU secretariat convened a meeting on JASPA for African delegates attending the ILC. COTU delegates apparently asked for representation in the high-level seminars discussed above and that missions 'should work in close co-operation with trade unions in the country examined'.[32] The federation also tried unsuccessfully in its comments on the report to have some recommendations included about decision-making structures for wages and incomes policy and employment creation that would involve input from trade unions.[33] That the politically marginalizing effects of the report were contested is significant – indeed, we can see in COTU's engagements here some effort at using international networks to work around avenues for political action that were 'blocked' at the national scale. Still, the concept of the 'informal' certainly obscured the power structures underlying relations of poverty in Kenya, and maybe more importantly in practice the particular ways in which the concept was rolled out had distinct implications for ongoing struggles over the course of Kenyan development and control of the country's political system.

This point can be underlined by examining the impacts of the report in Kenya. Partly in response to the WEP report, the Kenyan government did undertake a number of reforms to its development strategy; these are illustrative of the broader argument being made here. The Kenyan government published a sessional paper on employment in 1973 addressing the recommendations of the report (Republic of Kenya 1973). While most of the ILO's report was accepted 'in principle', many of the recommendations themselves were questioned. The Kenyan government's implementation of the recommendations, moreover, was highly selective. This in itself is indicative of the actual influence of the ILO over Kenyan policy-making in that the report was certainly not intended as a menu of choices:

> The ILO strategy, while perhaps not constituting a totally indivisible package, contains a core of mutually reinforcing recommendations. In particular, the recommendations on the structure of rewards, land policy, technology, protection, and the informal sector seem to be inextricably linked to each other . . . Thus, partial implementation is likely to be ineffective and may even in some respects make matters worse.
>
> (Godfrey 1978: 41)

Indeed, the Kenyan government's commitment to the 'have nots' seems particularly questionable in light of some of the recommended reforms that were *not* pursued: e.g. a progressive land tax and limits on individual landholding; the ending of demolition of slum housing (and consequently of informal business premises); redistributive incomes policy; and an end to harassment of traders, taxi-drivers, and vagrants (Godfrey 1978). The failure to address this latter issue, indeed, came in spite of the Sessional Paper's assertion that

> The Government acknowledges that there is much counterproductive harassment of the so-called informal sector. This harassment will cease and more

realistic standards and controls will be applied. The Government has already taken initial steps to ensure that the informal sector is provided with sufficient credit and management and technical services.

(Republic of Kenya 1973: 27)

As Sandbrook aptly summarized ten years after the ILO mission, the Kenyan government's 'action fell well short of its rhetoric, insofar as the government shied away from structural reform' (1983: 238). Leys (1973) noted at the time that the more 'structural' or redistributive reforms recommended in the ILO report seemed to depend on the assumption that Kenyan elites would act contrary to their own interests.[34]

In fact, the structure of WEP and JASPA inhibited the extent to which follow-through on recommendations was really possible in a number of ways. First, because the missions were led by 'outside' experts, there was often diminished commitment or capacity on the part of the ILO for follow-up. The ILO put a considerable effort into publicizing the Kenya report, but notably, this was rarely directed at Kenya itself, rather at promoting the work of the Kenya mission and especially the concept of the 'informal sector' in order to raise the ILO's profile in other parts of Africa. Second, WEP was financed primarily through bilateral donor agencies rather than the ILO's regular budget. Donor support was provided for the missions themselves, but generally without any additional funds committed for follow-up; this meant that 'any fresh projects to follow up on the recommendations of the comprehensive missions had to compete with existing projects or with proposals already in the pipeline' (Bangasser 2000: 7).

We might well note here that the Kenya mission report (and WEP's general approach, including the concept of the 'informal' more broadly) were problematic because they were relatively superficial reforms that fell well short of necessary structural changes. Indeed, Sandbrook, Leys, and others frequently made precisely this criticism in the decade or so following the publication of the report – prompting one official to respond (with annoyance) that

> international organizations have to work within the given framework of a country's economic, social, and political systems . . . it is not possible for us to refuse the request of a government on the ground that it should first change its political system or abolish the "real vested class forces".[35]

However, to stop our critiques here would overlook the utility of *the report itself* as a resource in the context of shifting patterns of political relations of force apparent in postcolonial Kenya. The report's usefulness in this sense, indeed, was *enhanced* by precisely the things Leys, Sandbrook, and others correctly note prevented it having much impact on actual relations of poverty in practice. In short, the fact that the 'informal/formal' dichotomy occluded the structural or relational dimensions of urban poverty, the constriction of space for trade union input, the 'technical' and 'non-political' nature of the report, the fact that the report came with a set of ambiguous policy recommendations, and the limited ability to follow-up on the

Irregular work in the postcolonial order 93

part of the ILO, all enabled the Kenyan government to use the report in efforts to legitimize an economic policy framework that rhetorically placed the government as the protector of the 'have nots' in Kenyan society (to the exclusion of opposition parties or trade unions) by claiming the moral sanction of the ILO. This despite the fact that many of the ILO's actual recommendations were either rejected or watered down.

Indeed, a dispute with the Kenyan government stemming from a WEP working paper written by a junior ILO staffer in 1975 serves to illustrate how important the limits to follow-up on the mission from the ILO really were. In brief, the working paper (drawing heavily on two influential radical analyses of Kenyan political economy published around the same time as the WEP report [Sandbrook 1975; Leys 1975]) argued that the Kenyan state was not implementing certain recommendations of the report because the Kenyan government continued to 'serv[e] the interests of the dominant classes' (Asp 1975: 2), and that it was specifically 'recommendations leading to fundamental structural change [that] have been rejected by the government' (Asp 1975: 7). The working paper itself was not presented with much nuance, and for the most part it reiterated arguments that had been made elsewhere (e.g. Leys 1973), but it should be obvious enough from the preceding that the argument was not entirely without merit. It was also, for fairly obvious reasons, rather objectionable to the Kenyan government that it should be published as a working paper with the implicit endorsement of the ILO. The Ministry of Labour wrote to the Director General's office to demand the retraction of the paper, which it described as 'poor and malicious . . . and written in bad taste'.[36] In response to the complaint, the Director General wrote a letter of apology to the Kenyan Government, the ILO stopped circulation of the paper in question, and the employment department changed its policies on working papers to prevent the circulation of working papers outside the department without approval.[37] In short, the Kenyan government took steps to preserve the limited, advisory character of the report by asking for the censure of a working paper that called into question its commitment to actually implementing it.

Conclusion

This chapter has traced out the emergence of 'informal' labour as a framework for the governance of irregular labour. I have argued that the emergence of the 'informal' in this sense should be situated in the wider context of struggles over the political organization of labour in postcolonial Africa, particularly in Kenya. These struggles were themselves shaped by the conflicts over the relationships between the state, 'stabilized' urban workers, and other irregular labourers that had largely been left unresolved by the process of decolonization.

The ILO's early articulations of the 'informal' sector share many of the shortcomings identified in other understandings of irregular labour elsewhere in this book. Namely, in the emphasis on encouraging the development of supposedly 'absent' linkages between 'formal' and 'informal' economies, the ILO's use of the concept both rhetorically cocooned the varied forms of precarious livelihood strategies through which the urban poor eked out a living from the broader workings of capitalist accumulation, and served to normalize the forms of exploitation present in the 'formal' sector. Indeed, such understandings could be mobilized as means of disciplining organized workers. Certainly, this is evident in the Kenyan example with respect to the ways in which the concept of 'informal' labour – and more generally the ILO's interpretation of unemployment in terms of a binary between 'modern' and 'traditional' economies – helped to minimize the political role of organized labour. WEP missions more generally often even proposed wage restraints for unionized workers (like the example from Ethiopia briefly discussed above).

It is well worth noting, though, that the particular complex of political relations of force into which the concept of 'informal' labour was initially rolled out did not last long. The postcolonial political-economic order was in severe crisis by the late 1970s. The reasons why don't necessarily need to detain us long here; suffice to say that postcolonial systems encompassed a range of internal contradictions (notably, the degradation of agriculture despite a reliance on primary exports, weak productivity in state-owned industrial activities often subsidized by primary exports, and resultant large and structural fiscal deficits) which were exacerbated by shifts in the global political economy including increasingly volatile commodity prices (which both undercut the value of many primary exports and during the oil shocks raised the cost of fuel imports and subsidies) and foreign debts that suddenly became much more difficult to repay in the context of the Volcker shocks (see Sandbrook 1983; van de Walle 1999; Young 2004). More important for present purposes is the fact that these crises in Africa and globally ushered in a period of neoliberalization that very much shifted the ground on which the governance of irregular labour took place. I turn to a discussion of these dynamics in the remaining two chapters.

Notes

1 The longer history of ILO engagements with African trade unions and of the complex political struggles involved is traced in greater detail in Bernards (2017c).
2 This history of political conflicts around differing visions of regional and international trade unionism is discussed further in Bernards (2017c).
3 Thorkil Kristensen, 'ILO Seminar at Kericho: Introductory Statement', n.d., ILOA WEP 159-3-02-2.
4 International Labour Office, 'Draft Project Document, Submitted to the United Nations Development Programme: Jobs and Skills Programme for Africa', 1972, ILOA WEP 159-3 (2).
5 Michel Doo-Kingué to Francis Blanchard, 24 March 1972, ILOA WEP 159-3 (2).
6 H.K. Nook minute to Jean Reynaud and A.A. Shaheed, 2 March 1973, ILOA WEP 159-3 (2); *cf.* Francis Blanchard to Michel Doo-Kingué, 21 April 1972, ILOA WEP 159-3 (2).
7 Kjeld Phillip, 'High-Level Meetings for Permanent Secretaries in African Governments', 20 April 1970, ILOA WEP-159-3-01.
8 'Notes on a Meeting between Dr. Ammar and Mr. Blanchard, Friday 13 February 1971', ILOA WEP 159-3-01-3.
9 Abbas Ammar Minute to Mr. Mendes 3 March 1971, ILOA WEP 159-3-227-1. There were eventually three separate field teams set up along with a group at the African

Irregular work in the postcolonial order 95

Regional Office in Addis Ababa – one for francophone Africa, which was often referred to by the French language acronym PECTA; one for Anglophone Africa; and in the late 1970s a related team was set up in Southern Africa, to give assistance to national liberation movements in the white-ruled states along with Botswana, Lesotho, and Swaziland.

10 'Jobs and Skills Programme for Africa: Proposals for Action in the 1972–1973 Biennium', pp. 4–8, ILOA WEP 159–3 (2).
11 S.B.L. Nigam, 'JASPA Activities During 1972', p. 3, ILOA WEP 159–3 (2).
12 R. Mayer 'Points for Discussion for Dr. Ammar with Professor Feldheim', n.d., ILOA WEP 159–3–01.
13 'Notes on Meeting Convened by Dr. Ammar on Wednesday, 1 April 1970, 9:00am', ILOA WEP 159–3–01, p. 2.
14 'Aide Memoire for Discussion with Mr. Blanchard with a view to submitting a concerted recommendation to the Director General on the advisability of inviting employers' or workers' organizations to the African WEP seminars'; see also 'Meeting on Employment Policy, Dakar, 6–12 December 1970', n.d., both in ILOA WEP 159–3–01–1.
15 Pierre Feldheim and Yves Sabolo 'Analyse Critique des Résultats du Séminaire de Dakar sur le Politique de l'Emploi', 21 December 1971, ILOA WEP 159–3–01–3. The report is misdated in the file, it was written in December of 1970 shortly after the conference; it is referenced in Francis Blanchard Minute to Director General, 6 January 1971, same file.
16 See for instance S. Zottos to Mr. Méndez, 'Progress Report on the Organization of the Kericho Meeting', 8 April 1971, ILOA WEP 159–3–02.
17 H.A. Dunning to Dr. Abbas Ammar, 19 August 1970, ILOA WEP-3–01–1.
18 Kjeld Phillip to Dr. Ammar, 27 August 1970, ILOA WEP 159–3–01–2.
19 Getahoun Tesemma to Mr. W. Jenks, 12 January 1970, ILOA WEP 159–3–78.
20 'Meeting with Mr. Jenks: Ethiopia', 3 February 1970, ILOA WEP 159–3–78.
21 Kjeld Phillips minute to Dr. Ammar, 26 February 1970, ILOA WEP 159–3–78.
22 Tsahafe Taezaz Aklilu Habte Wold to Mr. Wilfred Jenks, 3 July 1972, ILOA WEP 159–3–78.
23 Francis Blanchard to M.E. Ndisi, 28 July 1972, ILOA WEP 159–3–78.
24 H.A. Dunning minute to Mr. Aamir Ali, 13 February 1973, ILOA WEP 159–3–78–3.
25 S.B.L. Nigam, 'Ethiopia Employment Mission, Summary Record of Discussions Held at the Workshop Organized by the Government of Ethiopia on 9–10 July 1973', 14 July 1974, p. 14, ILOA WEP 159–3–78–3.
26 This section draws on material previously published in Bernards (2017a). The present version has been expanded to include considerably more supporting evidence, especially from archival materials relating to the mission.
27 'Basic Ideas for the High-Level Kenyan Mission', annex to Jorge Mendez minute to Dr. Ammar, 26 April 1971, ILOA WEP 159–3–227–1. Emphasis added.
28 Ironically, this sat at odds with the ILO's emphasis on free and independent trade unions. This dilemma was common in the ILO's work in the region at the time, see Bernards (2017c).
29 B.E.D. Komba-Kono 'Trade Union Organization – Kenya', 21 July 1971, ILOA WEP 159–3–227–1.
30 S. N'Diaye-Guirandou 'Notes on the Kenya Federation of Employers and Kenyan Employers' Associations in General', ILOA WEP 159–3–227–1.
31 'Kenya Employment Mission', Annex to Paul B.J. Chu minute to Mr. de Givry, Mr. Abbas Ammar, EPPD, 10 June 1971, p. 1., ILOA WEP 159–3–227–1.
32 'Summary of the main points raised by the African delegates attending the International Labour Conference, at the meeting convened by the General Secretariat of the Organization for African Unity on ILO strategy concerning the Jobs and Skills Programme for Africa', 2 July 1970, ILOA WEP 159–3.
33 Central Organization of Trade Unions (Kenya), 'Initial Comments on: Employment, Incomes and Equality in Kenya: A Report of UN-ILO Team of Experts (Geneva 1972)', ILOA WEP 159–3–227–1 (2).

96 *Irregular work in the postcolonial order*

34 This was, in fact, a common complaint about WEP/JASPA in general even within the ILO. For instance, in an early memo discussing the plans for JASPA, one official lamented the lack of consideration given to the political situation in different countries, noting that 'surely the employment problem cannot be tackled the same way in Brazzaville or Conakry and in Abidjan (assuming it can be tackled at all in the latter capital)?'. Rene Livchen minute to Abbas Ammar, 8 June 1970, ILOA WEP 159–3. See also below, p. 169.
35 Shyam B.L. Nigam to Mr. L. Richter, 4 May 1982, ILOA WEP 159–3 (9).
36 J.I. Othieno to F. Blanchard, 16 March 1976, ILOA WEP 159–3–227–3–1 (3).
37 A. Béguin minute to Mr. Emmerij and Mrs. Mosimann, 5 April 1976, ILOA WEP 159–3–227–3–1 (3).

5 Neoliberal crises and the politics of informality

As noted in the introduction, precarity and informality are often understood with reference to the roll-back of statutory protections for labour in the neoliberal era. I followed a number of recent commentators in dismissing these interpretations, perhaps exemplified by Standing's (2011) discussions of the 'precariat', as failing to account for the pervasive character of precarious livelihoods and violent coercion in the history of capitalism (*cf.*Munck 2013; Harris and Scully 2015). That said, neoliberal reforms have clearly made a difference in the form, scope, and extent of irregular labour in the global political economy. Simplistic narratives attributing irregular forms of work to neoliberal deregulation won't do, but it would be hard to give an adequate account of the present without thinking seriously about neoliberalism. The next two chapters thus take up the question of *how* processes of neoliberalization have shaped the contemporary governance of irregular labour. The short answer is: while the fundamental dynamics at play in the production and governance of irregular forms of labour have not necessarily changed, the particular characteristics of contemporary initiatives are usefully understood with reference to the contradictions of neoliberal reforms.

This argument obviously implies an understanding of the relationships between neoliberalism and labour that goes beyond the removal of labour market regulations. For present purposes, it is helpful to follow Brenner *et al.* (2010a: 184), who point to a contradictory series of dispersed, variegated 'neoliberalizing processes' which have 'facilitated marketization and commodification while simultaneously *intensifying* the uneven development of regulatory forms across places, territories and scales' (*cf.*Peck and Tickell 2002). Hence, we can point to a loosely configured, shifting, and partially contradictory series of policy reforms constituting a 'neoliberal project' in Africa (see Harrison 2010). This might be taken to include, in the initial phase of structural adjustment the liberalization of trade and investment, devaluation of currencies, austerity policies, and the privatization of state-owned enterprises, and subsequently farther-reaching reforms of property rights, labour market reforms, the reconstruction of public institutions under the guise of 'good governance', and the introduction of new forms of financial practices. Notably, these are processes that in Africa as elsewhere have been highly uneven, and have not resulted in a fixed neoliberal 'end-state' largely because they are contradictory and almost inherently prone to failures – 'they entail regulatory strategies that fundamentally undermine the very socio-institutional and political-economic conditions needed for their successful implementation' (Brenner *et al.* 2010b: 333; *cf.* Peck 2013). Neoliberalism can thus be understood as an intensification of the ongoing processes of primitive accumulation central to the theoretical framing of this book, wherein the production of 'free' labourers is a contradictory and deeply political process intimately bound up with ongoing transformations in property rights.[1] These processes have necessarily entailed substantive shifts in the material and political relations of force through which the governance of irregular labour has been carried out in practice.

The present chapter accomplishes two tasks. First, I briefly map out the context of neoliberal reforms and the growth of unemployment and precarious work in the region. While I examine some specific cases in greater detail over the next two chapters, in broad strokes we can point to some dynamics of neoliberalization that are relatively common. In particular, neoliberal reforms have reconfigured processes of primitive accumulation in ways that have generated an intensification of coercive and precarious labour relations, while undermining the political foundations of the postcolonial state. The undercutting of the organizational links between trade unions and ruling parties that had enabled a kind of fragile political stability in many cases in the 1970s was a particularly important consequence for present purposes. These dynamics, I argue, do a good deal to explain the character of subsequent shifts in the governance of irregular labour. Second, I trace out the ways in which these dynamics are reflected in shifting patterns of governance of 'informal' economies. The latter part of this chapter traces out analyses of two specific projects: an initiative around informal apprenticeships started in Tanzania, and an initiative aimed at developing markets for 'microinsurance' in francophone West Africa, particularly Senegal.

Two points are particularly important to underline. One is that, while the ILO's governance of informal economies has shifted in substantial ways with respect to both policy contents and the mechanisms by which policy is carried out, the basic framework of concepts and conventions developed in the earlier debates highlighted in previous chapters (i.e. in this case 'informal' labour) have generally persisted. Importantly, they retain the fundamentally residualist elements of previous understandings of irregular labour. The ILO continues to frame informality as the product of the exclusion of the majority of Africans from 'normal' markets and regulatory protections. Second, the specific character of contemporary interventions has been strongly shaped by the shifting relations of political force visible in neoliberal African political economies – dynamics which are helpfully captured by Gramsci's concept of 'organic crisis'. In particular, the shifting configuration of political power and state forms underlying processes of neoliberalization, particularly the changing relationships between the state and organized labour, have shaped the strategic incentives of states engagements with the ILO's programmes on informal labour.

The chapter proceeds as follows: The first section below maps out, in broad strokes, the trajectory of neoliberal reforms in sub-Saharan Africa. Next, the ILO's re-interpretation of 'informality' in the early 1990s, and particularly the turn to 'community'-level interventions, are situated in this context. The final two sections subsequently trace out the ways in which these dynamics are reflected in a pair of ILO projects: the development of microinsurance policy in Senegal and a project on 'upgrading informal apprenticeships' in Tanzania.

Irregular labour in neoliberal Africa

This section sets the context for subsequent discussions of efforts to govern the 'informal' and in the next chapter through a brief consideration of the contradictory dynamics of neoliberalism in Africa. As noted at the end of the previous chapter, the postcolonial order in sub-Saharan Africa was in severe political and economic crisis by the end of the 1970s. This period of crisis in Africa played a critical role in the shaping of neoliberal agendas more generally. The World Bank's (1981) report titled *Accelerated Development in Sub-Saharan Africa: An Agenda for Action* (World Bank 1981; most often referred to as the 'Berg Report' after its primary author) was a critical early statement of the emerging consensus that states were a hindrance to economic growth and needed to be scaled back. As Harrison has aptly noted, in the late 1970s and first years of the 1980s, 'it was *only* in regard to Africa that a region-wide representation of statist problems and marketized solutions was propounded' (2010: 18). The World Bank and IMF, along with other major donors, pursued a package of policy reforms along these lines throughout the 1980s: 'The reforms attempted to reduce the state's role in production and in regulating private economic activity ... they placed more emphasis on maintaining macroeconomic stability and avoiding overvalued exchange rates' (World Bank 1994: 34). Reforms focused on 'keeping inflation low, exchange-rates competitive, and budget deficits sustainable' (World Bank 1994: 35). In practice this meant widespread programmes of austerity, privatization, and currency devaluation. These programmes were unevenly implemented within and between countries (see van de Walle 1999; Woods 2006). But in any event, by the mid-1990s structural adjustment was widely considered to have failed even by the standards of economic growth set by the Bank itself – with the 1980s increasingly recognized as a 'lost decade' for development, perhaps particularly in sub-Saharan Africa but elsewhere as well (see Best 2013; 2016).

All of this has had distinctive implications for labour. These consequences are traced in some more detail with respect to the more specific examples from Tanzania, Senegal, and Niger considered in the following chapters. But a few general points are worth underlining. Structural adjustment programmes had two fairly immediate adverse effects. First, programmes of privatization and public sector retrenchment, in contexts where the majority of 'formal' jobs were either in parastatal businesses or civil service, created widespread unemployment. Second, the devaluation of currencies, along with the dismantling of food and fuel subsidies, often had a devastating effect on real wages and living costs. The Bank frequently emphasized that one of the merits of adjustment was the overcoming of a persistent bias against agriculture: 'One of the most fundamental shifts in the development strategy for Africa was to view agriculture not as a backward sector but as the engine of growth' (1994: 35). Yet the dismantling of marketing boards and credit cooperatives, trade liberalization, and currency devaluation, in the context of declining world agricultural prices, tended to diminish farm-gate returns, while renewed efforts to institute private property in land systematically dispossessed the rural poor (Gibbon *et al.* 1993; Woodhouse 2003). Working classes, in short, have disproportionately borne the brunt of adjustment.

Politically, the painful costs of adjustment had critical implications of their own. The impacts of retrenchment and declining real wages in particular frequently strained or undermined the relationships between ruling parties and trade unions (the former also often put a significant dent in union memberships). The organizational underpinnings of the postcolonial historic bloc (Bayart 2009) more widely – frequently taking the form of civil society organizations closely linked with the ruling party apparatus – were increasingly streamlined or dismantled altogether. There was widespread backlash against structural adjustment, starting with a wave of so-called 'IMF Riots' in the 1980s, and followed by more widespread and organized protest movements targeting national governments in the early 1990s (see Riley and Parfitt 1994; Seddon and Zelig 2005). This movement culminated in a series of experiments with 'democratization' – especially multiparty elections (see Bratton and van de Walle 1997; Abrahamsen 1997). As Seddon and Zelig note, 'In a four-year period, from 1990–1994, a total of thirty-five regimes had been swept away by a combination of street demonstrations, mass strikes and other forms of protest, and by presidential and legislative elections that were often the first held for a generation' (2005: 19).

This pattern of failure, backlash, and state restructuring is crucial to understanding the political relations of force that drove the re-articulation of policies towards 'informal' economies from the 1990s onwards. On one hand, neoliberal strategies of governance pushed towards more localized, community-level interventions dealing with health, education, and microfinance as mechanisms for poverty reduction (see Cammack 2004; Best 2013; 2016). On the other, problems of 'good governance' and institutional development have been increasingly central to neoliberal regulatory agendas, developments that have seen the World Bank, IMF, and major donors increasingly involved in the day-to-day practice of governance and administration in the region (see Abrahamsen 2000; Harrison 2004). Harrison is essentially correct that 'the history of neoliberalism in Africa has been of an expanding frontier, of increasingly broad-based and ambitious practices to make African countries in the neoliberal image' (2010: 34–35). This process of expansion has been driven forward (ironically) by a pattern of continual failure and ongoing contestation. Neoliberal reforms have continually failed to produce promised development outcomes, but the solutions to these failures have often involved more diffuse and varied policy responses that have nonetheless reinforced the logics of commodification and marketization underlying processes of neoliberalization. These subsequent rounds of interventions have, however, as is perhaps especially clear from the cases discussed below, created contradictions of their own.

Broader dynamics of neoliberalization also had a significant influence on the ways in which the concept of 'informal' work was redeployed in the 1980s and 1990s. They also do a good deal to help us understand the ILO's somewhat contradictory position in Africa and more generally. The crisis of Fordism, as Robert Cox had noted already in the 1970s, undercut the social foundations of the ILO (Cox 1977). The ILO's initial response was to try to resist the tide of neoliberal reforms. As discussed in more detail below, we can detect a fairly constant undercurrent of ILO involvement in efforts to defend and even expand postcolonial institutions for labour markets and social protection through the 1980s. But these efforts were, by and large, unsuccessful and undercut by structural-adjustment-era budgetary constraints. By the early 1990s, the ILO was casting about for alternatives, and increasingly pushed towards more localized interventions, emphasizing 'community autonomy' as an alternative to state and market-based programmes. This dynamic is clearly illustrated in the development of microinsurance, discussed further below.

A key juncture here was the decision to focus the Director General's report to the ILC in 1991 on the 'informal' sector. The report, of course, drew on a body of work 'on the ground' by ILO staff and consultants, especially under JASPA and the parallel Regional Employment Programme for Latin America and the Caribbean. The report, interestingly, acknowledged the ambiguity of the 'informal': 'even after two decades of investigation by scholars and international civil servants, there is still no generally accepted definition of the term "informal sector". All we know for certain is that it exists' (ILO 1991: 1). The report identified the 'dilemma' posed by the informal as 'whether to promote the informal sector as a provider of employment and incomes; or to seek to extend regulation and social protection to it and thereby possibly restrict its capacity to provide jobs and income for an ever expanding labour force' (ILO 1991: 2). The report concluded, somewhat implausibly, that it was possible to pursue both objectives at the same time. The DG's report laid out a broad plan of action based around four themes: improving productivity in the informal sector; improvements to welfare for the poor; establishing a regulatory framework and forms of social protection for the informal economy; and organizing informal workers.

Visible here in incipient form, then, is a kind of fragmentation of efforts to govern the 'informal' sector. What happened to the concept in the 1990s has been aptly described as a 'dispersion' of the 'informal' across virtually all the activities of the organization (Bangasser 2000). Nearly every department of the ILO, in one way or another, started some kind of programming related to the 'informal' at some point in the 1990s. Deliberately or not, this approach dovetailed well with the growing emphasis on community-level interventions and closer interactions with the day-to-say business of the state. The ILO's interventions – as the following two examples illustrate particularly clearly – have in practice often followed the neoliberalizing logic underlying what Breman and van der Linden (2014) have called the 'project of informalization'. That is, as with the de Soto-influenced interventions favoured by the World Bank (discussed in the introduction), they have emphasized the formalization of property rights and the development of access to credit, skills, and the like as means of facilitating 'successful' enterprises in the informal economy. But these programmes have also been bound up in significant ways by the changing political relations of force in neoliberalizing African political economies.

From social security to microinsurance for informal workers

There were a few ILO-linked efforts to promote the extension of coverage to various groups of non-standard workers from the late 1970s. Missions to Gabon (ILO 1982), Cameroon (ILO 1989), and Morocco (ILO 1990) dealt with the extension of social security to the 'self-employed', agricultural workers, or 'artisans'. The ILO's advisors were faced with a dilemma: contributory schemes would be near-impossible for workers with small and unpredictable incomes, and public subsidies were difficult to provide in the context of fiscal crisis and structural adjustment. A report to the Cameroonian government noted this problem explicitly (ILO 1989: 130). One solution to this dilemma was proposed in an article published by a pair of ILO officials in the late 1980s on the extension of social security to 'self-employed' workers in Africa (Mouton and Gruat 1989). The article makes particular note of 'traditional' institutions and village associations, tontines, harvest insurance, informal associations, and mutual benefit schemes as potential alternative means of providing social protection to self-employed workers (Mouton and Gruat 1989: 52). The notion that the best means of covering 'informal' workers or non-standard populations was through the design of alternate schemes – particularly the use of small-scale financial practices organized at the community level – played a considerable role in subsequent efforts to promote social protection.

After the 1991 ILC these activities were ramped up and brought under the rubric of the 'informal' sector. A major 'interdepartmental' project on the informal sector was organized in 1994–1995. The project was centered on three major cities in developing countries: Bogota, Manila, and Dar es Salaam, including an initiative to establish autonomous health insurance schemes through existing organizations of informal workers in Dar es Salaam (Aryee 1996: 51–52). The decision to focus on developing alternative insurance schemes through organizations of informal workers was reinforced after a study in Manila that found that 'indigenous' schemes were 'more appropriate and effective in meeting the needs of operators', but suffered from administrative weaknesses which could be remedied through technical cooperation (Aryee 1996: 51). The interdepartmental project solidified the emphasis on providing social security for informal workers through alternative channels, often 'community' organizations.

The Social Security department subsequently took up a pilot project applying a similar approach in four countries – Tanzania, Benin, India, and El Salvador. Based on the interdepartmental project, Social Security proposed three options for the extension of social protection: separate social insurance programmes designed for informal workers, the extension of formal social security schemes to the informal sector, and the provision of non-contributory social assistance (van Ginneken

1996). Separate social insurance schemes, in practice, were the major emphasis in the 1990s – neither other option seeming viable in the prevailing climate of austerity. The interventions in Benin and Tanzania, drawing heavily on the experience of the interdepartmental project, started by scouting out appropriate informal workers' organizations in target cities to run social insurance programmes. In Benin, the pilot project proposed involved using several informal workers' organizations to collect contributions, while drawing on a public-private microfinance institution, the Fédération des Caisses d'Épargne et de Credit Agricole Mutuel (FECECAM) to manage money. The basic model proposed was to have officials of informal sector organizations collect contributions and deposit them at an account with the local branch of FECECAM. Agreements would be established with local clinics to permit card-carrying members to draw on the funds to pay for medical care (Gauthé 1997: 24). The Beninois project was never implemented in full, but the basic model was carried forward. In Tanzania, the project proposed extending the model of the Dar es Salaam intervention to Arusha and Mbeya (Kiwara and Heynis 1997). It identified 'viable' groups of informal workers in the two cities, based on criteria including having upwards of 400 members, a common bank account, stable leadership, and the nearby availability of healthcare providers (1997: 75–76). The Tanzanian government also organized a similar pilot scheme in the rural Inguna region on the basis of the Dar es Salaam experiment – although in this case member contributions were augmented by matching funds from the World Bank (Kiwara 1999: 138–140).

The Social Protection Department of the ILO established an initiative on 'Strategies and Tools against Social Exclusion and Poverty' (STEP) in the late 1990s. Under STEP, the ILO carried out a major study of healthcare mutuals in nine countries in West and Central Africa, which recommended that governments needed to establish a regulatory and institutional context for the autonomous provision of health insurance, international donors should focus on training at the local level (Atim 1998). A pair of officials in the Social Protection Department would eventually advance the concept of 'microinsurance', referring to autonomous community-directed organizations linked together in larger corporate structures to facilitate the pooling of risk (Dror and Jacquier 1999), to describe such alternate 'community-based' forms of social protection the ILO increasingly sought to promote in the 1990s. They argued that existing solutions were inadequate: markets were unlikely to provide much in the way of health coverage to poor communities, and governments in the developing world had shown little capacity or willingness to provide universal healthcare. As an alternative, they proposed 'microinsurance' as a set of 'autonomous enterprises' operated at the community level, with 'networks to link multiple small area- and occupation-based units into larger structures that can enhance both the insurance function (through a wider pooling of risk) and the support structures needed for improved governance (through training, data banks, research facilities, etc.)' (1999: 77). In order to ensure that microinsurance would be able to accomplish this function in a way that would be relevant to communities excluded from healthcare, the authors argued that microinsurance would need to be 'simple, affordable, and located close to members' (1999: 82). The point, for present purposes, is that in its original articulation 'microinsurance' was understood as a 'community-' based alternative to both government and market provision of health coverage.

A pair of points are worth underlining about these programmes. In the first instance, they are usefully understood in the context of the political relations of force unleashed by the contradictory dynamics of neoliberalization introduced above. These programmes were efforts to manage the worst consequences of structural adjustment without fundamentally altering the dynamics of renewed primitive accumulation underpinning them. Importantly, as is discussed further below, this movement provided the basis for a subsequent round of neoliberalizing projects aimed at commercializing microinsurance markets in the 2000s. Second, the residualist thrust of earlier ILO understandings of informal economies is maintained, and even deepened, by the emergence of efforts to 'improve' the conditions of informal workers through dedicated social security schemes. 'Informal' economies were still understood in terms of the exclusion of workers from 'formal' jobs and regulatory protections, and the ILO's proposed solutions involved finding alternate means of providing some of the goods (e.g. risk management, financial services) that neither states or markets were providing at the time. The differentiation of normalized from irregular workers is reinforced by this move insofar as it is reinterpreted as a more or less permanent boundary. The structural conditions underpinning the growth of informal economies largely slip from view.

Microinsurance as financial inclusion[2]

Microinsurance never gained much traction in the ILO's Social Protection department. Most of the activity of the Department from the early 2000s was oriented towards a 'policy vision' based on universality, cemented in 2012 by the passage of the recommendation on 'Social Protection Floors'. A key report in 2009 suggested that 'governments remain the ultimate guarantors of social security . . . neither the market nor informal arrangements can guarantee adequate levels and universal access to effective social security' (ILO 2009b: 40). The Social Protection department has increasingly emphasized the need for non-contributory, universal social security – according to one official: 'The emphasis is clearly on the floor. So we called for avoiding narrow targeting, because when you target on the extreme pool, you leave out broader coverage'.[3] Microinsurance policy thus almost entirely passed over to the Social Finance branch of the ILO in the early 2000s, and was also rapidly taken up by a growing network of other international and regional regulatory institutions. The networks emerging around the idea of 'financial inclusion' were particularly significant. The ILO's Social Finance branch chaired a working group on insurance at Consultative Group to Assist the Poor (CGAP), which began collecting case studies on microinsurance in the early 2000s (see Churchill 2006). An early training guide on microinsurance for microfinance institutions was also published in 2003 (Churchill *et al.* 2003). The ILO institutionalized this loose movement linking microinsurance activities to 'financial inclusion' by establishing the Microinsurance Innovation Facility (MIF) in 2007. MIF was hosted at Social

Finance, with funding from the Munich Re and Gates Foundations, as well as the International Finance Corporation (IFC – the private lending arm of the World Bank).[4] This shift from Social Protection department to MIF and CGAP also drove some mutations in the practice of microinsurance itself. If the emphasis on community autonomy that dominated ILO activities in the 1990s never exactly went away, much of the practical work done by the MIF in promoting microinsurance has been carried out through engagements with insurance supervisors.

The International Association of Insurance Supervisors (IAIS) and the CGAP working group co-published an issues paper on regulatory frameworks for microinsurance in 2007. The paper highlights the role of regulation in promoting the expansion of commercial microinsurance. Parts of the paper hew very closely to the logic of the World Bank's work on microcredit or the G20 Principles for Innovative Financial Inclusion that would be issued a few years later (see Soederberg 2013). It suggests that regulatory frameworks for microinsurance need to balance 'how they can contribute towards developing and overseeing microinsurance activities while simultaneously continuing to promote safe and sound financial systems' (IAIS 2007: 38). There is a particularly important tension running through the guidelines, however, over the role of not-for-profit mutuals and cooperatives in relation to commercial insurance markets on the one hand and social protection functions on the other. The microinsurance paper notes the importance of clearly delineating the roles of public and market actors in providing social protection (2007: 15). Citing STEP publications on healthcare mutuals in Senegal and Mali, and echoing arguments raised in ILO research in the 1990s (e.g. Dror and Jacquier 1999), the paper argues that 'The experience in West African jurisdictions shows that public redistributive systems often do not function in the informal economy. The only way for the poor to be covered is to set up microinsurance mutuals that are very inexpensive' (2007: 21). Subsequent guidelines have also been published on the role of mutuals and cooperatives in delivering insurance. Here the role for community-based organizations in pooling risk is seen as a sort of 'stepping stone' towards the development of commercial insurance markets (IAIS 2010: 13). However, the range of other purposes for which mutuals can be used potentially complicates things:

> As [mutuals and cooperatives] can be part of a range of social and economic policy areas including financial services, agriculture, social welfare, health and community relations, the likely range of interested agencies can be greater than would be the case with . . . other forms of insurers. . . . It is also likely that arrangements for effective, complete, and coordinated oversight . . . will have to consider a wider range of potentially competing objectives that will require special attention.
>
> (2010: 14)

Mutuals and cooperatives are thus identified simultaneously as stepping-stones and/or substitutes for both conventional insurance markets and public redistribution and social protection. In the IAIS guidelines microinsurance is simultaneously linked with the public provision of social assistance, with community-level mutual or cooperative organizations, and with the development of commercial insurance markets.

These guidelines have been put in practice in West Africa through a series of complex engagements between the ILO, the World Bank, and the *Conférence Interafricaine des Marchés d'Assurances* (CIMA), a regional network of insurance regulators harmonizing standards in fourteen countries in West and Central Africa. CIMA passed a set of regulations on microinsurance and index insurance (*Livre VII*) in 2012 aimed at encouraging the development of microinsurance institutions in member countries. The rules themselves were based on a report commissioned from Desjardins International Development (DID) by the World Bank on the microinsurance market in the region. The report identified the prominent role of community groups in existing insurance markets – particularly healthcare mutuals – as a particularly salient feature of the West African market. The DID report emphasizes the need to bring mutuals under existing regulatory requirements as much as possible (DID 2011: 56).

However, the CIMA rules restrict the commercialization of microinsurance to a greater degree. The rules do seek to bring mutuals and community organizations under insurance regulations. Mutuals are subject to lower initial capital requirements than limited liability corporations (300 million F CFA rather than 500 million), but are otherwise required to follow the same rules. However, the CIMA rules relatively strictly segment microinsurance product lines from other financial services. They require microinsurance enterprises to seek a license from national regulators specifying which types of insurance they are permitted to offer. Organizations offering credit or savings services are restricted to life insurance; microinsurers offering health, crop, or property insurance are prohibited from offering savings or credit products. *Livre VII* similarly allows registered insurance providers to offer microinsurance products, but requires them to keep distinct accounts for their microinsurance operations. The regional regulations, then, are set up largely within the market-constituting logic laid out by the IAIS and DID, but leave a considerable role for community organizations and set limits on commercial activities. Indeed, they carve out certain (relatively unprofitable but politically significant) areas of activity – health and crop insurance in particular – as domains in which microinsurers must be set up as independent institutions.

Microinsurance and the politics of informality in Senegal

If we want to understand the particular shape of initiatives around microinsurance in Senegal, we need to recognize the particular strategic imperatives for government and trade unions created by the configuration of political relations of force prevailing in the context of the organic crisis of the postcolonial order in Senegal. As Boone (1992) describes particularly clearly, the political-economic order in postcolonial Senegal depended on the articulation of state monopolies over agrarian exports with local and foreign merchant capital, and with a series of mechanisms for securing the consent of subaltern groups, including urban employment in the civil service or in an industrial sector dominated by parastatals and agrarian cooperatives for rural workers. Importantly, as Bayart (2009: 182–192) has noted of postcolonial Africa more generally, this mode of extraverted development depended politically on the incorporation of substantial elements of subaltern social forces into the 'postcolonial historic bloc', often through the formation of a 'civil society' closely linked to the ruling party (as in e.g. the trade union politics discussed below). In practice, rural political economies, including the cooperatives, were dominated by clientelist relations organized around Sunni Islamic brotherhoods (see O'Brien 1971). These kinds of symbiotic relationships between (urban) states and (rural) 'traditional' authorities were common in postcolonial regimes in Africa – Mamdani (1996) has usefully described them as forms of 'decentralized despotism'. Agrarian markets were managed through 'triangular relationships' between Mouride merchant brotherhoods, 'traditional' Islamic authorities (Marabouts), and the state (Beck 2001). Boone suggests that this model was in crisis in the 1980s because it depended on the redistribution of rents from export markets that were increasingly volatile and threw up significant barriers to the development of production. The process of structural adjustment was truncated in practice, including in Senegal (see Woods 2006), but it did involve the ejection of many subaltern elements of the postcolonial historic bloc in the process of privatization of parastatals and the retrenchment of social programmes. Boone notes that the process of liberalization in the 1980s and 1990s led primarily to the solidification of the close relations of merchant capital and the state, while marginalizing other members of the postcolonial bloc (Boone 1994). Mouride merchants also became increasingly politically independent of Marabout authorities in the process (Beck 2001).[5] With more specific reference to labour, two developments are relevant.

First, trade unionism in postcolonial Senegal was premised on a particular model of relations between trade unions and the ruling party called 'responsible participation', which has also been thrown into question by structural adjustment (see Ndiaye 2010; Diop Buuba 1992). The *Confedèration Nationale des Travailleurs du Sénégal* (CNTS) was established in the early 1970s after the government abolished the leaderships of existing national trade union bodies. The government adopted a policy of 'responsible participation' that granted CNTS members in the *Parti Socialiste* a share of cabinet seats and made all salaried worker members of the party into CNTS members (and vice versa) in exchange for industrial peace. At least implicitly, the arrangement rested on the kind of rigid differentiation of salaried formal workers from the precarious urban poor discussed in greater detail in the previous chapter – particularly insofar as these policies meant that public servants and workers in publicly owned enterprises made up the considerable majority of CNTS' membership. This arrangement was undercut from the early 1980s onwards by dual processes of structural adjustment and political opening. Among other things, the devaluation of the regional currency (the CFA Franc) dramatically reduced real wages and retrenchment and privatization led to major job losses in the public sector. These costs of adjustment for workers led to intense debates within CNTS about whether or not to remain affiliated to the *Parti Socialiste*, and perhaps ironically, the political pluralism that resulted from protests against neoliberalization encouraged the formation of rival trade union confederations (see Diop Buuba 1992; Ndiaye 2010). These trends were accentuated when the *Parti Socialiste* lost the 2000 election, and CNTS subsequently opted to officially disaffiliate. The new government, meanwhile, encouraged the formation of new confederations out of rival tendencies in CNTS by greatly facilitating the registration of rival trade union centres. By 2010, CNTS remained the largest trade union body in the country with roughly 80 000 registered members, but there were eighteen officially recognized 'national' trade union confederations (see ILO 2010a: 28–34). The point here is that the political relations of force are marked by increased competition to organize a shrinking core of normalized workers; CNTS in particular has also made some efforts at organizing 'informal' and retrenched workers through credit cooperatives (see Bernards 2016). The dismantling of agrarian cooperatives and weakening of 'triangular' relationships between the state, Mourides, and Marabouts have created similar forms of fragmentation and political competition in rural settings.

Second, alongside this fragmentation of the union movement, the incidence of irregular forms of work has expanded considerably. Formal measures of unemployment have typically hovered around 10 percent (ILO 2013a; Diene 2014); but labour force participation rates for 'working age' individuals (15–64) are less than 50 percent. By most estimates the 'informal' sector accounts for the majority of value added across most sectors – petty street vending, then, is increasingly accompanied by the informalization of transport, manufacturing, fishing, and agriculture (Benjamin and Mbaye 2012: 48–58). Indeed, a different indication of the scope of irregular work comes from the fact that only 5 percent of the population participates in the national retirement fund – a contributory scheme into which formal salaried workers typically pay (ILO 2013a: 31). In any event, the broader point is that the expansion of irregular forms of labour threatens to undercut the legitimacy of neoliberal modes of governance, and the mechanisms by which subaltern social forces were incorporated into the postcolonial order have largely been dismantled in the process of structural adjustment. This broader context of political relations of force has profoundly shaped the development of microinsurance as a specific form of governing informal work. Notably, while the IAIS guidelines tended towards the promotion of commercial markets for microinsurance, the actual implementation of microinsurance policy in Senegal has been shaped strongly by struggles to remake the state's relations to irregular workers.

Activity specifically relating to the CIMA rules in Senegal originates in a World Bank report on index insurance for agriculture commissioned by a newly established public-private agricultural insurance provider. The report recommended that the provider establish a publicly subsidized 'social safety net' for small farmers based on yield-indexed insurance (World Bank 2009a). The ILO's Social Protection Department, meanwhile, was helping to develop a national policy framework for social security for informal workers. There was little specific discussion of microinsurance, but, as with many of the discussions under STEP in the late 1990s and early 2000s, finding alternative mechanisms for the delivery of social protection to informal workers was a main focus of the ILO's attention. A report

Neoliberal crises and informality 109

published in 2013 had identified insurance mutuals and microfinance institutions as potential delivery and payment channels for a national 'Simplified Regime for Small Contributors' (RSPC) (ILO 2013b: 40). Much of this work would subsequently end up being re-directed towards microinsurance policy in 2014, where funding from the IFC and organizational support from MIF were available.

The Senegalese Ministry of Finance and *Direction des Assurances*, MIF, and the UN Capital Development Fund, ran a national planning workshop on microinsurance policy in Dakar in August of 2014. The workshop settled on a policy framework for microinsurance that was noticeably tailored towards the mobilization of community organizations in the provision of social protection – especially health insurance. The ILO sent the specialists in social security who had helped draft the report on the RSPC along with specialists in microinsurance. The workshop report is explicit about the 'social protection' framework within which the country's microinsurance policy strategy was to be developed: 'Current social protection covers about 20 percent of the population, as against the majority of Senegalese citizens . . . working in the rural and informal sectors, who are excluded' (ILO 2014c: 3, author's translation). The conference settled on a plan of action including financial education, training for microinsurers, advocacy, and regulatory reforms to support the expansion of microinsurance (ILO 2014c: 7).

A follow-up workshop was held in September of 2014, again in Dakar, aimed at elaborating more specific courses of action. Workshop recommendations stressed the need for a state-led financial education programme with the explicit objective to 'stimulate demand in an ethical and responsible manner' (ILO 2014d: 7, author's translation). It also laid out a consumer protection role for regulators, in line with the CIMA rules, calling for the Senegalese *Direction des Assurances* to 'exercise a strict control over insurance companies and intermediaries, and to screen all insurance products that will be presented to the public' (ILO 2014d: 7, author's translation). In short, the segmentation evident in *Livre VII* of microinsurance products from both other financial services (i.e. credit and savings) and from more established forms of insurance is carried over into the Senegalese policy. The Senegalese plan, then, involves delegating social protection for informal and agricultural workers primarily to the voluntary sector, but in a way that is actively organized, through a variety of education programmes, subsidies, and regulatory mechanisms, by the state. Initiatives in the agrarian sector, where a publicly subsidized index insurance provider is already in place (see above), might be read in a similar way. Microinsurance is being rolled out in an effort of re-articulating the state's relationship to subaltern classes through the enrolment of existing community organizations in a state-supervised project for 'financial inclusion'. Of course, whether or not this will actually be successful remains to be seen.

As a means of reducing poverty and managing insecurity for 'informal' workers in urban settings and dispossessed agrarian populations, this framework leaves a good deal to be desired. Microinsurance undoubtedly downloads responsibility for the provision of social protection onto impoverished individuals and communities. It thus risks creating a decidedly two-tiered system of social protection, with a shrinking system of state pensions supporting a small core of normalized workers and subsidized markets for microinsurance covering others. This framework also performs many of the political functions that the wider differentiation of irregular from normalized workers often does – namely, it 'cocoons' irregular forms of work from the wider structural forces that create them by emphasizing the exclusion of informal workers from 'normal' modes of social protection. It thus lends itself at best to reducing some of the worst effects of ongoing processes of primitive accumulation. But at the same time, the specific roll out of microinsurance policies in Senegal has been profoundly shaped by the specific political relations of force – microinsurance policy has been shaped less by commercializing impulses and more by political imperatives to organize irregular workers and render them legible to the state in the context of the dismantling of the mechanisms by which relationships with subaltern populations had been managed in the postcolonial period.

Governing informal apprenticeships in Tanzania[6]

We can point to some similar dynamics to those outlined in the previous section in projects targeting skills and training programmes for informal workers. Skills and training in the informal economy were, to some extent, longstanding concerns of the ILO. The ILO conducted some research on apprenticeships in the informal sector in the 1970s under the auspices of WEP, but this was almost entirely stopped during the period of structural adjustment. The World Bank cut funding for vocational training in the 1980s and early 1990s, suggesting that governments should concern themselves with providing basic elementary and secondary education, while other training could be done more efficiently by private employers (World Bank 1991). By the early 2000s, however, in the context of a growing emphasis at the ILO on unemployment, especially youth unemployment, officials in the ILO's Skills and Employability Department (one of three branches of the newly re-organized Employment Sector) re-opened investigations into training practices in the informal sector, focusing in particular on apprenticeships. The ILO hosted a workshop on informal apprenticeships in Africa in Geneva in 2007 (ILO 2007a). The workshop was followed up by a large research project on informal apprenticeships in Mtwara and Lindi regions of Tanzania.

We usefully understand the way in which this project has played out with reference to the broader patterns of shifting political relations of force around irregular work in Tanzania. The history of 'informal' work in Tanzania echoes the trajectory in neighbouring Kenya discussed in the previous chapter to some extent. Casual dockworkers played a critical role in the early development of trade unions (Illife 1975). After independence, state-dominated 'formal' sectors of the economy were increasingly identified as terrains for trade union action and increasingly made distinct from 'informal' spaces. This separation was reinforced by government hostility to small-scale self-employment. This set of arrangements deteriorated in the context of structural adjustment in the 1980s and 1990s. Privatization and deregulation have led to widespread de-industrialization and retrenchments, and have thus often greatly expanded the place of 'informal' activities in workers' livelihoods. Currency devaluations that badly eroded real wages also encouraged increasing numbers of 'formal' sector workers to seek means of supplementing incomes through 'informal' activity. The result has been growing differentiation within the sphere of 'informal' work, and the growth of power relations within 'informal' economies between employers and employees (see e.g. Rizzo 2011). Relations between formal and informal sector workers' organizations remain difficult, with trade union interest in organizing informal workers varying widely by location and sector.[7]

The growing importance of 'informal' employment in Tanzania again poses a significant set of political challenges for the state. While hostility and harassment of informal workers by local authorities has often persisted (see Rizzo 2011: 1187–1188), the government has increasingly sought out means of organizing and regularizing the 'informal' economy. The government started a de Soto-influenced programme for 'Property and Business Formalization' (commonly called 'Mkurabita', based on the acronym in Swahili) in 2004. At its root, the programme is aimed at re-articulating the relationship of the state to subaltern populations in the wake of the transformations of 'informal' work highlighted above. This is most plainly visible in the growing emphasis on developing mechanisms for taxation of informal economies:

> Tanzania recognizes that a substantial amount of economic activities taking place in the small and medium business are not well recognized and regulated. Under the poverty reduction programs, Tanzania plans to increase the level of government expenditure and transfer payments to take care of the poorer sections of the population. Thus, government revenue may need to grow at a rate that exceeds the growth of national income. With the limited revenue generated from the formal sector unable to cope with expenditure requirements, the extension of the tax net becomes a necessity.
> (TRA 2010: 2)

On a very basic level, then, the 'formalization' drive should be read as an effort to stabilize the relationship between the state and a vast swath of the population living in its territory. This is, evidently, a very broad strokes picture of the evolution of the 'objective formation' of informal work in Tanzania, but it does highlight a number of salient tendencies.

This history of struggle over the regulation of 'informal' workers played a considerable part in shaping the trajectory of the ILO project. This is visible in the first instance in the simple fact that target populations in Mtwara were often initially suspicious of the ILO project:

> The informal master crafts people are very suspicious when someone comes from the government. They tried to hide their training because they thought it's an illegal system. So it took a lot of effort to convince these guys that we need to collaborate, it's okay, we want to improve this system.[8]

112 *Neoliberal crises and informality*

The project that took shape thus ended up depending very heavily on finding local collaborators, ranging from the national vocational training authority to (surprisingly) an order of Benedictine monks that had been established in the region under German colonial rule. A number of potential collaborators, including national trade union federations, were uninterested. Indeed, one ILO official interviewed suggested that the relative disinterest of trade unions played a significant part in preventing the pilot project findings on working conditions and exploitation in apprenticeships (see below) from being carried forward.

The findings of the ILO project were outlined in a working paper published in 2009 (Nübler *et al.* 2009). The emphasis was placed – as with a good number of other World Bank and ILO interventions (see Taylor 2010) – on improving the institutional context of apprenticeships. The general thrust of the ILO's proposals was that national and international policy interventions should proceed by 'building on the traditional institutional framework, so that the incentives of [master craftspeople] and apprentices to participate in apprenticeships are sustained' (Nübler *et al.* 2009: ix). This approach came with some significant limitations. A particularly indicative set of issues emerged around the unregulated nature of 'graduation' from apprenticeship. Simply put, it was normally up to the master craftsperson to determine when an apprentice had completed his or her apprenticeship; during the period of the apprenticeship, however, the apprentice continued to provide cheap or free labour for the master craftsperson. The project found that:

> There are some indications that MCs extend apprenticeship periods for some weeks or months in order to benefit longer from the difference between high productivity and low compensation of apprentices. A total of 42 per cent of MCs state that their apprentices are proficient some time before they terminate their apprenticeship . . . While apprentices undertake simple tasks during the first few months, and perform tasks requiring little skills during the following months, they are able to work independently with clients in the third stage of skills acquisition. At the third stage, apprentices demonstrate the productivity of a skilled worker, allowing the MC to recover training costs.
>
> (Nübler *et al.* 2009: 31)

The study drew somewhat ambivalent conclusions about this practice:

> MCs have the authority to determine the end of apprenticeship, thereby taking into account the ability and talent of apprentices. The advantage of this flexible arrangement is that MCs can adjust the period of cost recovery and ensure that apprentices achieve the desired standards of competence. The downside of flexibility, however, is the risk of MCs taking advantage of this situation in order to gain additional returns. Some interviews with apprentices indicated that apprentices did not always agree with the MC's decision on graduating the apprentice. This suggests that policies need to establish clear and transparent rules and criteria for termination of apprenticeship.
>
> (Nübler *et al.* 2009: 33–34)

Here the ILO's project comes in contact with power relations between 'informal' workers, and issues of potential or actual exploitation *within* the informal economy. The problem is still understood, however, in terms of an absence: that there are no clear regulatory criteria around graduation opens informal apprenticeship up to abuse. This is, no doubt, partially true. But the argument that upgrading institutions should solve the problem does little to address the power imbalance between master and apprentice, to say nothing of the broader structural context of widespread unemployment that facilitates this relation of power. A number of key areas for 'upgrading' were identified in the 2009 report: recognition of skills earned in informal apprenticeships in the broader economy, social security provisions for apprentices, and working conditions in informal workplaces.

As in the Kenyan case above, however, the actual emphases of subsequent interventions have reflected a relatively narrow subset of these concerns relatively well-aligned with ongoing state efforts at organizing subaltern populations, particularly emphasizing the recognition of skills. This is largely despite the broader efforts of the ILO. The Informal Apprenticeships project was oriented towards the delineation of common research methodologies, and a set of common training tools for policy-makers that would allow for a set of interventions that could be applied more widely (ILO 2012b). Similar studies were conducted in Malawi, Benin, and Zimbabwe. The emphasis of this broader project, as in Tanzania, is on 'strengthening the institutional framework' around informal training, by helping design policies aimed at 'strengthening incentives and benefits from apprenticeship training, improving the decent work component, and securing public funding to finance the training' (ILO 2012b: 1). The training guide aims to outline a set of 'best practices' for governing informal apprenticeships. Similar circulations of 'best practices' have also been carried out by more direct means, including by organizing study tours – in May of 2010, for instance, officials from the ILO's Pretoria office led a Zimbabwean delegation to Accra to study the existing arrangements for training in the informal economy in Ghana (ILO 2010b). The ILO's project, then, aims to secure the spread of a definite set of institutional forms throughout the region through the circulation of particular kinds of knowledge. The ILO, in short, continues to emphasize the broader agenda emerging from the initial report on Tanzania.

However, in terms of the actual implementation of follow-up initiatives, many of the concerns raised in the initial report about, say, exploitation and the rules around graduation have largely fallen from view. The most developed case in this respect is Tanzania. The main thrust of follow-up activity has been around 'Recognition of Prior Learning' (RPL) (see Aggarwal 2015). Broadly speaking, RPL programmes deal with the recognition and valuation of skills acquired in informal settings. As the Informal Apprenticeships project has progressed, the ILO has begun to pay increasing attention to the problems posed in this respect by the limited value often assigned to 'informal' learning by 'formal' employers – it is not enough for informal apprenticeships to simply produce better skilled workers, 'whatever skills they have acquired need to be assessed and also certified'.[9] In 2014 the Vocational Education and Training Authority (VETA) adopted a RPL

114 *Neoliberal crises and informality*

programme in collaboration with the ILO, in which VETA offers short courses to 'artisans' without formal credentials and certifies graduates (Mwakyusa 2016). In this sense it is the aspects of the ILO's project on Informal Apprenticeships that hew closest to the broader strategy implicit in Mkurabita have been carried over into specific programmes in Tanzania – in particular, the emphasis on translating 'informal' economies into legible spaces that can be governed effectively by the state. As in Kenya in the 1970s, this trajectory is best explained by the history of struggles over the mobilization and organization of subaltern populations in which it is enmeshed. As noted above, the kind of institutional economics through which the ILO project has been articulated is highly limiting in terms of its capacity to conceptualize relations of domination or exploitation in the workplace, but even this relatively narrow agenda has been further constrained by the dynamics of ongoing struggles to organize subaltern classes in Tanzania.

Again, as with the case of microinsurance policies in Senegal, we could justifiably question the usefulness of this approach in resolving relations of poverty. More skilled informal workers, even better recognized skills for informal workers, would seem to do little to address the dynamics of dispossession that have expanded the scope of the 'informal' economy in Tanzania since the 1980s. Again, the same set of residualist ideas about 'informality' is in evidence: 'informality' is understood in terms of the *absence* of recognition and regulation, and the resolution of poverty is accordingly framed in terms of fairly straightforward technical interventions. Reifying the boundary between 'formal' and 'informal' economies, in short, does important political work in cocooning informality from the broader dynamics of primitive accumulation within which it operates. At the same time, again as in Senegal, the efforts of the state to reposition itself in relation to irregular workers has played a critical role in shaping the actual implementation of the programme.

Conclusion

The foregoing discussion has sought to situate the shifting contours of ILO programming on 'informal' labour in the context of the contradictory dynamics of neoliberalization in sub-Saharan Africa. The critical point to underline here is that, as against an understanding of neoliberal reforms as *causes* of precarity through the removal of regulatory protections (e.g. Standing 2011), we can point to a number of shifts in the scope and form of precarious labour, coupled with shifting patterns of political relations of force, both rooted in the dynamics of neoliberalism, which together have engendered new patterns of governance of irregular labour. The relationships between neoliberalism and irregular work, in brief, are marked by far more complex patterns of continuity and change than are often assumed.

Recent efforts to mobilize the concept of 'informal' labour as a means of governing irregular forms of labour continue to share the underlying residualist understanding of irregular forms of labour with earlier iterations of the concept. They are, at the same time, profoundly linked with shifting patterns of political relations of force engendered by contradictory dynamics of neoliberalization. Processes of structural adjustment have undoubtedly, in many ways, changed the dynamics of irregular forms of work in practice, while simultaneously dismantling the political and organizational means by which the postcolonial historic bloc was held together. More targeted programmes for 'informal' workers have emerged in part as means of managing the political dynamics this has created. Managing irregular labour, in short, has been a crucial means through which contradictory processes of neoliberalization have played out in Africa. This point is underlined again in the following chapter, which turns to the problems posed by the revival of regulatory interest in 'forced labour'.

Notes

1 Related perspectives on neoliberalism and primitive accumulation, albeit less attentive to the place of labour, can be found in Harvey (2003) and Sassen (2010).
2 The remainder of this section draws extensively on Bernards (2016).
3 Author interview, ILO official, Pretoria, October 2014.
4 MIF has since been renamed the 'Impact Insurance Facility'.
5 The significance of the dismantling of these 'triangular relationships' is taken up further in the discussion of child trafficking in the following chapter.
6 This section draws on Bernards (2017a).
7 See the debate between Fischer (2013) and Rizzo (2013).
8 Author interview with ILO official, Geneva, July 2014.
9 Author interview, ILO official, Pretoria, October 2014.

6 Reviving the governance of forced labour

'Traditional slavery' and child trafficking in West Africa

As noted at the end of Chapter 2, despite the insistence of the ILO and of sympathetic academics that the ILO has treated the abolition of forced labour as a 'constant mission' from the 1920s onwards (e.g. Maul 2007) the governance of forced labour has in fact been rather sporadic. Not much happened on this front for the ILO in sub-Saharan Africa, between the early 1960s and the 1990s. In itself this is an indication of the deeply political nature of the governance of irregular labour – there is little argument that coercive labour recruitment of one kind or another persisted through the twentieth century (see Brass and van der Linden 1997). All the same, forced labour in the postcolonial world largely fell off the ILO's radar. Debates about forced labour in the 1950s and 1960s were dominated by concerns about the use of coercion in Soviet territories. There was a brief debate in the early 1960s about what kinds of coercion could be justified by the exigencies of 'national' development in the context of decolonization (see Maul 2012; 2007). But, by and large, global regulatory attention to the problem of forced labour was limited.

Questions around forced labour have, however, been strongly revived in the 1990s and 2000s. The ILO's conventions on forced labour are among of the 'core conventions' identified in the 1998 Declaration on Fundamental Principles and Rights at Work. The ILO established the SAP-FL in 2002 and has issued a series of major reports on forced labour in the last two decades (ILO 2001; 2005a; 2009a; 2012a; 2014b). Forced labour involving children has taken on a growing importance in this agenda; the ILO also passed a convention on the 'Worst Forms of Child Labour' (C182) in 1999 (and immediately identified it as a core convention), which placed a considerable emphasis on forced labour and trafficking. The ILO has also started to take steps to update existing rules on forced labour. In 2014, the ILC debated and passed a protocol updating C29. Notable provisions included the elimination of the 'transition period'; as well as provisions on technical assistance including the adoption of national tripartite plans of action for the elimination of forced labour and a commitment to 'release, protection, recovery and rehabilitation of people affected by forced labour'. This new set of routines and techniques connects the standard-setting role of the ILO much more to its other 'development' activities – 'the nature of modern forced labour calls for a truly global programme or awareness building, backed by meticulous research and development of appropriate statistical methods to identify problems and their solution' (ILO 2001: 90–91). In short, the ILO seeks to govern forced labour with a very different set of techniques than it did in the 1930s and 1940s.

The ILO has consistently presented these new initiatives as a revival of its 'historic mission' of combatting forced labour: 'The adoption of the ILO Declaration on Fundamental Principles and Rights at Work and its Follow-Up in 1998 signalled a renewed international resolve to relegate forced labour to history' (ILO 2001: 1). But this presentation disguises a number of important changes. The forms of directly state-backed forced labour that were explicitly targeted by the ILO's forced labour conventions (in colonial and communist contexts, respectively, for C29 and C105), are increasingly scarce. The present agenda is primarily concerned with private forms of forced labour, which are explicitly banned in virtually all countries. There have been a number of insightful critiques of these emergent frameworks published in recent years (e.g. Lerche 2007; Rogaly 2008; Phillips and Mieres 2015). The organization has paid increasing attention to the role of poverty in creating vulnerabilities to forced labour. However, it often continues to understand poverty in terms that will be familiar from the discussions of the informal economy in the previous chapter – that is, as a set of exclusions from 'normal' markets through lack of access to credit or training (*cf.* Phillips and Mieres 2015). The ILO's current activities primarily focus on improving the enforcement of laws banning forced labour, and on interventions to reduce poverty in vulnerable communities. The upshot of all of this is, as critics have correctly pointed out, an understanding of forced labour that is insufficiently attuned to the broader structural factors underlying coercive labour practices.

This is problematic because in practice, as previous authors have pointed out in more extensive detail (LeBaron and Ayers 2013; Phillips 2013; Manzo 2005; McGrath 2013b), processes of neoliberalization and the broader transformation of global production networks have dramatically altered both the extent and form of forced labour. There is little space with which to trace out these developments in any great detail here, but for the moment it should suffice to highlight a few points. The increasing importance of buyer-driven production networks dominated by global branded retailers in many sectors oriented around low-skill, labour intensive production (e.g. garments and textiles, electronics), has both contributed to the dramatic growth of subcontracted production and increased pressure on smaller contracting firms to cut costs (Phillips 2016). This has often led both to the intensification of labour discipline in the workplace by suppliers (see Pun and Smith 2007, on electronics firms in China) and to the growth of homeworking and subcontracting arrangements increasingly subject to various forms of forced and child labour (see Phillips *et al.* 2013, on the garment sector in Delhi; McGrath 2013b, on biofuels in Brazil). At the same time, neoliberal reforms to agrarian property structures emphasizing the solidification of private property rights in land have often intensified longer-running patterns of enclosure and dispossession that have often led to the intensification of various forms of exploitation. The most studied example here is probably bonded labour in India, which tends to be drawn from a broader population of dispossessed agrarian workers forming a 'huge reserve army of labour to be hired and fired according to the need of the moment, in agriculture but increasingly also in other economic sectors' (Breman and Guérin 2009: 3). But, as noted in greater detail below with respect to Niger in particular, related dynamics are sometimes associated with the transformations of property rights associated with broader patterns of neoliberal reforms, leading to notable patterns of intensification and transformation of ostensibly 'traditional' patterns of slavery and bondage. These effects are compounded by the rapid growth of unemployment in the context of programmes austerity and privatization. The point, in short, is that neoliberal reforms have increased the vulnerability of many workers to deepening forms of exploitation, including increasingly by overtly violent means (see LeBaron and Ayers 2013; Phillips and Mieres 2015). An understanding of forced labour premised on a residualist understanding of poverty and 'governance failures' is inadequate in this context – as, again, several critics have rightly pointed out (e.g. Lerche 2007; Rogaly 2008; Phillips and Mieres 2015).

As elsewhere in this book, however, I seek here to think through the sources and the implications of emerging tendencies in the ILO's approach to forced labour, rather than critique them in the abstract. The first section of this chapter traces out the new agenda around forced labour that has emerged at the ILO in the early twenty-first century. However, again as with the other examples discussed above, the ways in which the 'global' policy frameworks developed by the ILO have actually intersected with shifting patterns of relations of force at more localized scales have played a substantial role in shaping the outcomes of these programme in practice. This point is explored in the latter two sections by considering two examples of ILO efforts to govern forced labour in West Africa: a project dealing with the persistence of 'traditional slavery' in Niger, and a major sub-regional project on child trafficking across West Africa.

Governing unfree labour in the twenty-first century

A first point to underline here is that the revival of interest in unfree labour at the ILO should be understood in the context of the contradictory political dynamics unleashed by the neoliberal reforms of the 1980s and 1990s. As discussed in Chapters 4 and 5, and as Robert Cox (1977) had already noted in the late 1970s, the crisis of Fordist relations of production posed significant problems for the ILO. Simply put, it undermined the basic social relations and forms of state with which the organization had historically been closely entangled. These tensions were sometimes manifested quite directly – as in the American withdrawal from the organization in the 1970s – but more broadly they were reflected in the difficulty faced by the organization in re-shaping an agenda for international labour governance that could work in a context defined by declining trade union densities, the erosion of left parties, and the dismantling of the tripartite institutions central to the ILO's vision. The ILO was increasingly marginalized even from debates about international labour standards in the 1990s. Labour movements in core countries increasingly focused on other international organizations that might have more power to sanction violators – most notably the World Trade Organization (WTO).

The issue came to a head in 1996 at the WTO's Singapore Ministerial where the US and European delegations, under pressure from the ICFTU, pushed for a resolution incorporating labour standards into the WTO's rules (see O'Brien *et al.* 2000). The final resolution in Singapore did reaffirm the ILO's status as the appropriate institution to manage international labour standards. However, the position of the ILO at the time was such that the decision of the Singapore Ministerial might be attributed primarily to a desire among states and business actors to avoid enforceable labour standards.

The ILO's response was encapsulated in two closely linked moves in the late 1990s. On one hand, the organization moved towards an emphasis on a much narrower code of labour standards focused on a few 'Core Conventions' – prohibitions on discrimination, guarantees of freedom of association, and (critically for present purposes) conventions banning forced labour and child labour – in the 1998 'Declaration on Fundamental Rights and Principles at Work'. While conventions and recommendations relevant to child labour date to a convention on minimum ages for industrial work (C5) passed in 1919, the passage of C182 in 1999 in its emphasis on the 'worst forms' of child labour also clearly brought issues of child labour much closer to the ILO's agenda on forced labour. In 1999 the ILO followed this set of activities by announcing a new 'Decent Work' agenda with four main objectives: promoting employment, promoting rights at work (primarily the core conventions), promoting social protections, and promoting 'social dialogue' (ILO 1999). As a number of critics have noted, this agenda involved a re-focusing of the organization's efforts on managing the worst abuses of labour, without confronting the broader context of structural changes in which these abuses take place (see Standing 2008; Vosko 2002; Lerche 2012; Selwyn 2013). Indeed, the 'Decent Work Agenda' in this context has been interpreted as contributing to *legitimizing* neoliberal reforms by offsetting their worst effects without challenging their substance (Standing 2008; Vosko 2002; Bernards 2015).

Worth underlining for present purposes is the extent to which the boundary between normal modes of exploitation and irregular labour (in this case forced labour and the 'worst forms' of child labour) is central to this legitimating function. Here the argument raised in Chapter 1 about the role of boundary-drawing between 'normal' and 'irregular' modes of exploitation in naturalizing proletarian forms of exploitation is clearly illustrated. The ILO's repositioning of 'forced labour' and the 'worst forms' of child labour as lynchpins of its wider framework of international labour standards worked to re-situate the boundary between 'acceptable' and 'unacceptable' forms of exploitation around the question of violent coercion. Coupled with a growing emphasis on unemployment and informality (examined in the last chapter), this new agenda has often worked to sideline questions that might be raised about exploitation in 'normal' jobs. In Standing's perceptive critique 'Banning "the worst forms of child labour", banning "forced labour", campaigning against gender discrimination and defending freedom of association are matters of common and civil law. They do not constitute a . . . progressive agenda' (2008: 367). This is very much true, but we can push the argument further: the way in which the free/forced binary has been repositioned in the ILO's standard-setting activity since the 1990s has served to set the bar relatively low in terms of what constitute 'acceptable' forms of exploitation – those based on the 'silent compulsion' of the market get more or less a free pass. Indeed, this probably helps to explain the extent to which the ILO's core conventions have been adopted into private-voluntary codes of conduct for global supply chains.

The free/forced labour binary thus remains quite central to the ILO's work here. The ILO's definition of forced labour, in C29 relied heavily on liberal conceptions of consent when it defines forced labour as 'all work or service that is exacted from any person under the menace of any penalty and for which the said person has not offered himself voluntarily'. The colonial context in which C29 was negotiated has changed dramatically, as has the ILO's broader approach to forced labour, but this emphasis persists. A recent General Survey on the application of the ILO's forced labour conventions included the explicit qualification that 'the employer and the state are not accountable for all external constraints or indirect coercion existing in practice: for example, the need to work to earn one's living could become relevant only in conjunction with other factors for which they are answerable' (ILO 2007b: 20–21). Here the problematic demarcation of 'forced' labour from the forms of coercion implicit in 'free' labour is reiterated quite explicitly.

The ILO's contemporary agenda on forced labour places a much greater emphasis on the illegal or illicit character of forced labour. Until very recently the ILO's standards on forced labour were targeted primarily at legal requirements to work backed by state force. Rather than a question of ensuring that legislation adheres to C29 and C105, or restraining states' resort to coercive recruitment practices, eliminating forced labour becomes a question of strengthening state capacity to enforce the near-universal laws prohibiting forced labour. Of 20.9 million cases of forced labour counted by the ILO in 2012, the ILO finds that 2.2 million are instances of state-imposed forms of forced labour, while 4.5 million are 'victims of forced sexual exploitation' and another 14.2 million are found 'in economic activities such as agriculture, construction, domestic work, and manufacturing', the largest grouping of whom are in various forms of bonded labour in South Asia (ILO 2012a: 13). This shift has had significant political implications in practice. If forced labour is framed as a criminal problem, the primary solution is the better enforcement of laws. The ILO's (2001) report suggests that 'Attaining better enforcement of laws that ban forced labour forms a natural part of repairing failures in governance that characterize many manifestations for forced labour' (ILO 2001: 3). This has been a significant focus of interventions in practice. SAP-FL technical cooperation interventions have often involved training for judges and security officials on ILO standards on forced labour and the enforcement of laws prohibiting forced labour. Of course, most forms of labour recruitment that would fall under the ILO's definition of forced labour *are* in fact illegal, and those laws *are* often weakly enforced. But the growing emphasis on the criminality of forced labour, rather than, say, the myriad ways in which it is bound up in global production networks (Manzo 2005; McGrath 2013b), or broader patterns of agrarian transformation (Breman 2010), contributes to deepening the cocooning of forced labour.

122 *Reviving the governance of forced labour*

This emphasis has often been deepened by a growing emphasis on policing human trafficking elsewhere in the international system. As a number of authors have observed, discourses about 'human smuggling' or 'trafficking' contribute to the construction of migration as a 'security' problem requiring particular modes of policing and techniques for surveillance and classification (e.g. Mountz 2003; Bigo 2002; van Liempt and Sersli 2013). This global policy discourse about trafficking was cemented particularly clearly with the passage of the Protocol on Trafficking in Persons, especially Women and Children, to the United Nations Convention Against Transnational Organized Crime – the 'Palermo Protocol' – in 2002. The Palermo Protocol is first and foremost a 'security' instrument; it strongly emphasizes border controls and police cooperation, rather than, say, the rights of victims or the underlying causes of trafficking (Anderson and Andrijasevic 2008). The mainstream of the global governance of human trafficking is largely defined by the Palermo Protocol, so for the ILO to try to govern forced labour in this context has thus meant dealing increasingly with security governance. These 'security' and 'criminality' frames are sometimes an awkward fit with the ILO's emphasis on labour rights. One ILO official, for instance, notes of the Palermo protocol: 'It's a very strong instrument . . . but the focus is very much on prosecution, so there's not really a labour component to it' (Author interview, June 2014, Geneva). The prominence of this 'security' frame is still significant for present purposes insofar as it serves to deepen the emphasis on criminality and prosecution in governing forced labour.

The ILO has also made some significant gestures towards linking the incidence of forced labour (as defined by the ILO) to vulnerabilities engendered by poverty. A 2014 report, for instance, finds that:

> Income shocks that push households further into poverty, and often below the food poverty line . . . increase the likelihood of exposure to forced labour. These households are more likely to need emergency funds, eventually relying on third parties to support their families. This heavy dependence on other individuals can lead to manipulation, coercion, exploitation and deception, especially if a creditor is a recruiter or trafficker.
>
> (ILO 2014a: 45–46)

While the linkage drawn here between poverty and vulnerability to exploitation could potentially serve to link the incidence of forced labour to broader structures of accumulation, in practice – as Phillips and Mieres (2015) rightly argue – the ILO often falls back on conceptions of 'poverty' that tend to reinforce rather than weaken the 'cocooning' of forced labour. In particular, poverty is conceived of in terms of the 'exclusion' of poor people from access to training, credit, and markets. This is particularly visible in the ways in which poverty reduction has been incorporated into ILO programming on forced labour. It has been common practice in programmes in West Africa, for instance, to promote so-called 'Income Generating Activities' (IGAs) in communities vulnerable to forced labour or child labour, especially child trafficking (discussed further below). Similar efforts at promoting microcredit as a solution have also been pursued by the ILO since the mid-1990s – this is framed explicitly as an effort at using 'microfinance initiatives to improve the access to bonded labourers to financial markets' (ILO 2001: 80). A number of projects assessing the role of microfinance in this respect have been carried out, especially in South Asia (e.g. Premchander *et al.* 2014). In either case, the lack of access by the poor to credit or training – rather than the broader context of property rights and labour regimes – is ultimately identified as the root cause of forced labour. These approaches to poverty are closely related to the interventions in informal economies outlined in the previous chapter.

The binary between 'free' and 'forced' labour is thus ironically re-asserted insofar as 'forced' labour continues to be identified with residual spaces left 'outside' of global capitalism. This is true both in the sense that contemporary policy has tended towards an emphasis on improving law enforcement and in that efforts to link vulnerability to forced labour with poverty have relied on a relatively limited and residual conception of poverty itself in terms of 'exclusion' from markets. The criminalization of forced labour and the reliance of the ILO on residual understandings of poverty contribute to 'naturalizing' the 'silent compulsion' of the labour market. The ILO's approach to forced labour frames the elimination of forced labour as a product of the extension of the legal and economic systems underpinning 'normal' free labour relations, and indeed the ILO's technical interventions on law enforcement, IGAs, microfinance, and the like contribute (albeit in relatively minor ways) to the extension of those systems in practice. However, the translation of these broad frameworks into practice is seldom straightforward, it is deeply coloured by broader patterns of political relations of force, and hence highly variegated across time and space. The following sections, accordingly, highlights the importance of these dynamics by turning to a closer examination of the ILO's interventions on 'traditional slavery' in Niger and child trafficking in West Africa.

Governing 'traditional' slavery in Niger[1]

An interesting set of projects under SAP-FL for present purposes revolves around measures to prevent 'traditional slavery' in Niger and Mauritania. The present discussion focuses on the former. There is a good deal of debate even within the ILO about the extent of 'forced labour' and 'slavery' in Niger, and even about whether or not the forms of slavery that do exist actually constitute forced labour. Activist estimates (e.g. Abdelkader 2004) suggest that tens of thousands of people are still held as slaves in Niger. The Nigerien government has consistently disputed these numbers, and the ILO's research has often hedged on whether 'slavery' itself is at issue rather than discrimination against people of 'slave descent' (e.g. Sekou and Abdoukarimou 2009; ILO 2009a: 15). The reliance of these interventions, however, on the concept of 'traditional slavery' has tended to obscure the linkages between transformations in existing forms of unfree labour and the process of structural adjustment and neoliberalization. But at the same time, the politics of governing forced labour has been rather more complex than this critique implies, with ongoing struggles over the shape of the postcolonial state in the context of ongoing processes of primitive accumulation playing a critical role in shaping and delimiting the practice of ILO interventions.

The concept of 'traditional' slavery is common in popular assessments of forced labour in the Sahel (e.g. Bales 2008, on Mauritania). It is also repeated in most ILO assessments of forced labour (ILO 2001; 2005a; 2012a). The concept of 'traditional slavery' is problematic because it suggests an understanding of forced labour as a historically static cultural practice (LeBaron and Ayers 2013; Manzo 2005). Nonetheless, it *is* very much in keeping with the ways in which the ILO has understood 'forced labour', as discussed in the previous section, particularly the tendency to frame forced labour as a feature of residual spaces left out of global markets. Of course, the 'traditional' character of Nigerien slavery is questionable. Slavery in Niger, as elsewhere, is a dynamic institution – it is widely varied within the country and across time (see Rossi 2015). Contemporary processes of neoliberalization have impacted a good deal on the character and extent of unfreedom.

Slavery in Niger, while highly variable in terms of cultural form and between agrarian and pastoralist social formations, is historically very closely linked to questions of property and land use rights, which have been contentious political issues for Niger's entire postcolonial history (see Lund 1997). The country's legal system retains overlapping 'modern' and 'traditional' frameworks for ownership with national and local authorities often struggling over jurisdiction – themselves the legacies of the structure of 'decentralized despotism' of colonial rule mediated by 'traditional' authorities common across Africa (Mamdani 1996). The military regime sought to resolve these issues by decreeing in 1974 that all land should be the private property of the current user. This provoked a considerable degree of conflict around overlapping property claims, which the regime promptly sought to close off in 1977 by decreeing that local authorities had no authority to decide land claims. The resulting situation has usefully been described as one of 'precarious stability' (Lund 1997: 101) in which land users often paid informal tithes to land owners, while continuing to maintain use rights. Land tenure reform became a major cause for regime opponents, which the regime tried to head off in 1986 with a new Rural Code. Land reform remained a major issue in the process of political opening in the early 1990s, with the main opposition party campaigning in the first multiparty elections in 1993 on a platform that centered on challenging officials' abuse of power – which, in local iterations of the campaign in rural areas, often meant informal promises to overhaul the existing system of land tenure to return expropriated land or land that had been lost due to rigged trials by traditional chiefs (Lund 1997: 103). In the Gramscian terms introduced in Chapter 1, property rights became a crucial issue around which particular forms of class consciousness and 'corporate interests' were articulated in the process of democratization in Niger.

These forms of opposition to the military regime coincided with pressure from major donors – the US, France, and the World Bank in particular – to harmonize and privatize property rights in land. The United States Agency for International Development (USAID) approved a major agricultural development programme in 1990, which was premised on 'enhanc[ing] the ability of individual rural inhabitants to gain control over resources they habitually use, and to manage and profit from them in a sustainable manner' (USAID 1990: 2) – or, in short, on the privatization and formalization of individual land tenure rights. The programme also included conditionalities related to the implementation of the Rural Code (1990: 142–153). The security of property rights in land has continued to be a focus of interventions from the World Bank (2009b) and the country's most recent Poverty Reduction Strategy Paper (IMF 2013).

These processes were accompanied in urban centres by the erosion of labour market institutions and growing unemployment and casualization of work. The military regime had relied heavily on uranium exports to finance urban industrialization in the 1970s, and faced a growing budget crisis as uranium prices fell in the early 1980s. In the process of structural adjustment, this system was largely dismantled through the privatization of state-owned enterprises (Gervais 1995: 31). The resulting instability of employment has been compounded by a number of food crises (Olivier de Sardan 2008), which have spurred significant protest mobilizations around the cost of living (Maccatory *et al.* 2010). As elsewhere, these shifts have profoundly altered the relationships between organized labour and the state. Trade unions have participated in a number of major protest actions and strikes directed at the rising cost of living, public sector retrenchments, and against the military regime (Adji 2000).

These transformations have shifted the scope and forms of unfreedom visible in Niger, as well as the ways in which 'slavery' has been articulated politically. Hereditary slave status in many agrarian communities was often closely entwined with patterns of land use. 'Slavery' was historically often as much a cultural status as a form of economic servitude; many 'slaves' kept secure access to land by paying tithes to owners. The privatization of land, however, has often meant that conflicts over use rights and rents have been sharpened in ways that have led to the deepening expropriation of 'slaves' in agriculture (see Kelley 2008; Abdelkader 2004: 9–10; Sekou and Abdoukarimou 2009: 81). The effort to regularize and privatize land tenure, along with climatic shifts and increasingly prevalent droughts, have heightened strains on pastoral livelihoods, which have historically been dependent on regular migration and ongoing access to pasture and water which have increasingly been turned over to agriculture (Thébaut and Batterbury 2001). This seems to have led to the increased incidence of violent conflict (Thébaut and Batterbury 2001), and has coincided with reports of intensifying slavery for agricultural and domestic work in pastoral-nomadic communities (Abdelkader 2004; Sekou and Abdoukarimou 2009). These patterns of slavery are also deeply gendered, with domestic work in particular dominated by women.

The broader dislocations associated with privatization and structural adjustment have also increased vulnerability to certain forms of extreme exploitation – as LeBaron and Ayers (2013) argue, this is common elsewhere in sub-Saharan Africa as well. The expansion of the 'informal' economy has played a role here. For instance, there are some reports of slaves working in informal markets in some smaller urban centres (although rarely in the capital city Niamey) and turning over earnings to masters (Sekou and Abdoukarimou 2009: 80). The rapid expansion of unemployment and rural dispossession, coupled with the discovery of gold in the 1970s, has contributed to a boom in artisanal gold mining in the Liptako-Gourma region encompassing parts of Western Niger along with Mali and Burkina Faso. The use of child labour in these mines has been widely reported (ILO 2007c; ROTAB 2014). These developments to some extent parallel the dynamics Luxemburg notes in the late nineteenth and early twentieth centuries – where capitalist accumulation relies on raw materials produced through non-capitalist forms of production. (Similar dynamics are also visible in nearby parts of Eastern Senegal, see below).

These linkages between shifting forms of primitive accumulation on one hand and transformations in unfreedom on the other are largely obscured by the emphasis on 'traditional' slavery. However, the particular shape of governance targeting 'forced labour' in Niger has been deeply shaped by transformations in the political relations of force. The anti-government mobilization that took place around the end of the military regime, and which was strengthened by the backlash against structural adjustment (see Gervais 1995: 37–38) and growing cost of living (Maccatory et al. 2010; Mueller 2013), is a crucial development in this respect. Mobilizing against slavery has been an important avenue through which challenges to existing political structures have been articulated. The most prominent organization involved here is Timidria. This organization was originally established in the early 1990s context of democratization as a community development organization in Azawagh, and transitioned into campaigning against slavery later in the decade (see Jeanne 2008). The crisis of the postcolonial regime in Niger, and the concomitant emergence of various forms of political mobilization by subaltern social forces, has played a critical role in the politicization of slavery.

This politicization of slavery in Niger has coincided with renewed international efforts to govern unfree labour. The ILO commissioned a study on the prospects for the 1998 Declaration in Niger, which identified slavery as a problem (Oumarou 2001: 23–26). Anti-slavery advocates within and outside Niger sought to enrol the ILO to pressure the Nigerien government. Anti-Slavery International (ASI) financed a study of slavery in Niger, conducted in 2002 and 2003. Timidria did the bulk of the actual research. The study identified roughly 11 000 people as belonging to a hereditary 'slave caste', generally working for a master as shepherds, agricultural workers, or domestic workers. In some cases they performed wage work for others and were compelled to turn over their earnings to masters (Abdelkader 2004). ASI and the ICFTU began lodging protests with the ILO about slavery in Niger in 2003. Alongside the ILO, Timidria has also pursued a number of international legal avenues to press claims about slavery. Most notably, in 2008, the organization won a case at the Community Court of Justice for the Economic Community of West African States alleging that the state of Niger had failed to uphold its international obligations to protect its citizens from slavery (see Duffy 2009).

The initial response on the part of the Nigerien government was on one hand to argue that Timidria exaggerated the true extent of slavery in the country. Indeed, the head of Timidria was arrested and charged with fraud not long after the ASI report was published, with the government alleging that a ceremony at which 7 000 slaves were supposed to have been freed was based on false information intended to solicit money from foreign donors (he was released not long afterwards) (BBC 2005). The government in Niger did make some superficial moves toward reducing the extent of slavery, most notably by criminalizing the ownership of slaves in 2002. The Ministry of Labour also eventually created a national commission against forced labour and discrimination in 2006. The commission, however, only existed on paper. The ILO, through SAP-FL, has subsequently sought to provide financial and technical support to the commission. The ILO has also commissioned a good deal of research on slavery and forced labour in Niger, but has tended to hedge a good deal on the degree to which slavery actually persists in the country (e.g. Sekou and Abdoukarimou 2009). A joint study by the ILO and the Nigerien *Institut Nationale du Statistique* was also conducted in 2009 and 2011, but focused primarily on child labour and avoided dealing with forced labour (ILO-INS 2011).

In 2010, the government fell to a military coup spurred by civil unrest resulting from opposition to an effort to amend the constitution. The military turned power over to a new civilian government in 2011, which has been more willing to participate in the ILO project on forced labour.[2] The new government also created a second national committee, on human trafficking, in 2012. Niger was also the first country to ratify the ILO's 2014 protocol on forced labour, as part of the ILO's '50 for Freedom' campaign. The SAP-FL project currently taking shape, then, involves support for coordination between the two commissions, coupled with some public education activities. It should be noted that the succession of Nigerien governing regimes has exercised a considerable degree of agency in shaping these developments. SAP-FL efforts, as well as those of Timidria, ASI, and others, have been delayed, subverted, and diluted by a number of actions taken by the state. Niger now has two 'paper committees' dealing with forced labour, whose function will largely depend on the input of the ILO. Anti-slavery advocates in Niger have been able to bring a considerable degree of pressure to bear on the government by drawing on the resources connected to the ILO's governance of forced labour, but the government may be able to draw on the same organization to diffuse those pressures.

The general tendency of the ILO's interventions in Niger has been to reinforce the binary between 'slavery', 'human trafficking', and 'free' forms of labour. In this sense, it has contributed to depoliticizing the linkages between ongoing processes of primitive accumulation and the transformation of existing forms of exploitation, or indeed the extension of new ones. But Gramsci's conception of the political relations of force is useful here insofar as it highlights the fact that the process has hardly been smooth, uncontested, or unproblematic. The SAP-FL project has been driven in no small part by the mobilization of 'slavery' as a means of fostering solidarity among subordinate populations in rural areas by organizations like Timidria, drawing in part on links to transnational organizations, especially ASI. The cocooning of forced labour has been enacted through a series of controversies over the form and extent of unfreedom prevalent in the country.

These struggles have often been proxies for the broader legitimacy of the state and the tenuous hegemony of existing ruling classes. The ILO's interventions on 'traditional slavery' have thus been closely bound up with these broader struggles over the political relations of force and the authority of the state. Similar dynamics are visible in wider initiatives targeting child trafficking which have been ongoing in West Africa since the early 2000s, to which I turn in the next section.

Governing child trafficking in West Africa

Given the considerable emphasis on human trafficking and border security among major donor countries (Mountz 2003; van Liempt and Sersli 2013), it is perhaps not surprising that the policing of child trafficking has been a major area of the ILO's emphasis in governing forced labour in practice. The first major regional project on trafficking specifically was funded by the USAID and the US Department of State, as well as the Danish International Development Agency. The project was called 'Combatting the Trafficking of Children for Labour Exploitation in West and Central Africa', (hereafter referred to by the French acronym LUTRENA), and covered Cameroon, Mali, Côte d'Ivoire, Gabon, Burkina Faso, Benin, Togo, and Ghana as 'core' countries, along with activities in Senegal, Niger, Guinea, and Nigeria. The programme encompassed a number of different interventions, but two sets of activities carried out under LUTRENA are particularly significant for present purposes. They are very clearly reflective of the broader areas of emphasis introduced above: namely, LUTRENA focused to a considerable degree on poverty reduction in regions identified as vulnerable to trafficking and on improving the enforcement of laws against child trafficking.

LUTRENA approached questions of poverty by promoting 'income generating activities' (IGAs) in high risk areas. Very frequently these programmes involved training from ILO 'experts' or outside consultants in some kind of handicraft production. The logic behind IGAs is clear enough – if poor populations are vulnerable to child trafficking, it follows that providing parents with alternative income streams is likely to reduce the extent of trafficking – but the programmes were largely unsuccessful in practice. Here we can see the practical realization of the ILO's particular understanding of poverty as a cause of trafficking. Of course, this has more than a faint echo of the emphasis on training and skills development for informal workers discussed in the previous chapter. It shares most of the latter's shortcomings – namely the avoidance of dealing with the underlying structural causes of poverty in favour of minor interventions aimed at upgrading the 'skills' of poor people. Even when programmes were targeted to the most vulnerable populations, it would be difficult or impossible to carry out such localized IGA programmes on a wide enough scale to significantly impact the underlying conditions behind child trafficking. Moreover, there were frequent instances where people were trained in how to make products for which there was simply no local market and no possibility of selling elsewhere (ILO 2007d: 14–15).

By far the more substantive focus of LUTRENA's work was on law enforcement. LUTRENA involved efforts to train security forces to recognize trafficked children and differentiate them from benign forms of mobility. For instance, a training workshop for security agencies in Ghana and Nigeria was held in Accra as early as October of 2003. The workshop was organized by the ILO, and attended by the American ambassador to Ghana, officials of the ILO, and high-ranking security officials along with a few front-line personnel including customs and border agents from both countries. Discussions at the workshop centered on international and domestic legal frameworks governing trafficking, and on research on the extent of trafficking and on major internal and trans-border trafficking routes in the region (see ILO 2005b). In short, workshop organizers sought to enrol security actors into the broader project of policing child trafficking with information on known trafficking routes and the reiteration of international laws.

Recognizing the limited capacities of conventional police and border forces, the formation of 'village vigilance committees' (VVCs) was a central feature of the project. This was in part a response to the difficulties in enrolling security agencies into policing child trafficking – 'local' actors, it was assumed, would have a better understanding of localized trafficking routes and be better able to differentiate trafficked children from mobile children more generally. There are no published numbers on the number of VVCs that were actually established, although they were set up in Benin, Burkina Faso, Togo, Mali, Ghana, and Côte D'Ivoire (ILO 2010c: 1). In two regions in Mali, Kolondieba and Koutiala (both near the border with Côte d'Ivoire), twenty-six VVCs with 222 members were established (ILO 2010c: 2). They were, however, undoubtedly a central component of LUTRENA. VVCs were typically organized by handing out a very specific set of equipment (ILO 2010c: 3). Badges for VVC members and bicycles were distributed as means of securing the visibility of the programme. And maybe more importantly, a set of forms was issued to facilitate the collection of information on cases of trafficking: 'Across the region, the [VVCs] collect the same minimum information about a child who is retrieved, using registers and forms. The forms document particulars about the child and include photographs if available' (ILO 2010c: 3). In theory, LUTRENA was meant to enrol a complex network of governments, NGOs, community groups, IOs, and security forces spanning most of West and Central Africa into a singular project aimed at 'combatting child trafficking'.

In practice, achieving this kind of cooperation was often rather difficult, given the particular complex of relations of force within which it operated. African states have, for the most part, struggled to control the entire scope of their territory – with uneven geographies of state power often mirroring the 'arterial' modes of power present in colonial Africa (Cooper 1994). These limitations were compounded by austerity measures adopted during the period of structural adjustment. An evaluation of LUTRENA in 2007, for instance, makes clear that very basic material problems often inhibited the coordination of state security forces: 'Whereas LUTRENA offices use simple, but very efficient, internet models for internet telephone and local network zones, all government partners and many NGO implementers have no access to internet, even the most rudimentary' (2007d: 28). Of government services in the field, including security forces and customs officers, the report notes that 'if they want to play an effective role, [they] need to be equipped with some means of transportation (off road motorcycles) and communication (telephone/fax, PC and access to the internet in the near future)' (2007b: 29). This echoes concerns that Nigerian and Ghanaian security forces had raised in the 2003 workshop (ILO 2005b). Downloading responsibility to local communities through VVCs, though, posed similar problems. In the first instance, the VVCs were inherently 'geographically limited' (ILO 2007d: 17) – they worked only in the patchwork of communities in which they were installed. Further, the systematic registering of child trafficking cases was never really fully implemented. Here again, the materials mobilized through LUTRENA proved limited in practice:

> In some countries, a special index card has been developed in order to document cases and harmonize the recording system. However, from discussions with security forces and local authorities, it became clear that these cases are not documented comprehensively enough, and are only signalled within a routine manner by usual procedures between police and authorities.
> (ILO 2007d: 17)

Police and security forces, in short, either were never given or never paid much attention to the index cards.

One of the responses to these difficulties encountered in LUTRENA – many of which were also experienced in a number of analogous projects elsewhere – was to try to systematize a set of common guidelines for the combat of child trafficking. Between 2007–2009, the ILO developed a series of training modules on combatting child trafficking. IPEC issued a 'resource kit' on child trafficking for policy-makers in 2008 (ILO 2008). The kit pulls together a set of 'best practices' in combatting child trafficking. These practices include the VVCs established under LUTRENA. The ILO also issued a training programme, largely based on this resource kit, in conjunction with UNICEF and the UN Global Initiative to Fight Human Trafficking, the following year (ILO 2009c). Here the 'best practice' guidelines in the resource kit are distilled down into a series of training modules, including a five-day lesson plan and even an activity book for participants. These documents and teaching techniques have been fed back into 'local' and 'regional' initiatives to combat trafficking. LUTRENA ended in 2008. The ILO and UN Office on Drugs and Crime (UNODC) both started new projects on child trafficking in West Africa in 2010, with funding from Spain and France and Monaco, respectively. These projects have been somewhat more *ad hoc*, providing various kinds of support on a national basis to different actors and institutions with some kind of commitment to policing child trafficking, although the ILO, UNODC, and to a lesser extent the International Organization for Migration have coordinated their programmes to a considerable extent. These did not necessarily do much to address the more fundamental issues underlying the focus on law enforcement – the example of one country, Senegal, should suffice.

Child trafficking in Senegal

Senegal was part of the LUTRENA project, and more broadly subject to long-standing political controversies about child trafficking. These have centered most prominently on children who have travelled to Dakar or other secondary cities in Senegal to attend Koranic schools led by Senegalese Marabouts. A good number of these children – referred to as *talibés* – come from elsewhere in West Africa (see Einarsdottír *et al*. 2010; Einarsdottír and Boiru 2016; Department of State 2016: 327; Kielland and Gaye 2010). *Talibés* do engage in well-documented forms of unfree labour on behalf of Marabouts – especially forced begging, but also occasionally agricultural labour. The US Department of State's Trafficking in Persons (TIP) report for 2016 estimated that upwards of 30 000 such children were engaged in forced begging in Dakar alone (Department of State 2016: 327). It is probably worth underlining that this issue has consistently been presented, much as with slavery in Niger, as a question of unacceptable 'traditional' practices.

This is, of course, a questionable premise. The growth of forced begging needs to be understood in the context of the wider shifts in political and economic structures noted in the previous chapter. It is useful here again to expand on the shifting frameworks of economic organization and property rights in rural Senegal that have taken place through processes of neoliberalization. In the first instance, the dismantling of agrarian cooperatives has undermined the economic foundations of clientelist networks dominated by marabouts (on which see O'Brien 1971), and helped to shift the balance of power within the 'triangular' relationships described in the previous chapter towards merchant capital. These dynamics have been amplified by shifts towards private property-based systems for land tenure and decentralized land administration. These have both amplified political conflicts over the administration of land disputes (Sow 2014; Niang *et al*. 2015). This has been accompanied at the national level by a number of government initiatives to facilitate foreign investment in land. These have led in a number of instances led to the displacement and dispossession of rural populations in favour of land grabs and/or for mining rights (Kesseler and Tine 2004). These dynamics seem likely to be amplified in agrarian regions as well, as the country's agricultural policy framework is increasingly negotiated with major donors and the private sector through the 'New Alliance for Food Security and Nutrition' and Millennium Challenge Corporation and premised on the liberalization of investment in land and involvement of private companies (see NAFSN 2012; GRAIN and AFSA 2015).

At the same time, public austerity in Senegal and elsewhere in West Africa have created a growing population of parents willing to send children to schools in Dakar or elsewhere in Senegal – partly out of a desire for children to obtain a religious education, but also partly because access to decent public schooling has been gutted by austerity measures, particularly in more remote rural communities (Einarsdottír *et al*. 2010; Einarsdottír and Boiru 2016). These dynamics, in another parallel to Niger, have been reinforced by patterns of climate change, especially in the North of the country through increasingly frequent droughts in the semi-arid Sahel (Kielland and Gaye 2010). In the absence of formal and informal state-led mechanisms for securing against drought, child mobility (including sending children to schools in Dakar or other rural centres) has taken on increased importance in household security strategies. The practice of forced begging by *talibés*, in short, has been (like 'traditional' slavery in Niger) profoundly shaped by the intersections of processes of neoliberalization with gendered and ethnic relations and changing ecological conditions.

More important, though, in terms of the role of the ILO and other global institutions are the legacies of the political role of the Marabouts in the colonial and postcolonial period. The economic and political foundations of Marabout authority have undoubtedly been weakened in the processes of structural adjustment and democratization, they have nonetheless not been displaced altogether (see Beck 2001; Boone 1992). The state continues to work through complex patterns of ethnic politics and alliances with local elites – indeed, this political dependence is perhaps heightened by donor-supported moves towards decentralized administration and tax-collection (see Beck 2001; Juul 2006). This persistence of the culturally and politically significant role of Islamic education has contributed to making controversies around child trafficking into politically sensitive issues.[3] Here again, then, the governance of irregular labour is closely bound up with shifting patterns of political relations of force and the organization of subaltern populations.

Successive Senegalese governments have, in this context, largely sought to evade taking concrete actions against child trafficking. As in Niger, creating a committee to study the problem was adopted as a kind of stalling tactic. 'The National Council on Combatting Trafficking in Persons' was created by a presidential decree in 2008. No one was actually appointed to the council until 2010, and even then, no budget or support staff were allocated. As with 'traditional slavery' in Niger, international organizations did much of the work of fleshing out the committee – in this case very literally by renting office space in a building near the UNODC offices in Dakar and supplying computers, printers, internet connections, and the like.[4] The point here is that interlinked ethnic and religious considerations have, as in Niger, strongly shaped the implementation of international programmes aiming to govern child trafficking.

While the issue of *talibés* and forced begging has remained politically more or less off limits, the focus of interventions has largely shifted away from Dakar and towards Senegalese borderlands – particularly the borders with Mali and Guinée. The ILO and UNODC have started carrying out targeted training of border guards in locations along major trafficking routes, especially near Kédougou – in the southeast of the country (near the former borders) – where child labour is widely used in artisanal gold mining. The patterns of rural dispossession, increased exposure to climate change, and privatization of land rights noted above play a considerable role in shaping the availability of children from Senegal and neighbouring countries for these purposes, much the same as with talibés. The focus of the ILO and UNODC's interventions, however, remains on detection and law enforcement, with training for border guards and local NGOs on spotting trafficked children.[5] In practice training for border guards have been the main focus of interventions. The ILO's training materials have been adapted slightly, mainly by shortening the training programme from five days to two or three, but these form the basis of training for Senegalese border guards and in similar programmes underway in Mali. They are also used to train local civil society organizations on means of recognizing trafficked children in communities around the Kédougou gold mines.

Here again, the potential effectiveness of this set of programmes is checked by the broader structural context in which it operates. The articulation of a regulatory boundary between free and 'forced' labour – in this case quite literally by training law enforcement and local civil society to spot the differences between trafficked children and others – serves as a means of naturalizing the broader context of exploitation and dispossession implicit in gold mining in Kédougou and more broadly in patterns of neoliberalization in West Africa. But it is worth noting that the direction of even these modes of intervention is profoundly shaped by more localized patterns of political relations of force. It is children working in artisanal gold mining in Kédougou, rather than those begging in Dakar, who are the primary targets of international interventions on the ground, this even though both sets of activities get equal billing as concerns in, say, the US Department of State's TIP report (2016: 327).

Conclusion

The overarching point of this chapter is that the re-articulation of the binary between 'free' and 'forced' labour is a crucial component of the governance of irregular labour in the twenty-first century. The ILO has made the enforcement of 'fundamental rights' at work – including a prominent emphasis on the elimination of forced labour – into a core component of its efforts to reposition itself as a significant actor in the global political economy in the context of the erosion of the Fordist compromise with which the organization was historically integrally linked (see Cox 1977; Standing 2008). This move, by focusing on the boundary between acceptable and unacceptable forms of exploitation, has served to normalize forms of exploitation that do meet these relatively minimal standards, and sidelined questions around the role of changing global production networks and broader patterns of ongoing primitive accumulation in the context of processes of neoliberalization in creating new forms of unfreedom. The ILO's activities directly targeting forced labour have tended to prioritize relatively thin efforts at poverty reduction by remedying 'exclusions' from credit markets, training, and the like on the one hand – many of which have strong parallels to the projects targeting 'informal' economies discussed in the previous chapter – and the improved enforcement of existing laws on the other. These points of emphasis have re-articulated, but certainly not dismantled, the boundary between 'free' and 'forced' labour implicit in the older framework of conventions discussed in Chapter 2. Actually-existing patterns of unfreedom, however, as was demonstrated in the cases of Niger and Senegal, have been profoundly altered by ongoing processes of primitive accumulation – particularly neoliberal reforms to property rights and austerity measures.

At the same time, variations in political relations of force across territories have been vital in shaping the actual implementation of ILO programmes in at least two ways. In the first instance, real patterns of irregular labour in Niger and Senegal are deeply inflected with relations of social difference and shifting patterns of state authority. 'Slavery' in Niger has been closely bound up with the politics of land use rights, with race and ethnicity, as well as resistance to military rule. The governance of child trafficking in Senegal is bound up both with religious practice and shifting patterns of citizenship and political authority. Unfree forms of labour in both cases are strongly gendered. Second, this fact has shaped both the political salience of unfreedom and the ways in which it has proven possible to enrol local and national authorities in global regulatory projects. The salience of 'slavery' in Niger remains deeply contested, and ILO projects have been rolled out through a series of controversies over what forms of unfree labour should be covered, as well as their scope and extent in practice. Child trafficking for some purposes and in some places in Senegal has received far more practical attention than others.

Notes

1 This section is drawn from Bernards (2017b).
2 The following draws on author interviews with ILO officials in Geneva (June 2014) and Dakar (November 2014).
3 This diagnosis was repeated to me in interviews with UNODC and ILO officials working on child trafficking.
4 Author interview, UNODC Official, Dakar, November 2014.
5 *Ibid.*

Conclusion

The core arguments presented in the preceding chapters can be summarized as follows:

(1) Precarity and violence are endemic under capitalism. Their incidence is, no doubt, historically and geographically uneven, but if we look from a global perspective there is arguably no point in the past 500 years where supposedly irregular forms of labour have not been widespread.
(2) The differentiation of normalized, acceptable forms of exploitation from these persistent forms of precarity and coercion is both political and contingent on the one hand and vital to ongoing processes of primitive accumulation and proletarianization on the other. There is no abstract or *a priori* dividing line between 'free' and 'forced' labour, 'informal' and 'formal', 'precarious' and 'standard' working relations – rather, such binaries are artefacts of ongoing political struggles. Governing irregular labour is in this sense intimately linked to the political management of 'normal' labour relations.
(3) These processes of differentiation, in practice, are carried out simultaneously across multiple scales of action and mediated by broader patterns of political relations of force, including patterns of global governance, state-building, and over the political mobilization of subaltern populations more broadly.

I won't repeat the empirical claims that have been laid out in Chapters 2–6 here. The kinds of struggles with which this book has concerned itself have clearly played out in different ways at different points in time, conditioned by colonial and postcolonial hegemonic projects, shifting patterns of production, and changing patterns of global governance and world order. The variable emphases and understandings through which the ILO and others have approached 'forced labour', 'informal' economies, and rural-urban migration in sub-Saharan Africa underline the arguments made about the contingency and political character of the governance of irregular labour.

By way of conclusion, I want to highlight a few arguments that follow from the issues raised in the previous chapters. My focus here is particularly on the critical implications of the arguments and approach presented in this book in terms of the study of work in IPE and more broadly for the politics of labour. Three points in particular are important. First, while we can point in the past few years to very welcome (and badly needed) revivals of interest in questions about labour, and more broadly in class as an analytical category, the *politics* of class – and particularly the making of class – have so far largely been overlooked. This issue is, of course, central to the argument of this book. The present argument points to the need for a wider research agenda exploring the historical construction of class, and the ways in which these processes intersect with broader political relations of force; perhaps most importantly around struggles over race, gender, nationality, and citizenship. Second, this book has important implications for our understandings of the scope and limits of neoliberalism in the global political economy. Arguments like Standing's (2011) account of the 'precariat', attributing the rise of precarious labour to regulatory roll-backs, can relatively easily be dismissed. However, the more important take away points from much of the material presented in this book are that, while neoliberalism undoubtedly matters, we need more fine-grained analyses of the ways in which labour and irregular work are bound up in contradictory processes of neoliberalization. Finally, and relatedly, the existential challenges emerging for global labour in the present day (van der Linden 2016), are results of much longer-run failure on the part of the international labour movement to grapple explicitly with processes of primitive accumulation, and particularly with the naturalization of proletarian modes of exploitation. This is a strategic failure that has been compounded at times by failures to challenge colonial constructions of race and the very gendered terms of the standard employment relationship (Vosko 2010). There are some promising tendencies apparent in this respect – as in, for instance, gestures towards the organization of informal workers (see Gallin 2001) and the increasing attention by the international trade union movement to questions around forced labour in global supply chains. But these remain fraught and somewhat limited. Labour in the twenty-first century needs a politics that will more explicitly challenge ongoing processes of primitive accumulation and the bifurcation of 'normal' from irregular forms of exploitation. The remaining pages of this book take up each of these points in turn.

IPE, work, and the making of class

As noted in the introduction, IPE and related disciplines have had a somewhat ambivalent relationship with studies of labour. Questions around labour and production played an enormous role in the establishment of critical IPE, particularly through the work of Robert Cox (1977; 1987; Harrod 1987; *cf.*Phillips 2016). However, labour issues have often been pushed to the background (see Moore 2012). There have been notable exceptions (e.g. Amoore 2002; Moore 2010), including analyses of global labour governance and the troubled progress of transnational solidarity (O'Brien *et al.* 2000; Taylor 2011; Bieler 2012). But until recently labour, and particularly irregular work or forms of labour in the global south, has largely been overlooked – although a recent growth in studies of various forms of unfree labour (e.g. LeBaron and Ayers 2013; LeBaron 2014a; 2014b; Phillips 2013; Phillips and Mieres 2015), or more broadly of labour in global production networks (e.g. Selwyn 2012; Mayer and Phillips 2017) is promising. There has also been a recent revival of interest in class-based analyses of IPE, particularly around questions of development (e.g. Selwyn 2014; 2015; Campling *et al*. 2016).

Yet this turn to labour and to class-based analyses coincides with increasing anxiety in global labour studies and in practice about how exactly to understand class – and in particular how to define and situate 'the working class' in the context of the seeming collapse of the institutions that have underpinned the global labour movement since the nineteenth century – particularly trade unions, social welfare systems, and socialist parties (e.g. Breman and van der Linden 2014; van der Linden 2016) and more broadly the failure of the organized 'working class' to appear as a transcendental political subject in the way that much Marxist thought in the nineteenth and twentieth centuries seemed to expect. We can put the problem here fairly simply: What does it mean to talk of the 'class-based' character of any phenomenon in the global political economy, especially if we want to understand the latter in terms of the confrontation between capital and labour, in a context in which we find it increasingly hard to pin down know what the 'working class' is?

I would suggest that this book shows that part of the answer is to recognize that class is a fundamentally historical and *political* phenomenon. That is, we can argue all we want about who is and isn't part of the working class in any abstract sense, but for 'labour' or the 'working class' to be a meaningful actor in the workplace or in wider political arenas, it needs to be mobilized and organized. Gramsci's (1971) observation that any particular configuration of 'objective' configurations of class relations in the process of production might make possible a number of very different moments of political relations of force is pertinent. We might add, following Hall (1980); McNally (2016); and others, that such political constructions of class have historically always been mediated by racialized and gendered imaginaries. And, vitally, I argue, these processes of political construction of class have often involved political struggles over what the relationships are between proletarian and other forms of exploitation. The bigger point, though, is that analyses of labour, and class-based analyses of other phenomena in IPE, need to be attentive to the *politics* through which working classes are made and unmade as salient political actors. Workers' organizations are, of course, key actors in this process. Working classes are, in E. P. Thompson's (1966) justly famous phrase, 'present at their own making'. These processes of construction are also, however, deeply bound up with patterns of state-making and international order. Exploring these contested processes of 'class-making' is, in itself, a vital avenue to pursue. The multi-scalar nature of these processes – which inevitably have global or international dimensions, but take place simultaneously in a variety of local sites – is perhaps especially important to examine.

Neoliberalism and its limits

One of the core questions addressed directly in the last two chapters, and more implicitly throughout the book, concerns the relationship between neoliberalism and precarity. It is common to attribute the contemporary growth of precarity to the rise of neoliberalism – or at least, neoliberalism understood as a deregulatory political agenda. Standing's *Precariat* (2011) probably remains the highest profile such analysis. I have insisted throughout that precarity and violent forms of coercion long predate neoliberalism. The historically pervasive character of irregular forms of labour belies explanations of their existence based in conjunctural factors. In a word, they are fundamental components of capitalist relations of production.

At the same time, it remains hard to deny that the scope of precarity has increased, and that new forms of precarious work and violently coercive exploitation are indeed emerging in part as a result of neoliberal reforms. Neoliberalism has been described, not inaccurately, as an 'attack' on workers (Bhattacharya 2014; Breman and van der Linden 2014), and neoliberal policies credited for a 'global development crisis' marked by deepening inequality and increasing vulnerability and poverty (Selwyn 2014). Different methods of confronting, challenging, or offsetting neoliberal reforms have, accordingly, occupied a good deal of analysis in global labour studies (e.g. Webster *et al.* 2008; Fraile 2010). The present analysis suggests that neoliberalism matters, but it is a fundamentally fraught and contradictory agenda. In any case, neoliberalization has reshaped and deepened rather than created precarious labour.

Neoliberal reforms, in short, are a distinctive episode in a much longer history of ongoing primitive accumulation. Irregular labour, in various forms, cropped up throughout twentieth-century Africa. Managing the boundaries between precarious, casualized, and migrant labour on the one hand and stable, permanent settlement in cities was a major political challenge for colonial governments from the 1930s onwards – as processes of rural dispossession, in part through the use of forced labour, proceeded far enough that precarious livelihoods became increasingly common.[1] It certainly persisted after decolonization as a major political challenge in the 1970s, as evidenced in this book by the ways in which the Kenyan state enrolled the ILO's arguments about 'informal' labour in longer-running struggles over the political role of organized labour and the relations between organized workers and other subaltern classes. If neoliberal reforms have indeed led to the emergence of new forms of precarity and violence, the latter are nonetheless deeply coloured by the legacies of longer-running processes of primitive accumulation. Mechanisms for managing irregular labour in the neoliberal era, moreover, reflect political dynamics that have distinct echoes of previous eras. Neoliberal understandings of informality or forced labour are different in form from 1920s debates about colonial forced labour or 1970s debates about the informal, but all ultimately serve to 'cocoon' irregular labour from the workings of capitalism.

The book also points to an understanding of neoliberalism as a contradictory and fraught process in its own right. In this sense, this book would seem to support previous scholarship that has framed neoliberalization as a contradictory and invariably incomplete process, rather than an epochal end-state (e.g. Brenner *et al.* 2010a; Peck 2013). The contemporary governance of irregular labour is difficult to describe or explain without reference to neoliberalism (or at the very least, structural adjustment), but the incomplete, contested, and politically fraught nature of these processes is especially salient. Neoliberal reforms in Africa created contradictory political dynamics that needed to be managed, in part, through the fraught articulation of new mechanisms of governing irregular labour. This book has highlighted a number of such examples – including the need to find new means of rendering 'informal' economies legible, as in the Senegalese microinsurance and Tanzanian apprenticeships programmes discussed in Chapter 5, or the use of ILO programming on forced labour to offset the mobilization of opposition to slavery as a broader challenge to political regimes undercut by structural adjustment as in the Nigerien example discussed in Chapter 6.

The point of all of this is twofold. First, attributing contemporary precarity solely to neoliberalism probably takes us down a problematic road politically. Rolling back or 'blunting' (Fraile 2010) neoliberal reforms is not a bad thing *per se*, but it won't rid us of precarious work, forced labour, and the like unless accompanied by a deeper and wider challenge to capitalist relations of production and underlying processes of primitive accumulation. I return to this point in the following section. Second, in more academic terms, there is a need for more investigation of the specific ways in which irregular forms of labour are bound up with ongoing iterations of neoliberal development frameworks. Labour has very often been on the losing end of neoliberal reforms, but the politics of irregular forms of labour in particular are often at the root of some of the most acute contradictions underlying processes of neoliberalization.

As an example of what this kind of analysis might mean, we can point to the example of microinsurance, discussed briefly in Chapter 5. A number of critics have pointed to the problematic neoliberal character of microinsurance (e.g. Isakson 2015; Johnson 2013). Insofar as the deeply individualized and market-based modes of risk management underlying commercial microinsurance are, in fact, deeply limited as means of alleviating poverty, they make an important point. But, as the discussion of the Senegalese case in Chapter 5 suggests, this critique of microinsurance as 'too neoliberal' doesn't quite do justice to the more complex politics of actually rolling out microinsurance policies in the context of the longer-run political dynamics unleashed by processes of structural adjustment and their attendant impacts on labour markets (see also Bernards 2016). Particularly salient here is the contemporary remaking of relative surplus populations across much of the global south through processes of neoliberalization – and the challenges posed by the latter for the political means by which the postcolonial state had managed the political role of labour. The point, in short, is that the governance of irregular labour is a site at which the contradictory nature of neoliberalizing processes are particularly acute. We miss an important analytical opportunity to examine the ways in which these processes play out if we limit ourselves either to attributing the emergence of precarity to neoliberalism or seek to critiquing the 'neoliberal' contents of this or that policy framework.

Precarious politics?

I conclude this book by returning to one of the questions with which it opened. Namely, the suggestion that the increased incidence of precarity in the neoliberal age has undone the possibilities for progressive politics (Standing 2011; Bourdieu 1998). The argument, central to this book, that precarity and coercion are pervasive and even structural features of capitalism calls the more histrionic fears of precarious workers falling prey to nativist demagoguery in Standing's (2011) analysis into question. This might be an especially important point to underline given that this line of argument been taken up more vigorously in popular discussions in the past few years against the backdrop of the rise of the far right in Europe and the United States. That widespread precarity is normal suggests that there is no necessary connection between precarity and any particular political tendency. That said, it doesn't seem initially to suggest a particularly optimistic forecast of the prospects for workers' lives and livelihoods to argue that brutal forms of exploitation are part of the normal run of things under capitalist systems of production and accumulation. The present argument does, however, have distinctive implications for the possibilities for labour in the twenty-first century.

Most importantly, the arguments presented in this book suggest a somewhat different diagnosis of the contemporary challenges facing the global labour movement. Present-day labour is, no doubt, increasingly faced with a crisis because of the loss of 'standard employment relations' (van der Linden 2016). On the basis of the material presented in this book, though, this difficulty seems to be less the product of changing patterns of employment in themselves, and more of a much longer-term failure on the part of labour movements centered to challenge the naturalization of proletarian forms of exploitation. This is particularly visible when the latter was bound up with racialized colonial imaginaries. We can point, for instance, the failure of the Leeds Conference in 1916 to recognize 'Zulus and Cingalese' (see Chapter 2) as potential trade unionists. The precarious and irregular forms of work that cause so much anxiety today are not new. We can, no doubt, point to an increase in their frequency, alongside continuing neoliberal attacks on trade unions (or maybe better, partially as a result of the latter); and certainly the coincidence of these trends has complicated the capacity of the labour movement to mobilize political pressure (Bieler 2012). But given that the 'standard' employment relationships rooted in long-lost Fordist political economies were never a reality for most workers in the world, we better understand the present challenges as a century-old strategic miscalculation coming back to bite the present-day labour movement.

These are also questions that are acutely present for unions in the global south, not least in the African examples discussed in this book. The historical formation of trade unions, traced out in Chapters 3 and 4 in particular, came to rest in large part on the differentiation of a relatively small strata of permanently unionized workers from casualized or 'informal' urban workers and from rural populations. Of course, these are processes which some unions contested, to a greater or lesser degree, and the lived experiences of rank and file workers often crossed these boundaries. Normalized wage workers shared communities and households with irregular workers (or even shared their own time between 'formal' and 'informal' jobs). The political actions of organized labour both in colonial and early postcolonial times – as in the Ghanaian railway strike in 1961 discussed in Chapter 4 and AOF railway strike and Mombasa port strike discussed in Chapter 3 – depended on solidarities between organized workers and casualized temporary workers, the unemployed, 'market women', and others in the wider working classes. Nonetheless, the development of 'non-political' trade unions in the 1960s and 1970s ultimately depended heavily on maintaining a rigid boundary between formalized wage work and irregular work – which often came to be organized and governed under the rubric of the 'informal' sector – wherein workers' organizations could easily be confined to the technical tasks of collective bargaining. This already tenuous arrangement did not survive the economic and political crises of the postcolonial order that started towards the end of the 1970s. Close links to governing parties, though always politically fraught (Bernards 2017c), became impossible to sustain in the context of processes of neoliberalization – trade union memberships were decimated by privatization, retrenchment, and de-industrialization; workers' nominal wages were undercut by austerity, their real wages (along with the value of pension and insurance entitlements held by some workers) by currency devaluation. Casualized jobs, petty self-employment, and various forms of unfree labour have proliferated in this context. Politically, workers' organizations have largely been ejected from the postcolonial historic bloc and pushed into more oppositional relationships with states and governing parties. These processes have been accompanied by the pluralization of trade union centres – sometimes actively encouraged by governments, sometimes as a result of internal struggles over responses to neoliberalization. The result, noted in the analyses of microinsurance in Senegal in particular, has often been heightened competition between a growing number of unions for a shrinking core of members in normalized wage work. So, the question of how to connect normal and irregular workers politically would seem to be of growing strategic importance around the region.

So where to from here? Efforts to incorporate informal workers or the unemployed into existing trade unions are a very welcome start, fraught as these processes often are (see Gallin 2001; Rizzo 2013; Webster and Bischoff 2011). Much the same could be said for efforts by trade unions working to combat unfree labour and hyper-exploitation in global supply chains. Indeed, for unions seeking to remain relevant in the context of growing precarity and casualization on one hand and declining union densities on the other, such efforts are probably essential. In the context of widespread questions about internal democracy and the responsiveness of union leaderships to rank and file members, though, the organization of informal or precarious workers in and of itself is not a panacea. It is not even necessarily all that beneficial for irregular workers (see Theron 2010). A pair of broader considerations, I argue, are perhaps more important regardless of the specific organizational forms through which organized workers try to forge solidarities with informal workers.

In the first instance, to reiterate, it is a strategic as well as an analytic mistake to attribute the widespread nature of coercion and precarity in contemporary capitalism entirely to contemporary conjunctural factors. As a first cut, then, any proposed solution to precarious work, unfreedom, and the like that fails to fundamentally alter the underlying dynamics of primitive accumulation, particularly the widespread disciplining of labour through the 'silent compulsion' of the market, is liable at best to displace irregular forms of labour to other territories or into illicit spheres of activity. There are plenty of examples of such half-measures in this book. Perhaps most notably here we can point to the persistence of various forms of unfree labour despite near-universal legal prohibitions on coercive labour recruitment and slavery (*cf.* Brass 2010: 32–33), of which the contemporary transformations of slavery in Niger are a good example. Interventions that more fundamentally sever workers' reliance on the market to meet the needs of social reproduction are needed.

More fundamentally, it is a mistake for labour and progressive social movements to operate on the assumption that 'informal', 'forced', or precarious labour are fundamentally discrete from the forms of exploitation implicit in more normalized forms of work. As highlighted by a number of the examples discussed in this book, this can too-easily lead to an overly constrained view of the political role of workers' organizations. The clearest example here is likely the close connection traced in Chapters 3 and 4 between efforts to create 'non-political' workers' organizations both by postwar colonial regimes and by postcolonial states and the delineation of normal and irregular workers. My point here is not that we should ignore the considerable diversity of working relations, or the ways in which working practices are mediated by culture, race, gender, and politics. The point is, however, that the cocooning of irregular labour is unproductive. It is not reflective of the realities of work (past or present) – in which individual workers are liable to move between 'formal' and 'informal' jobs, or use informal earnings to supplement formal wages; coercive or fraudulent recruitment practices target the same vulnerable and dispossessed populations who also perform many forms of 'free' (if very cheap) labour. Indeed, it is quite common for many households in the global south and elsewhere to contain both normalized and irregular workers, and households are emerging as increasingly important units of social reproduction and sites of politics in many neoliberal contexts (LeBaron 2010; Scully 2016b).

The overarching point here is that the intimate linkages between irregular forms of labour and normal forms of wage labour, especially through ongoing processes of primitive accumulation, has to be a starting point for a politics of labour suited to the twenty-first century. Indeed, the failure of labour movements in both the global north and south to acknowledge and accommodate these linkages is arguably at the root of some of the crucial failures of labour politics in the twentieth century. Most notably, in the context of this book, we can point to the reassertion of neocolonial political economies in the 1960s and 1970s – after a period of political opening around the end of colonial rule in which, as Frederick Cooper (2005; 2014) has astutely pointed out, hopes of fundamental transformation were high and other outcomes were possible. The vital question, then, is how to foster what Gramsci might call the 'integral autonomy' of subaltern classes, normalized and irregular workers alike, in neoliberal times.

Note

1 This argument echoes Harris and Scully (2015), who locate the historical origins of precarious labour in colonial and postcolonial 'development' projects.

References

Abdelkader, G.K. (2004) *Étude sur le Dénombrement des Victimes de l'Esclavage au Niger*, Niamey: ASI and Association Timidria.

Abrahamsen, R. (1997) 'The Victory of Popular Forces or Passive Revolution? A Neo-Gramscian Perspective on Democratisation', *Journal of Modern African Studies* 35 (1): 129–152.

Abrahamsen, R. (2000) *Disciplining Democracy: Development Discourse and Good Governance in Africa*, London: Zed Books.

Adji, S. (2000) 'Globalization and Union Strategies in Niger', *International Institute for Labour Studies Discussion Paper DP/122/2000*, Geneva: ILO.

Agarwala, R. (2013) *Informal Labour, Formal Politics, and Dignified Discontent in India*, Cambridge: Cambridge University Press.

Aggarwal, A. (2015) *Recognition of Prior Learning: Key Success Factors and the Building Blocks of an Effective System*, Pretoria: ILO.

Amnesty International (2013) *The Dark Side of Migration: Spotlight on Qatar's Construction Sector ahead of the World Cup*, London: Amnesty International.

Amnesty International (2016) *New Name, Old System? Qatar's New Labour Law and Abuse of Migrant Workers*, London: Amnesty International.

Amoore, L. (2002) *Globalization Contested: An International Political Economy of Work*, Manchester: University of Manchester Press.

Amsden, A.H. (1971) *International Firms and Labour in Kenya: 1945–1970*, London: Frank Cass.

Anderson, B. and Andrijasevic, R. (2008) 'Sex, Slaves and Citizens: The Politics of Anti-Trafficking', *Soundings* 40: 135–145.

Aryee, G. (1996) *Promoting Productivity and Social Protection in the Urban Informal Sector: An Integrated Approach*, Geneva: ILO.

Asp, C. (1975) 'Social Classes and the Government in Kenya: A Comparison between the ILO Report and the Government's Response', *World Employment Programme Comprehensive Employment Strategies Working Paper no. 3*, Geneva: ILO.

Atim, C. (1998) *The Contribution of Mutual Health Organizations to Financing, Delivery, and Access to Health Care: Synthesis of Research in Nine West and Central African Countries*, Geneva: ILO.

Bales, K. (2008) *Disposable People: The New Slavery in the Global Economy*, Berkeley: University of California Press.

Banaji, J. (2003) 'The Fictions of Free Labour: Contract, Coercion, and So-Called Unfree Labour', *Historical Materialism* 11 (3): 69–95.

Bangasser, P.E. (2000) 'The ILO and the Informal Sector: An Institutional History', *ILO Employment Paper 2000/9*, Geneva: ILO.

Bayart, J.F. (2009) *The State in Africa: The Politics of the Belly*, 2nd English ed., New York: Polity.

BBC (2005) 'Niger Anti-Slavery Activist Charged', 5 May 2005, available: http://news.bbc.co.uk/2/hi/africa/4515857.stm.

Beck, L. (2001) 'Reining in the Marabouts? Democratization and Local Governance in Senegal', *African Affairs* 100 (401): 601–621.

Benjamin, N. and Mbaye, A.A. (2012) *The Informal Sector in Francophone Africa: Firm Size, Productivity, and Institutions*, Washington: Agence Française de Développement and World Bank.

Bernards, N. (2015) 'The Internationalization of Labour Politics in Africa', *Critical African Studies* 7 (1): 7–25.

Bernards, N. (2016) 'The International Labour Organization and the Ambivalent Politics of Financial Inclusion in West Africa', *New Political Economy* 21 (6): 606–621.

Bernards, N. (2017a) 'The Global Governance of Informal Economies: The International Labour Organization in East Africa', *Third World Quarterly* 38 (8): 1831–1846.

Bernards, N. (2017b) 'The Global Politics of Forced Labour', *Globalizations* 14 (6): 944–957.

Bernards, N. (2017c) 'The ILO and African Trade Unions: Tripartite Fantasies and Enduring Struggles', *Review of African Political Economy* 44 (153).

Best, J. (2013) 'Redefining Risk as Poverty and Vulnerability: Shifting Strategies of Liberal Economic Governance', *Third World Quarterly* 34 (1): 109–129.

Best, J. (2016) 'When Crises Are Failures: Contested Metrics in International Finance and Development', *International Political Sociology* 10 (1): 39–55.

Bhattacharya, S. (2014) 'Is Labour Still a Relevant Category for Praxis? Critical Reflections on Some Contemporary Discourses on Work and Capitalism', *Development and Change* 45 (5): 942–962.

Bieler, A. (2012) 'Workers of the World Unite? Globalization and the Quest for Transnational Solidarity', *Globalizations* 9 (3): 365–378.

Bienefield, M.A. (1975) 'Socialist Development and the Workers in Tanzania', in Sandbrook, R. and Cohen, R., eds., *The Development of an African Working Class: Studies in Class Formation and Action*, Toronto: University of Toronto Press, 239–260.

Bigo, D. (2002) 'Security and Immigration: Towards a Critique of the Governmentality of Unease', *Alternatives* 27 (1): 63–92.

Boone, C. (1992) *Merchant Capital and the Roots of State Power in Senegal, 1930–1985*, Cambridge: Cambridge University Press.

Boone, C. (1994) 'Trade, Taxes and Tribute: Market Liberalizations and the New Importers in sub-Saharan Africa', *World Development* 22 (3): 453–467.

Bourdieu, P. (1998) 'La précarité est aujourd'hui partout', in Bourdieu, P., *Contre-Feux*. Grenoble: Liber-Raisons d'Agir.

Brass, T. (1999) *Towards a Comparative Political Economy of Unfree Labour*, London: Frank Cass.

Brass, T. (2010) 'Unfree Labour as Primitive Accumulation?', *Capital & Class* 35 (1): 23–38.

Brass, T. (2014) 'Debating Capitalist Dynamics and Unfree Labour: A Missing Link?', *The Journal of Development Studies* 50 (4): 570–582.

Brass, T. and van der Linden, M. (1997) *Free and Unfree Labour: The Debate Continues*, Berlin: Peter Lang.

Bratton, M. and van de Walle, N. (1997) *Democratic Experiments in Africa: Regime Transitions in Comparative Perspective*, Cambridge: Cambridge University Press.

Breman, J. (2010) 'Neo-Bondage: A Fieldwork-Based Account', *International Labor and Working Class History* 78 (1): 48–62.
Breman, J. (2013) 'A Bogus Concept?', *New Left Review* 84: 130–138.
Breman, J. and Guérin, I. (2009) 'Introduction: On Bondage Old and New', in Breman, J., Guérin, I., and Prakash, A., eds., *India's Unfree Workforce: Of Bondage Old and New*, New Delhi: Oxford University Press, 1–20.
Breman, J. and van der Linden, M. (2014) 'Informalizing the Economy: The Return of the Social Question at a Global Level', *Development and Change* 45 (5): 920–940.
Brenner, N., Peck, J., and Theodore, N. (2010a) 'Variegated Neoliberalism: Geographies, Modalities, Pathways', *Global Networks* 10 (2): 182–222.
Brenner, N., Peck, J., and Theodore, N. (2010b) 'After Neoliberalization?', *Globalizations* 7 (3): 327–345.
Buell, R.L. (1928a) *The Native Problem in Africa*, Vol. 1, New York: Macmillan.
Buell, R.L. (1928b) *The Native Problem in Africa*, Vol. 2, New York: Macmillan.
Bush, B. (1999) *Imperialism, Race, and Resistance: Africa and Britain, 1919–1945*, New York: Routledge.
Byrne, D. (1999) *Social Exclusion*, Milton Keynes: Open University Press.
Cammack, P. (2004) 'What the World Bank Means by Poverty Reduction and Why It Matters', *New Political Economy* 9 (2): 189–211.
Campling, L., Miyamura, S., Pattenden, J., and Selwyn, B. (2016) 'Class Dynamics of Development: A Methodological Note', *Third World Quarterly* 37 (10): 1745–1767.
Chamberlain, J.P. (1933) 'Forced Labor', *Annals of the American Academy of Political and Social Science* 166: 80–85.
Chanock, M. (2001) *The Making of South African Legal Culture, 1902–1936: Fear, Favour, and Prejudice*, Cambridge: Cambridge University Press.
Chun, J.J. (2016) 'The Affective Politics of the Precariat: Reconsidering Alternative Histories of Grassroots Worker Organizing', *Global Labour Journal* 7 (2): 136–147.
Churchill, C., ed. (2006) *Protecting the Poor: A Microinsurance Compendium*, Geneva: ILO.
Churchill, C., Liber, D., McCord, M., and Roth, J. (2003) *Making Microinsurance Work for Microfinance Institutions: A Technical Guide to Developing and Delivering Microinsurance*, Geneva: ILO.
Cooper, F. (1994) 'Conflict and Connection: Rethinking African Colonial History', *American Historical Review* 99: 1516–1545.
Cooper, F. (1996a) *Decolonization and African Society: The Labor Question in French and British Africa*, Cambridge: Cambridge University Press.
Cooper, F. (1996b) '"Our Strike": Equality, Anticolonial Politics and the 1947–1948 Railway Strike in French West Africa', *The Journal of African History* 37 (1): 81–118.
Cooper, F. (2005) *Colonialism in Question: Theory, Knowledge, History*, Berkeley: University of California Press.
Cooper, F. (2006) 'A Parting of the Ways: Colonial Africa and South Africa, 1946–1948', *African Studies* 65 (1): 27–43.
Cooper, F. (2014) *Africa in the World: Capitalism, Empire, and Nation-State*, Cambridge: Harvard University Press.
Cox, R.W. (1973) 'ILO: Limited Monarchy', in Cox, R.W. and Jacobson, H., eds., *The Anatomy of Influence: Decision Making in International Organizations*, New Haven: Yale University Press, 102–138.
Cox, R.W. (1977) 'Labor and Hegemony', *International Organization* 31 (3): 385–424.
Cox, R.W. (1983) 'Gramsci, Hegemony, and International Relations: An Essay in Method', *Millennium: Journal of International Studies* 12 (2): 162–175.

148 References

Cox, R.W. (1987) *Production, Power and World Order*, New York: Columbia University Press.

Cox, R.W. (1996) 'The Idea of International Labour Regulation', in Cox, R.W. and Sinclair, T., *Approaches to World Order*, Cambridge: Cambridge University Press, 41–48.

Cutler, C. (2003) *Private Power and Global Authority*, Cambridge: Cambridge University Press.

Daughton, J.P. (2013) 'ILO Expertise and Colonial Violence in the Interwar Years', in Kott, S. and Droux, J., eds., *Globalizing Social Rights: The International Labour Organization and Beyond*, New York: Palgrave Macmillan, 85–97.

Davis, M. (2006) *Planet of Slums*, London: Verso.

De Angelis, M. (2004) 'Separating the Doing and the Deed: Capital and the Continuous Character of Enclosures', *Historical Materialism* 12 (2): 57–87.

Department of State [US] (2016) *Trafficking in Persons Report 2016*, Washington: Department of State.

Desai, V. and Loftus, A. (2013) 'Speculating on Slums: Infrastructural Fixes in Informal Housing in the Global South', *Antipode* 45 (4): 798–808.

de Soto, H. (2001) *The Mystery of Capital: Why Capitalism Triumphs in the West and Fails Everywhere Else*, London: Black Swan.

DID (2011) *Étude sur la Microassurance Dans la Zone CIMA: État des Lieux et Recommandations*, Lévis, Quebec: Desjardins.

Diene, M. (2014) 'Inequalities in the Context of Structural Transformation: The Case of Senegal', *Development* 57 (3–4): 540–546.

Diop Buuba, B. (1992) 'Les syndicats, l'État et les partis politiques', in Momar-Coumba Diop, ed., *Sénégale, Trajéctoires d'un État*, Dakar: CODESRIA, 479–500.

Dror, D. and Jacquier, C. (1999) 'Micro-Insurance: Extending Health Insurance to the Excluded', *International Social Security Review* 52 (1): 71–97.

Duffy, H. (2009) 'Hadijatou Mani Korua v. Niger: Slavery Unveiled by the ECOWAS Court', *Human Rights Law Review* 9 (1): 151–170.

Du Toit, A. (2004) 'Social Exclusion Discourse and Chronic Poverty: A South African Case Study', *Development and Change* 35 (5): 987–1010.

Einarsdottír, J. and Boiru, H. (2016) 'Becoming Somebody: Bissau-Guinean *Talibés* in Senegal', *International Journal of Human Rights* 20 (7): 857–874.

Einarsdottír, J., Boiru, H., Geirsson, G., and Gunnlaugsson, G. (2010) *Child Trafficking in Guinea-Bissau: An Explorative Study*, Reyjavik: UNICEF Iceland.

Ekers, M., Hart, G., Kipfer, S., and Loftus, A., eds. (2014) *Gramsci: Space, Nature, Politics*, West Sussex: Wiley-Blackwell.

Fall, B. (1993) *Le travail force en Afrique Occidentale Française (1900–1945)*, Paris: Karthala.

Fall, B. (2002) *Social History in French West Africa: Forced Labour, Labour Markets, Women and Politics*, Amsterdam and Calcutta: SEPHIS and CSSSC.

Featherstone, D. (2014) '"Gramsci in Action": Space, Politics, and the Making of Solidarities', in Ekers, M., Hart, G., Kipfer, S., and Loftus, A., eds., *Gramsci: Space, Nature, Politics*, West Sussex: Wiley-Blackwell.

Fischer, G. (2013) 'Revisiting Abandoned Ground: Tanzanian Trade Unions' Engagements with Informal Workers', *Labour Studies Journal* 38 (2): 139–160.

Fox-Bourne, H.R. (1900) *Slavery and Its Substitutes in Africa*, London: Aborigines Protection Society.

Fox-Bourne, H.R. (1903) *Forced Labour in British South Africa: Notes on the Condition and Prospects of South African Natives under British Control*, London: P.S. King & Son.

Fraile, L., ed. (2010) *Blunting Neoliberalism: Tripartism and Economic Reforms in the Developing World*, New York: Palgrave Macmillan.

Gallin, D. (2001) 'Propositions on Trade Unions and Informal Employment in Times of Globalization', *Antipode* 33 (3): 531–549.

Gauthé, B. (1997) 'Sécurité Sociale pour le Secteur Informel au Bénin', in van Ginneken, W., ed., *Social Security for the Informal Sector: Investigating the Feasibility of Pilot Projects in Benin, India, El Salvador, and Tanzania*, Geneva: ILO, 15–32.

Germain, R.D. and Kenny, M. (1998) 'Engaging Gramsci: International Relations Theory and the New Gramscians', *Review of International Studies* 24 (1): 3–21.

Gervais, M. (1995) 'Structural Adjustment in Niger', *Review of African Political Economy* 22 (63): 27–42.

Gibbon, P., Havnevik, K., and Hermele, K. (1993) *A Blighted Harvest: The World Bank and African Agriculture in the 1980s*, London: James Currey.

Gide, A. (1927) *Voyage au Congo: carnets de route*, Paris: Gallimard.

Gill, S. (1995) 'Globalisation, Market Civilization, and Disciplinary Neoliberalism', *Millennium* 24 (3): 399–423.

Glassman, J. (2006) 'Primitive Accumulation, Accumulation by Dispossession, Accumulation by "Extra-Economic" Means', *Progress in Human Geography* 30 (5): 608–625.

Godfrey, M. (1978) 'Prospects for a Basic Needs Strategy: The Case of Kenya', *Institute for Development Studies Bulletin* 9 (4): 41–44.

Goudal, J. (1929) 'The Question of Forced Labour before the International Labour Conference', *International Labour Review* 19 (5): 621–638.

GRAIN and AFSA (2015) *Land and Seed Laws under Attack: Who Is Pushing Changes in Africa?* Barcelona: GRAIN.

Gramsci, A. (1971) *Selections from the Prison Notebooks*, trans. Q. Hoare and G.H. Smith, London: Lawrence and Wishart.

Gramsci, A. (1977) *Selections from Political Writings (1910–1920)*, trans. Q. Hoare, London: Lawrence and Wishart.

Gramsci, A. (1985) *Selections from Cultural Writings*, trans. W. Boelhower, London: Lawrence and Wishart.

Gray, K. (2014) *Labour and Development in East Asia: Social Forces and Passive Revolution*, New York: Routledge.

Grimshaw, H.A. (1928) 'The Mandates System and the Problem of Native Labour', in *Problems of Peace: Lectures Delivered at the Geneva Institute of International Relations, Third Series*, Geneva: Geneva Institute of International Relations, 127–155.

Haan, H. (1933) 'Scientific Management and Economic Planning', *Annals of the American Academy of Political and Social Science* 166: 66–74.

Haas, E.B. (1964) *Beyond the Nation State: Functionalism and International Organization*, Stanford: Stanford University Press.

Hall, D. (2013) 'Rethinking Primitive Accumulation: Theoretical Tensions and Rural Southeast Asian Complexities', *Antipode* 44 (4): 1188–1208.

Hall, S. (1980) 'Race, Articulation, and Societies Structured in Domination', in *Sociological Theories: Race and Colonialism*, Paris: UNESCO, 305–343.

Hall, S. (1986) 'Gramsci's Relevance for the Study of Race and Ethnicity', *Journal of Communication Inquiry* 10 (2): 5–27.

Harris, K. and Scully, B. (2015) 'A Hidden Counter-Movement? Precarity, Politics, and Social Protection before and Beyond the Neoliberal Era', *Theory and Society* 44 (5): 415–444.

Harrison, G. (2004) *The World Bank and Africa: The Construction of Governance States*, New York: Routledge.

References

Harrison, G. (2010) *Neoliberal Africa: The Impact of Global Social Engineering*, London: Zed Books.
Harrod, J. (1987) *Power, Production, and the Unprotected Worker*, New York: Columbia University Press.
Hart, G. (2006) 'Denaturalizing Dispossession: Critical Ethnography in the Age of Resurgent Imperialism', *Antipode* 38 (5): 977–1004.
Hart, K. (1973) 'Informal Income and Urban Employment in Ghana', *Journal of Modern African Studies* 11 (1): 61–89.
Harvey, D. (2003) *The New Imperialism*, Oxford: Oxford University Press.
Hughes, S. and Haworth, N. (2011) *The International Labour Organization: Coming in from the Cold*, New York: Routledge.
IAIS (2007) *Issues in Regulation and Supervision of Microinsurance*, Basel: IAIS.
IAIS (2010) *Issues Paper on the Regulation and Supervision of Mutuals, Cooperatives and Other Community-Based Organizations in Increasing Access to Insurance Markets*, Basel: IAIS.
Illife, J. (1975) 'The Creation of Group Consciousness: A History of the Dockworkers of Dar es Salaam', in Sandbrook, R. and Cohen, R., eds., *The Development of an African Working Class: Studies in Class Formation and Action*, Toronto: University of Toronto Press, 49–72.
ILO (1927a) *Native and Colonial Labour in 1926*, Geneva: ILO.
ILO (1927b) *Proceedings of the International Labour Conference, Tenth Session, 1927*, Geneva: ILO.
ILO (1929) *Proceedings of the International Labour Conference, Twelfth Session, 1929*, Geneva: ILO.
ILO (1930) *Forced Labour*, Geneva: ILO.
ILO (1935a) *The Recruiting of Labour in Colonies and in Other Territories with Analogous Labour Conditions*, Geneva: ILO.
ILO (1935b) *The Regulation of Certain Special Systems for Recruiting Workers*, Geneva: ILO.
ILO (1937a) *Report of the Governing Body of the International Labour Office upon the Working of the Convention (no. 29) Concerning Forced or Compulsory Labour*. Geneva: ILO.
ILO (1937b) *Regulation of Contracts of Employment for Indigenous Workers*, Geneva: ILO.
ILO (1939) *International Labour Conference, Twenty-Fifth Session, Geneva, 1939: Regulation of Contracts of Employment for Indigenous Workers*, Geneva: ILO.
ILO (1944) *Social Policy in Dependent Territories*, Montreal: ILO.
ILO (1945) *Minimum Standards of Social Policy in Dependent Territories (Supplementary Provisions), Fifth Item on the Agenda, Twenty-Fifth International Labour Conference*, Montreal: ILO.
ILO (1947) *Committee of Experts on Non-Metropolitan Territories, First Session – London – March 1947: Report of the Committee*, Geneva: ILO.
ILO (1950a) *Conférence d'Elizabethville, 4me Rapport: stabilisation et migration des travailleurs*, Geneva: ILO.
ILO (1950b) *Conférence d'Elizabethville, 5me Rapport: le rendement de la main d'oeuvre et la question des salaires minima*, Geneva: ILO.
ILO (1952) *Commission d'experts sur la politique sociale dans les territoires non- metropolitains, deuxieme session, Géneve, 26 novembre – 8 décembre 1951, Point III de l'ordre du jour: Poursuite de l'étude de la question des travailleurs migrants*, Geneva: ILO.

References 151

ILO (1953a) *Report of the Committee of Experts on Social Policy in Non-Metropolitan Territories (Third Session, Lisbon, 7–19 December 1953)*, Geneva: ILO.
ILO (1953b) *Economic and Social Aspects of Workers' Housing in Non-Metropolitan Territories, with Special Reference to Responsibilities for Its Provision*, Geneva: ILO.
ILO (1953c) *Speech Delivered by Mr. C. Wilfred Jenks, Assistant Director General, International Labour Office, at the Opening Meeting of the Committee of Experts on Social Policy in Non-Metropolitan Territories, Lisbon, 7.12.53*, Geneva: ILO.
ILO (1956) *International Labour Conference, Thirty-Ninth Session, Sixth Item on the Agenda (Forced Labour) – Supplement: Report of the ILO Committee on Forced Labour*, Geneva: ILO.
ILO (1966) *The ILO and Africa*, Geneva: ILO.
ILO (1972) *Employment, Incomes, and Equality: A Strategy for Increasing Productive Employment in Kenya*, Geneva: ILO.
ILO (1973) *Employment and Unemployment in Ethiopia*, Geneva: ILO.
ILO (1982) *Rapport au Gouvernement de la République Gabonaise sur la Restructuration et l'Extension de la Protection Sociale*, Geneva: ILO.
ILO (1989) *Rapport au Gouvernement de la République Camérounaise sur l'Extension de la Protection Sociale aux Populations non-Salariées*, Geneva: ILO.
ILO (1990) *Maroc: Extension de la Protection Sociale au Secteur de l'Artisanat: Rapport de Mission*, Geneva: ILO.
ILO (1991) *Report of the Director General, Pt. 1: The Dilemma of the Informal Sector*, Geneva: ILO.
ILO (1999) *Report of the Director General: Decent Work*, Geneva: ILO.
ILO (2001) *Stopping Forced Labour*, Geneva: ILO.
ILO (2002) *Decent Work and the Informal Economy*, Geneva: ILO.
ILO (2005a) *A Global Alliance against Forced Labour*, Geneva: ILO.
ILO (2005b) *International Training Workshop on Child Trafficking for Security Agencies in Ghana and Nigeria: Accra (Ghana) – October 2003*, Geneva: ILO.
ILO (2007a) *Apprenticeship in the Informal Economy in Africa: Workshop Report, Geneva, 3–4 May 2007*, Geneva: ILO.
ILO (2007b) *General Survey Concerning the Forced Labour Convention, 1930 (no. 29), and the Abolition of Forced Labour Convention, 1956 (no. 105)*. Geneva: ILO.
ILO (2007c) *Girls in Mining*. Geneva: ILO.
ILO (2007d) *IPEC Evaluation: Combatting the Trafficking of Children for Labour Exploitation in West and Central Africa*. Geneva: ILO.
ILO (2008) *Combatting Trafficking in Children for Labour Exploitation: A Resource Kit for Policy-Makers and Practitioners*, Geneva: ILO.
ILO (2009a) *The Cost of Coercion*, Geneva: ILO.
ILO (2009b) *Social Security for All: Investing in Social Justice and Economic Development*, Geneva: ILO.
ILO (2009c) *Training Manual to Fight Trafficking in Children for Labour, Sexual, and Other Forms of Exploitation*, Geneva: ILO.
ILO (2010a) *Trade Union Pluralism and Proliferation in French-Speaking Africa*, Geneva: ILO.
ILO (2010b) *Mission Report: DWT Pretoria, 29 November 2010*, Pretoria: ILO.
ILO (2010c) *Going the Distance to Stop Child Trafficking: Local Vigilance Committees*, Geneva: ILO.
ILO (2012a) *ILO Global Estimate of Forced Labour: Results and Methodology*, Geneva: ILO.

ILO (2012b) *Upgrading Informal Apprenticeships: A Resource Guide for Africa*, Geneva: ILO.
ILO (2013a) *Profil pays du Travail Décent: Sénégal*, Dakar: ILO.
ILO (2013b) *Extension de la Protection Sociale à l'Économie Informelle: Vers un Régime Simplifié pour les Petits Contribuables (RSPC) au Sénégal*, Dakar: ILO.
ILO (2014a) *Transitioning from the Informal to the Formal Economy*, Geneva: ILO.
ILO (2014b) *Profits and Poverty: The Economics of Forced Labour*, Geneva: ILO.
ILO (2014c) *Rapport de l'Atelier Pour la Création d'une Stratégie Nationale de Développement de la Microassurance au Sénégal*, Dakar: ILO.
ILO (2014d) *Rapport de la Session d'Apprentissage sur les Nouvelles Opportunités de la Micro-Assurance*, Dakar: ILO.
ILO-INS (2011) *Rapport de l'Enquête Nationale sur le Travail des Enfants au Niger*, Niamey: ILO.
ILR (1941a) 'Wartime Policy in British Colonial Dependencies', *International Labour Review* 43 (3): 299–308.
ILR (1941b) 'Problems of British Colonial Trusteeship', *International Labour Review* 44 (5): 538–546.
ILR (1942) 'Social Problems on the Northern Rhodesian Copperbelt', *International Labour Review* 45 (5): 542–551.
ILR (1956) 'Social Policy in Non-Metropolitan Territories', *International Labour Review* 73 (6): 619–633.
IMF (2013) *Niger: Poverty Reduction Strategy Plan*, Washington: International Monetary Fund.
Isakson, S.R. (2015) 'Derivatives for Development? Small-Farmer Vulnerability and the Financialization of Risk Management', *Journal of Agrarian Change* 15 (4): 569–580.
Jeanne, M. (2008) 'La mise en scéne de l'esclavage dans l'espace saharo-sahélien: discours, actions, et profits de l'association Timidria au Niger', *Archive Orientale* 80 (2): 191–206.
Jeeves, A. (1975) 'The Control of Migratory Labour on the South African Gold Mines in the Era of Milner', *Journal of Southern African Studies* 2 (1): 3–29.
Jeffries, C. (1943) 'Recent Social Welfare Developments in Tropical Africa', *Africa: Journal of the International African Institute* 14 (1): 4–11.
Jeffries, R.D. (1975) 'Populist Tendencies in the Ghanaian Trade Union Movement', in Sandbrook, R. and Cohen, R., eds., *The Development of an African Working Class: Studies in Class Formation and Action*, Toronto: University of Toronto Press, 261–280.
Jessop, B. (2005) 'Gramsci as a Spatial Theorist', *Critical Review of International Social and Political Philosophy* 8 (4): 421–437.
Johnson, L. (2013) 'Index Insurance and the Articulation of Risk-Bearing Subjects', *Environment and Planning A* 45 (11): 2663–2681.
JRAS (1929) 'The Conference on Forced and Contract Labour', *Journal of the Royal African Society* 28 (111): 281–287.
Juul, K. (2006) 'Decentralization, Taxation, and Citizenship in Senegal', *Development and Change* 37 (4): 821–846.
Kelley, T. (2008) 'Unintended Consequences of Legal Westernization in Niger: Harming Contemporary Slaves by Reconceptualizing Property', *The American Journal of Comparative Law* 56: 999–1038.
Kesseler, S. and Tine, V. (2004) 'Un Mal Nécessaire? Influences Industrielles à l'Interface Urbain-Rurale: l'Impact des ICS sur la Zone de Mboro, Sénégal', *Johannes Gutenburg*

Universität, Mainz, Department of Anthropology and African Studies Working Paper no. 49.

Kielland, A. and Gaye, I. (2010) *Child Mobility and Rural Vulnerability in Senegal: Climate Change and the Role of Children in Household Risk Management Strategies in Rural Senegal*, Dakar: World Bank Group.

Kiwara, A.D. (1999) 'Health Insurance for the Informal Sector in the Republic of Tanzania', in van Ginneken, W., ed., *Social Security for the Excluded Majority: Case Studies of Developing Countries*, Geneva: ILO, 117–144.

Kiwara, A.D. and Heynis, F. (1997) 'Health Insurance for Informal Sector Workers: Feasibility Study on Arusha and Mbeya, Tanzania', in van Ginneken, W., ed., *Social Security for the Informal Sector: Investigating the Feasibility of Pilot Projects in Benin, India, El Salvador, and Tanzania*, Geneva: ILO, 73–94.

Lambert, R. and Herod, A., eds. (2016) *Neoliberal Capitalism and Precarious Work: Ethnographies of Accommodation and Resistance*, Cheltenham: Edward Elgar.

LeBaron, G. (2010) 'The Political Economy of the Household: Neoliberal Restructuring, Enclosures, and Daily Life', *Review of International Political Economy* 17 (5): 889–912.

LeBaron, G. (2014a) 'Unfree Labour Beyond Binaries: Social Hierarchy, Insecurity, and Labour Market Restructuring', *International Feminist Journal of Politics* 17 (1): 1–19.

LeBaron, G. (2014b) 'Reconceptualizing Debt Bondage: Debt as a Class-Based Form of Labour Discipline', *Critical Sociology* 40 (5): 763–780.

LeBaron, G. and Ayers, A. (2013) 'The Rise of a "New Slavery"? Understanding African Unfree Labour through Neoliberalism', *Third World Quarterly* 34 (5): 873–892.

Lee, J.M. (1967) *Colonial Development and Good Government*, Oxford: Clarendon Press.

Lerche, J. (2007) 'A Global Alliance against Forced Labour? Unfree Labour, Neoliberal Globalization, and the International Labour Organization', *Journal of Agrarian Change* 7 (4): 425–452.

Lerche, J. (2012) 'Labour Regulations and Labour Standards in India: Decent Work?', *Global Labour Journal* 3 (1): 16–39.

Lewis, W.A. (1954) 'Economic Development with Unlimited Supplies of Labour', *The Manchester School* 22 (2): 139–191.

Leys, C. (1973) 'Interpreting African Underdevelopment: Reflections on the ILO Report on Employment, Incomes, and Inequality in Kenya', *African Affairs* 72 (289): 419–429.

Leys, C. (1975) *Underdevelopment in Kenya*, Heinemann: London.

Li, T. (2009) 'To Make Live or Let Die? Rural Dispossession and the Protection of Surplus Populations', *Antipode* 41 (s1): 66–93.

Lund, C. (1997) 'Land, Legitimacy, and Democracy in Niger', *Review of African Political Economy* 24 (71): 99–112.

Luxemburg, R. (2003) *The Accumulation of Capital*, New York: Routledge.

Maccatory, B., Oumarou, M.B., and Poncelet, M. (2010) 'West African Social Movements "Against the High Cost of Living": From the Economic to the Political, from the Global to the National', *Review of African Political Economy* 37 (125): 345–359.

Maloney, W.F. (2004) 'Informality Revisited', *World Development* 32 (7): 1159–1178.

Mamdani, M. (1996) *Citizen and Subject: Contemporary Africa and the Legacy of Late Colonialism*, Princeton: Princeton University Press.

Mandel, E. (1968) 'Introduction', in Mandel, E., ed., *Fifty Years of World Revolution, 1917–1967: An International Symposium*, New York: Pathfinder.

Manzo, K. (2005) 'Modern Slavery, Deproletarianisation and Global Capitalism in West Africa', *Review of African Political Economy* 32 (106): 521–534.

Marx, K. (1990) *Capital: A Critique of Political Economy*, Vol. 1, New York: Penguin.

Marx, K. and Engels, F. (2004) *The Communist Manifesto*, ed. G.S. Jones, London: Penguin.

Maul, D.R. (2007) 'International Labour Organization and the Struggle against Forced Labour from 1919 to the Present', *Labor History* 48 (4): 477–500.

Maul, D.R. (2012) *Human Rights, Development, and Decolonization: The International Labour Organization, 1940–1970*, New York: Palgrave Macmillan and International Labour Organization.

Mayer, F. and Phillips, N. (2017) 'Outsourcing Governance: States and the Politics of a "Global Value Chain World"', *New Political Economy* 22 (2): 134–152.

Mboya, T. (1967) *Incomes Policies for Developing Countries*, Geneva: International Institute for Labour Studies.

McGrath, S. (2013a) 'Many Chains to Break: The Multi-Dimensional Concept of Slave Labour in Brazil', *Antipode* 45 (4): 1005–1028.

McGrath, S. (2013b) 'Fuelling Global Production Networks with Slave Labour? Migrant Sugar Cane Workers in the Brazilian Ethanol GPN', *Geoforum* 44: 32–43.

McIntyre, M. and Nast, H. (2011) 'Bio(necro)politics, Surplus Populations and the Spatial Dialectics of Reproduction and "Race"', *Antipode* 43 (5): 1465–1488.

McMichael, P. (1991) 'Slavery in Capitalism: The Rise and Demise of the US *Ante-Bellum* Cotton Culture', *Theory and Society* 20 (3): 321–349.

McNally, D. (2016) 'The Dialectics of Unity and Difference in the Constitution of Wage Labour: On Internal Relations and Working Class Formation', *Capital & Class* 39 (1): 131–146.

Meagher, K. (2005) 'Social Capital or Analytical Liability? Social Networks and African Informal Economies', *Global Networks* 5 (3): 217–238.

Mendiola, F. (2016) 'The Role of Unfree Labour in Capitalist Development: Spain and Its Empire, Nineteenth to the Twenty-First Centuries', *International Review of Social History* 61 (1): 187–211.

Moore, P. (2010) *The International Political Economy of Work and Empoyability*, New York: Palgrave.

Moore, P. (2012) 'Where Is the Study of Work in Critical IPE?', *International Politics* 49 (2): 215–237.

Morse, D. (1968) 'The World Employment Programme', *International Labour Review* 97 (6): 517–524.

Morton, A.D. (2007) 'Waiting for Gramsci: State Formation, Passive Revolution, and the International', *Millennium: Journal of International Studies* 35 (3): 597–621.

Mountz, A. (2003) 'Human Smuggling, the Transnational Imaginary, and Everyday Geographies of the Nation-State', *Antipode* 35 (3): 622–644.

Mouton, P. and Gruat, J.V. (1989) 'The Extension of Social Security to Self-Employed Persons in Africa', *International Social Security Review* 88 (1): 40–54.

Mueller, L. (2013) 'Democratic Revolutionaries or Pocketbook Protesters? The Roots of the 2009–2010 Uprisings in Niger', *African Affairs* 112 (448): 398–420.

Munck, R. (2013) 'The Precariat: A View from the South', *Third World Quarterly* 34 (5): 747–762.

Murphy, C. (1994) *International Organization and Industrial Change: Global Governance since 1850*, Oxford: Polity.

Mwakyusa, A. (2016) 'VETA to Train 5000 Artisans in Special Programme', *Tanzania Daily News*, 16 January 2016, available: http://dailynews.co.tz/index.php/home-news/46062-veta-to-train-5-000-artisans-in-special-programme.

NAFSN (2012) *Cooperation Framework to Support the "New Alliance for Food Security and Nutrition" – Senegal*, Dakar: NAFSN.

Ndiaye, A.I. (2010) 'Autonomy or Political Affiliation? Senegalese Trade Unions in the Face of Political and Economic Reforms', in Beckman, B., Buhlungu, S., and Sachikonye, L., eds., *Trade Unions and Party Politics: Labour Movements in Africa*, Cape Town: HSRC Press, 23–38.

Neilson, B. and Rossiter, N. (2008) 'Precarity as a Political Concept, or, Fordism and Exception', *Theory, Culture & Society* 25 (7–8): 51–72.

Niang, A., Sarr, N.F.M., Hathie, I., Diouf, N.C., Ba, C.O., and Ka, I. (2015) *Comprendre les Changements dans l'Access et l'Utilisation de la Terre par les Populations Rurales Pauvres en Afrique sub-Saharienne: Cas du Sénégal*, Dakar: Initiative Prospective Agricole et Rurale, IFAD, and IIED.

Nkrumah, K. (1961) *Tragedy in Angola: An Address by Osagyefo the President to the National Assembly of Ghana*, Accra: Government Printer.

Nübler, I., C. Hoffman, and C. Grenier (2009) 'Understanding Informal Apprenticeship: Findings from Empirical Research in Tanzania'. *ILO Employment Sector Working Paper, Employment #32*, Geneva: ILO.

Nyerere, J. (1969) 'The Role of African Trade Unions', in Sigmund, P.E., ed., *The Ideologies of the Developing Nations*, London: Praeger.

Oberst, T. (1988) 'Transport Workers, Strikes, and the "Imperial Response": Africa and the Post-World War II Conjuncture', *African Studies Review* 31 (1): 117–133.

O'Brien, D.C. (1971) *The Mourides of Senegal*, Oxford: Clarendon Press.

O'Brien, R., Goertz, A.M., Scholte, J.A., and Williams, M. (2000) *Contesting Global Governance: Multilateral Economic Institutions and Global Social Movements*, Cambridge: Cambridge University Press.

Olivier de Sardan, J.P. (2008) 'La Crise Alimentaire Vue d'En Bas: Syntheses des Recherches Menees sur Sept Sites en Niger', *Afrique Contemporaine* 225 (1): 217–294.

O'Meara, D. (1975) 'The 1946 African Miners' Strike and the Political Economy of South Africa', *The Journal of Commonwealth and Comparative Politics* 13 (2): 146–173.

Oumarou, M. (2001) *Défis et Opportunités pour la Déclaration au Niger*, Geneva: ILO.

Peck, J. (2013) 'Explaining (with) Neoliberalism', *Territory, Politics, Governance* 1 (2): 132–157.

Peck, J. and Tickell, A. (2002) 'Neoliberalizing Space', *Antipode* 34 (3): 380–404.

Perrings, C. (1977) 'The Production Process, Industrial Labour Strategies and Worker Responses in the Southern African Gold Mining Industry', *The Journal of African History* 18 (1): 129–135.

Phillips, N. (2011) 'Informality, Global Production Networks and the Dynamics of "Adverse Incorporation"', *Global Networks* 11 (3): 380–397.

Phillips, N. (2013) 'Unfree Labour and Adverse Incorporation in the Global Economy: Comparative Perspectives on Brazil and India', *Economy and Society* 42 (2): 171–196.

Phillips, N. (2016) 'Labour in Global Production: Reflections on Coxian Insights in a World of Global Value Chains', *Globalizations* 13 (5): 594–607.

Phillips, N. and Mieres, F. (2015) 'The Governance of Forced Labour in the Global Economy', *Globalizations* 12 (2): 244–260.

Phillips, N., Bhaskaran, R., Nathan, D. and Upendranadh, C. (2013) 'The Social Foundations of Global Production Networks: Towards a Global Political Economy of Child Labour', *Third World Quarterly* 35 (3): 428–446.

Posel, D. (1992) *The Making of Apartheid, 1948–1960: Conflict and Compromise*, Oxford: Clarendon Press.

Premchander, S., Prameela, V., and Chidambaranathan, M. (2014) *Prevention and Elimination of Bonded Labour: The Potential and Limits of Microfinance-Led Approaches*, Geneva: ILO.

Pun, N. and Smith, C. (2007) 'Putting Transnational Labour Process in Its Place: The Dormitory Labour Regime in Post-Socialist China', *Work, Employment and Society* 21 (1): 27–45.

Read, J. (2002) 'Primitive Accumulation: The Aleatory Foundation of Capitalism', *Rethinking Marxism* 14 (2): 24–49.

Republic of Kenya (1970) *Report of the Select Committee on Unemployment*, Nairobi: Government Printer.

Republic of Kenya (1973) *Sessional Paper no. 10 of 1973 on Employment*, Nairobi: Government Printer.

Riley, S. and Parfitt, T. (1994) 'Economic Adjustment and Democratization in Africa', in Walton, J. and Seddon, D., eds., *Free Markets and Food Riots: The Politics of Global Adjustment*, Oxford: Basil Blackwell, 135–170.

Rioux, S. (2013) 'The Fiction of Economic Coercion: Political Marxism and the Separation of Theory and History', *Historical Materialism* 21 (4): 92–128.

Rizzo, M. (2011) '"Life Is War": Informal Transport Workers and Neoliberalism in Tanzania 1998–2009', *Development and Change* 42 (5): 1179–1205.

Rizzo, M. (2013) 'Informalisation and the End of Trade Unionism as We Knew It? Dissenting Remarks from a Tanzanian Case Study', *Review of African Political Economy* 40 (136): 290–308.

Rogaly, B. (2008) 'Migrant Workers and the ILO's Global Alliance against Forced Labour: A Critical Appraisal', *Third World Quarterly* 29 (7): 1431–1447.

Roitman, J. (1990) 'The Politics of Informal Markets in sub-Saharan Africa', *Journal of Modern African Studies* 28 (4): 671–696.

Rojas, C. (2015) 'The Place of the Social at the World Bank (1949–1981): Mingling Race, Nation, and Knowledge', *Global Social Policy* 15 (1): 23–39.

Ross, E.A. (1925) *Report on the Employment of Native Labour in Portuguese Africa*, New York: Abbott Press.

Rossi, B. (2015) *From Slavery to Aid: Politics, Labour, and Ecology in the Nigerien Sahel, 1800–2000*, Cambridge: Cambridge University Press.

ROTAB (2014) *Étude de Référence sur les Entreprises et les Droits de l'Homme: Cas des Industries Extractives au Niger*, Niamey: Réseau des Organisations pour la Transparence et l'Analyse Budgetaire.

Russell, W.A., Cartmel-Robinson, H.F., Goodhart, H.L., and Moffat, M. (1935) *Report of the Commission Appointed to Enquire into the Disturbances in the Copperbelt, Northern Rhodesia*, Lusaka: Government Printer.

Saith, A. (2005) 'Reflections: Interview with Louis Emmerij', *Development and Change* 36 (6): 1163–1176.

Sandbrook, R. (1975) *Proletarians and African Capitalism: The Kenya Case, 1960–1972*. Cambridge: Cambridge University Press.

Sandbrook, R. (1983) *The Politics of Basic Needs: Urban Aspects of Assaulting Poverty in Africa*, London: Heinemann.

Sassen, S. (2010) 'A Savage Sorting of Winners and Losers: Contemporary Versions of Primitive Accumulation', *Globalizations* 7 (1–2): 23–50.

Scully, B. (2016a) 'Precarity North and South: A Southern Critique of Guy Standing', *Global Labour Journal* 7 (2): 160–173.

Scully, B. (2016b) 'From the Shop Floor to the Kitchen Table: The Shifting Centre of Precarious Workers' Politics in South Africa', *Review of African Political Economy* 43 (148): 295–311.

Seddon, D. and Zelig, L. (2005) 'Class and Protest in Africa: New Waves', *Review of African Political Economy* 32 (103): 9–27.

Sekou, A.R. and Abdoukarimou, S. (2009) 'The Legacy of Slavery in Niger', in Andrees, B. and Belser, P., eds., *Forced Labour: Coercion and Exploitation in the Private Economy*, Geneva: Lynne Rienner and ILO, 71–88.

Selwyn, B. (2012) *Workers, the State, and Development in Brazil: Powers of Labour, Chains of Value*, Manchester: University of Manchester Press.

Selwyn, B. (2013) 'Social Upgrading and Labour in Global Production Networks: A Critique and Alternative Conception', *Competition and Change* 17 (1): 75–90.

Selwyn, B. (2014) *The Global Development Crisis*, Cambridge: Polity.

Selwyn, B. (2015) 'Twenty-First Century International Political Economy: A Class-Relational Perspective', *European Journal of International Relations* 21 (3): 513–537.

Sembene, O. (1960) *Les bouts de bois de Dieu*, Paris: Le Livre Contemporain.

Senghor, L. (2012) 'La question negre devant le Congres de Bruxelles: la lutte contre l'oppression coloniale et l'imperialisme', in Murphy, D., ed., *Lamine Senghor: La violation d'un pays et autres écrits anticolonialistes*, Paris: L'Harmattan.

Shotwell, J.T. (1933) 'The International Labour Organization as an Alternative to Violent Revolution', *Annals of the American Academy of Political and Social Science* 166: 18–25.

Shotwell, J.T., ed. (1934) *The Origins of the International Labour Organization, Vol. 1: History*, New York: Columbia University Press.

Soederberg, S. (2013) 'Universalising Financial Inclusion and the Securitisation of Development', *Third World Quarterly* 34 (4): 593–612.

Soederberg, S. (2014) *Debtfare States and the Poverty Industry: Money, Discipline and the Surplus Population*, New York: Routledge.

Soederberg, S. (2017) 'Governing Stigmatised Space: The Case of the "Slums" of Berlin-Neukölln', *New Political Economy* 22 (5): 478–495.

Sow, A.A. (2014) *Note sur la Gouvernance Foncière a l'Aune de la Nouvelle Politique de Décentralisation et d'Aménagement du Territoire au Sénégal*, Dakar: Initiative Prospective Agricole et Rurale.

Standing, G. (2008) 'The ILO: An Agency for Globalization?', *Development and Change* 39 (3): 355–384.

Standing, G. (2011) *The Precariat: The New Dangerous Class*, London: Bloomsbury.

Steinfeld, R. (2001) *Coercion, Contract, and Free Labour in the Nineteenth Century*, Cambridge: Cambridge University Press.

Stoakes, E., Kelly, E., and Kelly, A. (2015) 'Revealed: How the Thai Fishing Industry Trafficks, Imprisons and Enslaves', *The Guardian*, 20 July 2015, available: www.theguardian.com/global-development/2015/jul/20/thai-fishing-industry-implicated-enslavement-deaths-rohingya.

Stopford, J.G.B. (1902) 'A Neglected Source of Labour in Africa', *Journal of the Royal African Society* 1 (4): 444–451.

Taylor, M. (2010) 'Conscripts of Competitiveness: Culture, Institutions, and Capital in Contemporary Development', *Third World Quarterly* 31 (4): 561–579.

References

Taylor, M. (2011) 'Race You to the Bottom . . . and Back Again? The Uneven Development of Labour Codes of Conduct', *New Political Economy* 16 (4): 445–462.

Thébaut, B. and Batterbury, S. (2001) 'Sahel Pastoralists: Opportunism, Struggle, Conflict, and Negotiation: A Case Study from Eastern Niger', *Global Environmental Change* 11 (1): 69–78.

Theron, J. (2010) 'Informalization from Above, Informalization from Below: The Options for Organization', *African Studies Quarterly* 11 (2–3): 87–105.

Thompson, E.P. (1966) *The Making of the English Working Class*, London: Vintage.

TRA (2010) *Review of Informal Sector for Taxation Purposes*, Dar es Salaam: Tanzania Revenue Authority.

Tyner, J. (2016) 'Population Geography I: Surplus Populations', *Progress in Human Geography* 37 (5): 701–711.

UN/ILO (1953) *Report of the Ad-Hoc Committee on Forced Labour*, Geneva: United Nations and ILO.

USAID (1990) *Agriculture Sector Development Grant II – Project Approval Document, Vol. 1: USAID-Niger*, Washington: United States Agency for International Development.

van der Linden, M. (2016) 'Global Labour: A Not-So-Grand Finale and Perhaps a New Beginning', *Global Labour Journal* 7 (2): 201–210.

van de Walle, N. (1999) *African Economies and the Politics of Permanent Crisis, 1979–1999*, Cambridge: Cambridge University Press.

van Ginneken, W. (1996) 'Social Security for the Informal Sector: Issues, Options, and Tasks Ahead', *Interdepartmental Project on the Urban Informal Sector Working Paper*, Geneva: ILO.

van Liempt, I. and Sersli, S. (2013) 'State Responses and Migrant Experiences with Human Smuggling: A Reality Check', *Antipode* 45 (4): 1029–1046.

Vosko, L. (2002) '"Decent Work": The Shifting Role of the ILO in the Struggle for Global Justice', *Global Social Policy* 2 (1): 19–46.

Vosko, L. (2010) *Managing the Margins: Gender, Citizenship, and the International Regulation of Precarious Work*, New York: Oxford University Press.

Webster, E. and Bischoff, C. (2011) 'New Actors in Employment Relations in the Periphery: Closing the Representation Gap amongst Micro and Small Enterprises', *Relations Industrielles/Industrial Relations* 66 (1): 11–33.

Webster, E., Lambert, R., and Bezuidenhout, A. (2008) *Grounding Globalization: Labour in the Age of Insecurity*, Oxford: Blackwell.

Weisband, E. (2000) 'Discursive Multilateralism: Global Benchmarks, Shame, and Leaning in the ILO Labour Standards Monitoring Regime', *International Studies Quarterly* 44: 643–666.

Wolpe, H. (1972) 'Capitalism and Cheap Labour in South Africa: From Segregation to Apartheid', *Economy and Society* 1 (4): 425–456.

Wood, E.M. (2002) *The Origin of Capitalism: A Longer View*, London: Verso.

Wood, G. (2003) 'Staying Secure, Staying Poor: The "Faustian Bargain"', *World Development* 31 (3): 455–471.

Woodhouse, P. (2003) 'African Enclosures: A Default Mode of Development', *World Development* 31 (10): 1705–1720.

Woods, N. (2006) *The Globalizers: the IMF, the World Bank, and Their Borrowers*. Ithaca: Cornell University Press.

World Bank (1981) *Accelerated Development in sub-Saharan Africa: A Programme for Action*. Washington: World Bank Group.

World Bank (1991) *Vocational and Technical Education and Training: A World Bank Policy Paper*, Washington: World Bank Group.

World Bank (1994) *Adjustment in Africa: Reforms, Results, and the Road Ahead*, New York: Oxford University Press.

World Bank (2009a) *Index Based Crop Insurance for Senegal: Promoting Access to Agricultural Insurance for Small Farmers*, Washington: World Bank Group.

World Bank (2009b) *Republic of Niger: Impacts of Sustainable Land Management Programs on Lang Management and Poverty in Niger, Environmental and Natural Resources Management Africa Region, Report no. 48230 NE*, Washington: World Bank Group.

Wright, E.O. (2000) 'Working-Class Power, Capitalist-Class Interests, and Class Compromise', *American Journal of Sociology* 105 (4): 957–1002.

Wright, E.O. (2016) 'Is the Precariat a Class?', *Global Labour Journal* 7 (2): 123–135.

Young, C. (2004) 'The End of the Postcolonial State in Africa? Reflections on Changing African Political Dynamics', *African Affairs*, 103 (410): 23–49.

Zeleza, P.T. (1987) 'Trade Union Imperialism: American Labour, the ICFTU, and the Kenyan Labour Movement', *Social and Economic Studies* 36 (2): 145–170.

Index

AOF 42, 49, 65–66, 70–71
apprenticeships 110–114

Ballinger, William and Margaret 53
Belgium 49; *see also* Congo Free State
Benin 102–103
Benson, Wilfred 44, 45, 61–62, 67
bonded labour 22, 118, 121, 123

C29: 2014 Protocol to 117; contemporary relevance 5, 121; establishment 43–47; impacts 48–49, 54; and 'indirect' compulsion 50; transitional period 47, 117; *see also* C105; Declaration on Fundamental Principles and Rights at Work (1998)
C105 53, 54, 118, 121
C182 117, 120
CDWA 61–62
CGAP 104–105
CGT 40, 66
child labour 117, 120, 132
child trafficking 122, 126, 127, 128–133
CIMA 106, 108–109
class *see* working class
CNTS 107–108
colonialism 41–43, 60–64
Communist Manifesto 18
communist parties 45–46, 66, 67
Congo Free State 2–3, 41, 42–43
Core Conventions *see* Declaration on Fundamental Principles and Rights at Work (1998)
COTU (Kenya) 88–89, 91
Cox, Robert W. 11, 26, 31, 39, 79, 83, 101, 136

Dakar 65, 66, 72, 85–86, 109, 131, 132
Dar es Salaam 65, 102–103

Decent Work 120
Declaration on Fundamental Principles and Rights at Work (1998) 117, 120, 126
decolonization 74–75, 79–82
devaluation *see* structural adjustment; wages
dockworkers 65, 110
du Bois, W.E.B. 43–44

ECOSOC 53
Ethiopia 63, 87

financial inclusion 104–105
forced begging 131–132
forced labour: ambiguity of 20–21; communist views on 45–46; and colonial 'labour shortages' 41–42; critical perspectives on 9; debates in 1920s 43–45; in global production networks 118–119; in history of capitalism 2–3, 21–22; ILO definition of 5, 46–47; and law enforcement 121–122; and migrant labour system in South Africa 49–54; and neoliberalism 118–121; in Niger 125–126, 127; popular attention to 1–2; and residualism 9, 123; salience of for ILO 55–56, 117–118; tension with abolitionism in colonial territories 42–43; *see also* C29; C105; child labour; child trafficking; free labour; slavery
formalization 8–9, 111
France 48–49; *see also* AOF
free labour: contested nature of 22, 25–26, 49; crucial to capitalism 18–19; and formation of non-working populations 24; and recruitment agencies 50–51

Ghana 56, 80–81, 113, 129
governance 10, 11, 25–26, 27–28, 31, 33–34

162 *Index*

Gramsci, Antonio: on colonial forced labour 46, 55; economic-corporate interests 124; hegemony 28; in IPE scholarship 26, 31; organic crisis 28, 98; passive revolution 33; political relations of force 27–28, 55, 127; and race 29–30; space and scale 31–33; subaltern 28–29, 142–143
Great Britain 48; British colonies 41, 65, 71, 74; Colonial Office 60–62
Great Depression 60

Hall, Stuart 4, 28, 29–30, 137
Housing 71–72

IAIS 105–106
IALC 68–70, 72–74, 79, 83
ICFTU 66, 81, 120, 126
IFC 105, 109
IGAs 122, 128
ILO: and anti-communism 39–40; Committee of Experts on Social Policy in Non-Metropolitan Territories 68–73; International Labour Conference 44, 46–47, 51, 56, 91, 101, 117; International Labour Review 47, 60–61, 62; Native Labour Code 50; Native Labour Section 43–44, 48; Philadelphia Conference of 1944 62, 67; Social Finance 104; Social Protection Department 103–104, 108; *see also* C29; C105; Declaration on Fundamental Principles and Rights at Work; LUTRENA; R035; SAP-FL; WEP
IMF riots 100
Independent Labour Party (UK) 53
informal labour: critical perspectives on 9, 77; ILO and popularization of 5; in Kenya 89–93; and neoliberalism 100–102; residualist conceptions of 7–8; in Senegal 108–109; social protection for 102–104; in Tanzania 110–111; and trade unions 91, 108, 110, 141; and training 110, 112–114; and unfree labour in Niger 125–126; World Bank and 8, 110; *see also* Kenya; microinsurance; Senegal; Tanzania; WEP
IPE 3, 9, 11–12, 136–137
irregular labour 3–4, 10, 17, 25–26, 138–140

JASPA *see* WEP
Jenks, Wilfred 73, 87

Kenya 66, 84, 88–93

labour shortage 41–42, 52, 56
land: access to and 'silent compulsion' in colonial Africa 41; privatization of tenure in Senegal 131; reserves in South Africa 53, 67; restriction of use rights as 'indirect compulsion' 48, 49; and structural adjustment 100, 118; use rights and slavery in Niger 124–125
League of Nations 38; *see also* LNU; Temporary Slavery Commission
LNU 44–45
LUTRENA 128–130
Luxemburg, Rosa 3, 21, 45, 126

marabouts 107–108, 131–132
Marx, Karl: ambivalence of free labour 20–21, 24; coercion 21, 24, 42, 48; 'General Law of Capitalist Accumulation' 23; and Gramsci 26–27; naturalization of 'free' labour 25, 55, 77; and proletarianization 18–19; 'silent compulsion' 21, 23, 38, 121, 142; *see also* primitive accumulation; relative surplus population
Mboya, Tom 82
microinsurance: development of 102–104; and financial inclusion 104–105; and neoliberalism 139; regulation of 105–106; in Senegal 108–110
migrant labour: and forced labour 1–2, 34n2, 51–54; and gold mining in South Africa 49–50; and metropolitan labour conditions 40; stabilization of 64–65, 69; and strikes 61, 66, 67; *see also* child trafficking; migrant labour, stabilization; urbanization; wages
migration 42, 122; *see also* migrant labour
mining: child labour in artisanal 125–126, 132; in Northern Rhodesia 60–61; political significance of unions in 80; in South Africa 49–52, 67
modern slavery 1; *see also* child labour; child trafficking; forced labour
Mombasa 60, 65–66
Morse, David 75n3, 82–83

neoliberalism: in Africa 99–100; and ILO 101, 119–120; and irregular labour 6–7, 97, 114–115, 137–139; and primitive accumulation 98; and unfree labour 118–119, 124, 131

new slavery 9; *see also* forced labour; modern slavery
Niger 123–128
Nigeria 41, 65, 129
Nkrumah, Kwame 81
Northern Rhodesia 60–61
Nyerere, Julius 80

Palermo Protocol 122
penal sanctions 26, 51
Portugal 46, 49, 56; Portuguese territories 42–43, 44, 53
precariat 6–7, 15n2, 136, 138, 140
precarity: historical prevalence 2–3; neoliberalism and 7, 97–98, 137–139; political implications 1, 140–143; residualist conceptions of 6–7; *see also* precariat
primitive accumulation: and coercion 20–22, 41; in colonial Africa 41, 48; and labour movement 136; and naturalization of exploitation 25–26, 55; and neoliberalism 98; in Niger 124; and proletarianization 18; and relative surplus population 23–24; in Senegal 126; in South Africa 49; *see also* Marx, Karl
prison labour 54
privatization *see* structural adjustment
property rights 8, 21, 26, 41, 111, 118, 124–125, 131; *see also* land

R035 47–48, 50
race 4, 29–30; and naturalization of exploitation 40–42, 60, 63
railways 41, 65, 74
recruitment 42, 46–47, 49, 50–52, 121
relative surplus population 23–25; and colonial social order 70; formation of 42, 49; and informal work 77; and neoliberalism 139; and organized labour 82; and race 61, 64; in South Africa 67
residualism 6–10
RPL 113–114

SAP-FL 117, 121, 123, 127–128
scale 10, 30–33
Senegal 106–110, 131–133
Senghor, Lamine 45–46
skills 8, 110–115, 128
slavery: abolition of in colonial Africa 41–43; and history of capitalism 2–3; Marx on 20–22; *see also* forced labour; modern slavery; new slavery; traditional slavery
social protection: and informal economy 101–102; and microinsurance 103–104, 105, 108–109; and stabilization debates 70–71
Soto, Hernando de 8, 111
South Africa 49–54, 66–68, 71
Soviet Union 53, 75n5
STEP 103
strikes: AOF railway 1947–48 65; and British colonial imaginaries 60–62; as challenge to colonial authority 70; on Copperbelt 60–61; Mombasa general strike 1947 65–66; postwar wave 65; as response to structural adjustment 100, 125; Sekondi-Takoradi railway 1961 81; Witwatersrand gold mines 1946 67
structural adjustment 99–100, 102, 104, 107–108, 110–111, 125
subaltern *see* Gramsci, Antonio

Tanzania 80, 102–103, 110–114
TAP 63, 73
Temporary Slavery Commission 44
Thomas, Albert 44, 45
trade unions: African unions and irregular labour 140–141; and anticolonial movements 74; debates about suitability of Africans for 40, 60–61; and establishment of international labour standards 39; internationalism and postwar colonialism 66; in Kenya 88–89; and postcolonial nationalism 80–82; and structural adjustment 100, 107–108, 110, 125; structural power in postcolonial economies 79–80
traditional slavery 123–124
training *see* apprenticeships; skills

UN-ILO *Ad Hoc* Committee on Forced Labour 53–54
United States: Department of State 128, 131; relationship with ILO 83–84; USAID 128
UNODC 130, 132–133
urbanization 63; *see also* migrant labour, stabilization

Versailles, Treaty of 39
VVCs 129, 130

wages: confiscation of slaves' 126; debates about wages as motivation to work for Africans 42, 46; devaluation and 99–100, 107; falling real wages and informal work 78, 111; family 70; migrant labour as threat to 40; and relative surplus populations 23, 64, 90; wage restraint policies 87, 89, 94; withheld to cover transport costs 22n2, 50, 51–52; worker demands for 65–66, 74, 91

WEP: context for 83, 85; criticisms 9, 87; 'discovery' of unemployment 82–83; in Ethiopia 87; in Kenya 88–93; 'non-political' nature of 85–86; organization of 85, 92; and popularization of 'informal' 5

working class: naturalization of 25; as political agent 4, 74, 136–137; and proletarianization 18–19; racialized ideas about 30, 42, 60; and relative surplus populations 23–24, 68, 77; and structural adjustment 100

World Bank: approach to informal labour 8–10; and development governance in 1970s 83; and financial inclusion 105; and microinsurance in Senegal 106–109; and neoliberalism in Africa 99–102; and property rights in Niger 124–125; and vocational education 110

WTO 119–120

WWII 49, 61